WESLEYANS HELP WOMEN'S SUFFRAGE

WESLEYANS HELP WOMEN'S SUFFRAGE

TEDDY BADER, M.D.

Revive Publishing
Oklahoma City, Oklahoma

WESLEYANS HELP WOMEN'S SUFFRAGE

TEDDY F. BADER, M.D.

Revive Publications
17 East Janice, Suite 102
Yukon, Oklahoma 73099

Forward

I grew up attending a Wesleyan Church in Boulder, Colorado where women did everything men did including preaching. I supposed that all churches were similar in treating women equally. The only denigration I heard of women was in secular society. My eyes were opened to an alternative vision during medical school where a Protestant friend told me women did not preach in his church because "they followed the Bible."

As an eventual specialist in liver diseases and liver transplantation, my enjoyment of reading history led me to the largely ignored organization, the Woman's Christian Temperance Union. More study tied the issues of women's suffrage, the alcohol industry and slavery together. The idea for a book began. As a physician and medical researcher, I have sought numbers to quantitate or to describe reality as much as possible. It seems to me, that where ideas can be quantified, we are more apt to come closer to reality.

The book chapters proceed in a loosely chronological progression. General ideas about Wesleyan influence culminate in a specific time and locale in Colorado. Four chapters show how Wesleyans helped to bring about an unusual victory for women's suffrage in the Centennial state. The time reviewed ends largely with the formation of the Church of the Nazarene in 1908. The last decade before the 19th amendment passed is not closely examined here as it would take another volume. It is not that Wesleyans stopped supporting suffrage, but that they were joined by many other groups that made their efforts less visible. For example, the General Federation of Women's Clubs threw their hat into the ring for suffrage in 1914; whereas before they had either opposed it or remained neutral.

Included are two essays that the reader may find useful. These are Appendices A and B. The first is the comparison of Quakers and Wesleyan Methodists. The second is on Soviet communism and women.

A few points to clarify. The terms "Wesleyan" and "Methodist" are largely synonymous in this book. If a church is intended, it is specified.

Regarding historical eras, the "AD, BC" terms are selected. Professor John Hale, a working archeologist and academic, states these terms are much less confusing when excavating a site than the similar sounding "CE, BCE" names. AD when written before the date traditionally meant *anno domini*, whereas when written after a date now means "advancing dates;" BC now means "backward count."

I have chosen the terms "white" and "black" and "Indian" to refer to races in this text. I am influenced by large polling data wherein those of African descent or the first inhabitants of America prefer those terms as opposed to "African-American" or "native American." No disrespect is intended in any case.

The singular and plural of "woman" bedevils the reader and author. Usage has changed. Nineteenth century usage often has "woman" as a plural where we would prefer the word "women." I use "women" when writing. However, in direct quotes I have retained the plural as woman.

We are now in the era of electronic books. Because of the different sizes of pages on viewing devices, one must assign a percentage location rather than page number in the bibliography.

Few books mention the influence of religion upon women's suffrage. The Wesleyan tradition, as defined in chapter three, has been one of the most supportive of all the branches of Christianity. I have undoubtedly made mistakes in this volume. I would appreciate those who would correct me in a charitable spirit.

Teddy Bader
tedbader@cox.net

Contents

July 1848. Americans were relieved and restless. Relieved that War with Mexico was over. Restless that gold had been discovered at Sutter's Mill. Thousands of men were scurrying to California to pick up nuggets of gold. People were moving faster with the railroad and steamboat. Women and men were wearing sleeves and shoulders tailored close to the figure. Dresses were still full length but with a lower and tighter waist.

In Seneca Falls, New York on July 19, 1848, women were streaming into the Wesleyan Methodist Church to join the First Women's Rights Convention. With three balconies, the Chapel was considered a large ecclesiastical structure for the time.[1] Even so, with 300 people attending, the crowd flowed out of doors on a hot and sunny day. The advertising had been only local in the form of posted signs and a notice in local newspapers,

> "WOMEN'S RIGHTS CONVENTION--
> a convention to discuss the social, civil, and
> religious condition and rights of women, will
> be held in the Wesleyan Chapel at Seneca
> Falls, New York on Wednesday and
> Thursday, the 19th and 20th of July, current;
> commencing at 10:00 AM. During the first
> day the meeting will be exclusively for
> women, who are earnestly invited to attend.
> The public generally are invited to be present
> on the second day, when Lucretia Mott, of
> Philadelphia, and other ladies and gentlemen
> will address the convention."

Lucretia Coffin Mott, a 55-year-old mother of six children, was the principal organizer for the convention. Elizabeth Cady Stanton, a 33 year old mother of seven children, was the primary author of a paper, *Declaration of Sentiments,* which was discussed, and amended, during the meeting.[a]

Most of the women attending the convention were active in the Quaker or evangelical Methodist movements. In retrospect, the most famous person present may have been Frederick Douglass, the 31-year-old black abolitionist. Standing six feet tall and weighing more than 200 pounds, he created a noticeable presence. Contemporaries recognized him as a great lecturer and writer. Douglas credited his development as an orator from his early days as a lay minister in the African Methodist Episcopal Zion Church, where he learned to speak in front of friendly black audiences. He maintained his status in his Methodist church throughout his lifetime. His story of escaping from the brutality of slavery was a gripping one. Douglass' first autobiography in 1845, *Narrative of the Life of Frederick Douglass, an American Slave Written by Himself*, became very popular in the North.

The meeting continued for two days, with breaks, into candlelit evenings. Each half-day session was begun with the famous statement from the *Declaration of Independence* modified as, "We hold these truths to be self-evident, that all men and women are created equal."

Patterned after the famous 1776 document, the *Declaration of Sentiments*, listed 18 grievances and 11 resolutions. The grievances for women centered on the lack of property rights, denial of education and

---

[a] Born in wealth, Stanton, obtained a secondary school education unusual for a woman of the time. She had a gifted intellect and liked to read in her father's law library. Short and stout, her figure suggested she preferred short walks rather than long ones; in addition, she loved naps and consuming muffins, cream and sugar. She could not understand the asceticism of her Quaker friends. Both her personality and appearance were pugnacious. Struggling with veracity, she told a story of being converted as a young woman by the hellfire preaching of the famous evangelist Charles Finney; only later to be talked out of it by the rational reasoning of her relatives. The trouble is that for the time in question, Finney's itinerary does not show him to be in Troy, New York, her hometown. (see Ginzberg, An American Life: Elizabeth Cady Stanton, 2010, p 7, 24-25).

employment, and a subordinate status in the Church by the male establishment.

The *Sentiments* expressed two theological concerns about men. The first was that "He allows her in church, as well as State, but a subordinate position, claiming apostolic authority for her exclusion from the ministry, and, with some exceptions, from any public participation in the affairs of the Church." And the second, "He has usurped the prerogative of Jehovah himself, claiming it as his right to assign for her a sphere of action, when that belongs to her conscience and God."

The resolutions were clearly concerned with one major issue: the lack of Christian ordination for women, or that is, the formal full ministerial authority to teach and preach in public (especially when men were present). The fourth resolution was clear on this: "[it is man's duty] to encourage her to speak and teach . . . in all religious assemblies." The tenth resolution stated "[the need] for the overthrow of the monopoly of the pulpit." The eleventh resolution continued "In regard to the great subjects of morals and religion . . .her right to participate with her brother in teaching them, both in private and in public, by writing and by speaking."

The last resolution added by the leadership in the pre-convention committee, almost did not make it to the first public draft and that was resolution nine: "That it is the duty of women of this country to secure to themselves their sacred right to the elective franchise." Some of the leadership felt the idea too radical. Lucretia Mott (and likely the other three Quaker women leaders) were doubtful that it should be included, as Quakers eschewed political activity. Not only did some of the governance group think the idea of voting rights too drastic, many of the participants also took exception. When the time came for vote on the motion, it appeared to be the only resolution which might fail to be approved by the attendees.

Frederick Douglass was stirred to speak. Feeling he could not claim the right to suffrage if he did not support the same right for women, he rose and said in part: "In this denial of the right to participate in government, [it is] not merely the degradation of woman and the perpetuation of a great injustice [that] happens, but the maiming and repudiation of one-half of the moral world and intellectual power for the government of the world."[2] His arguments seemed to help sway the convention that suffrage was an essential need for women.

The convention proceeded to approve the suffrage resolution by a majority vote, but it was the only resolution that did not pass unanimously.

While all attendees were invited to sign the *Declaration of Sentiments* and its resolutions, only about one in three did so. Sixty-eight women and 32 men appended their names. Ten people affiliated with the Seneca Falls Wesleyan Methodist church signed the document, including the pastor, Saron Phillips.[b] Seven more from the local Methodist Episcopal Church also signed the document. A quarter of the signatories were Quaker.[3,4] Only one Baptist, a man, signed the *Sentiments*. Local Catholics and Presbyterians were not in attendance at the convention.[5]

The national newspaper reaction to the convention was mixed. It was called "dull and uninteresting" by the *Rochester* [New York] *Advertiser*. The *Lowell* [Massachusetts] *Courier* worried that the eventual outcome of the ideas would lead to a reversal in gender roles. On the other hand, Horace Greeley, editor of the *New York Tribune*, admitted that if "all men are created equal," then Americans must endorse the right of women to vote.

The *St Louis Daily Reveille* was enthusiastic,

---

[b] The pastor's name was far more likely Samuel Phillips. See chapter six.

> "The flag of independence has been hoisted
> for the second time on this side of the
> Atlantic, and a solemn league and covenant
> has been entered into by a convention of
> women at Seneca Falls, New York."[5]

Appeals for women's rights in the mid-19th century were considered radical at the time, but not by today's standards. They were simply fundamental human rights for women. In 1848 women could not vote or hold elective office. In most states, married women could not own property in their own names or sign a legal contract; in the case of divorce, they forfeited nearly all custody rights. Few jobs were open to women. When they did find employment, women were often paid half what men earned for the same work. Few colleges and universities of the time admitted female students, and women could not serve on a jury. Individually, the limitations were blatantly unfair; together, they were an unjust system of discrimination. An entire gender was marginalized both by law and custom.[6]

> "Historian Gerda Lerner has pointed out that
> religious ideas provided a fundamental source
> for the *Declaration of Sentiments*. Most of the
> women attending the convention were active
> in Quaker or evangelical Methodist
> movements. The document itself drew from
> writings by the evangelical Quaker Sarah
> Grimke to make biblical claims that God had
> created woman equal to man and that man
> had usurped God's authority by establishing
> absolute tyranny' over woman."[7]

Why did this meeting take place in Seneca Falls, New York? Seneca Falls, located in central New York State had 4,000 citizens in 1848. With connections to the railroad and the Erie Canal, the town had more business and influence than one might think today. Apart from the fact that the five organizers lived in the local area, one can only speculate as to why they located their first meeting here. Perhaps, they wanted to avoid the glare of the media and certain opposition they might encounter in a larger city. Perhaps, they wanted a practice run. The latter reason seems to be logical since detailed planning for the meeting started only after the notices about the convention appeared. The *Declaration of Sentiments* had not yet been composed.

It is significant that Seneca Falls was very reform minded with both active antislavery and temperance societies. Abolition was a hot topic in the town, though the support was not unanimous. It may surprise the current reader that Northern abolitionists often faced bitter opposition and even persecution. The Wesleyan Methodist church was well known for its opposition to slavery. An example occurred in1843, the year the Wesleyan Chapel was built when Seneca Falls was consumed by controversy. Abby Kelley, an organizer for the American Anti-Slavery Society, announced her intention to create a local chapter in the village. Rhoda Bement, a local woman, asked her minister to announce a future Kelley lecture during their Presbyterian Church service.

Unfortunately, this request resulted in the public trial and excommunication of Bement from the congregation for her not following church protocol by having her husband speak for her. Later in 1844, Bement and her supporters searched for a new church community and converted to Wesleyan Methodism. They began worshiping in the Wesleyan Chapel.[8,9]

Similarly, a temperance paper, the *Water Bucket*, began publication in Seneca Falls in February 1842. Two months later, the town voted to prohibit the sale of alcohol. According to McMillen, the ban created, "an immediate and positive impact on the community. Drinking and crime dropped significantly. Most businessmen and factory owners welcomed the new law, which promised greater worker productivity and a sober citizenry."[10]

Seneca Falls illustrates the contemporaneous intertwining of two main topics that predate women's rights; namely, the abolitionist crusade and the temperance movement. Prior to 1848, women's rights advocates had been steeped in antislavery and anti-alcohol positions. For example, both Lucretia Mott and Elizabeth Cady Stanton were well known for speaking for abolition and temperance. Conversely, a person who was either pro-alcohol or pro-slavery, was invariably anti-women's rights. Thus, for much of the 19th century, it was often impossible to separate out women's right to vote from the other two issues.

Sally McMillen reflects:

> "The Seneca Falls convention of 1848 and its *Declaration of Rights and Sentiments* could have been of little consequence. Instead, this meeting and its articulated concerns became a springboard, generating an enormous effort by determined activists who dedicated their lives to the cause of women's rights."[11]

Why did the meeting take place in the Wesleyan Methodist church? This church, now preserved by the United States National Parks Service, is called the "Wesleyan Chapel." In 1848, it was the largest religious sanctuary in Seneca Falls. A current park monument refers to the historical women's rights structure as the "great lighthouse." The congregation of the church was known for its willingness to allow speakers with a commitment to social and moral reform. Shortly before the women rights convention, Frederick Douglass had spoken against slavery on May 4, 1848. He would speak many more times at the Wesleyan Chapel. It was not by accident that the venue for the first women's rights convention was held in a Wesleyan Methodist Church.

References
Chapter One

1. Black R, Drury K. The Story of the Wesleyan Church. Indianapolis: Wesleyan Publishing House; 2012, p. 52.
2. Douglass, F. The Life and Times of Frederick Douglass. New York City: Start Publishing; 1882, 93% location.
3. McMillen, SG. Seneca Falls and the Origins of the Women's Rights Movement. (Pivotal Moments in American History) The University of Chicago Press. 2008, location 29%.
4. Black, p 54.
5. Wellman, J. The Road to Seneca Falls: Elizabeth Cady Stanton and the First Women's Rights Convention. Chicago: University of Illinois Press; 2004, location 67%.
6. Black, p 53.
7. Seneca Falls Convention. Page Version ID: 683627756 ed: Wikipedia, The Free Encyclopedia; 2015.
8. nps.gov/wori/learn/historyculture/wesleyan-chapel-rehabilitation-project.htm [accessed 10-8-2015].
9. Altschuler, GC, Saltzgaber, JM. Revivalism, Social Conscience, and Community in the Burned-over District: The Trial of Rhoda Bement: Cornell University Press; 1983.
10. McMillen, location 26%.
11. McMillen, location 59%.

The Roman Empire existed for a thousand years, spanning 500 BC to 500 AD. The literature and archeology are voluminous. The examples in this chapter illustrate the attitudes towards Roman girls, women and slaves. The low status of women in the Empire is greatly improved by Christianity in the first century AD and continues to progress through the High Middle Ages. Slavery also disappears in Christian lands from 500 AD to 1500 AD.

WOMEN IN THE ROMAN EMPIRE

"If it is a boy, rear it; if it is a girl, throw it out." The Roman Empire historian William Harris asserts, "There cannot be any more striking quotation from the world of [Roman] papyri."[1]

The *patria potesta,* or father's power over the Roman family was complete and absolute. This domain extended to his children and wife. The father exercised complete control over all his family members, even the right of capital punishment. If they angered him, he had the legal right to disown his children, sell them into slavery or even kill them. The father also decided whether to keep newborn babies. Shortly after birth, the midwife would bring the newborn and lay it at his feet. If accepted, good and well; if not, the baby was exposed – deliberately abandoned outside. Roman culture was adamant that corpses not exist within city walls, so the baby would be taken outside the city to the municipal dump by a slave and left to die. Absurdly, Roman law forbid a father from killing his child; but it did not act against parents who allowed their baby to die from exposure.

Some babies so discarded were taken and raised for sale as a slave. Roman law was on the side of the rescuers having legal control of the baby. If the adult raising the child was a freeman or freewoman, the baby could be raised as slave or free, with the state recognizing the final decision.

The practice of infanticide in the Roman Empire has instigated many debates and has nearly developed into its own academic subject.[2] Some historians have tried to distinguish abandonment of newborns from the possible outcome of infanticide.[2] However, the current author raises a logical objection: if the family believed the baby was going to be picked up by someone else and not die, they would have referred to the process as "surreptitious adoption" not "abandonment." It seems commonsense to consider abandonment and infanticide as two sides of the same coin.

There is no doubt infanticide took place in the Roman Empire. Rather, was it common? Or uncommon? (10%, or one in ten births, defining the threshold for the prevalence of abandonment as "common").[2] Again, numbers are elusive, but Harris has argued the practice was common. Picking up abandoned newborns was a major source of resupplying the large number of slaves required by the Roman Empire.[3]

With 200,000 inhabitants, Ephesus was the second largest city in the Empire, after Rome, in the first and second centuries AD. Its city trash dump must have occupied several square miles where fires smoldered, and odors nauseated. There was rotting debris unfit for dogs. It was here that Ephesians left their unwanted newborns to die of exposure. Mostly females, some normal, some deformed, but all left to suffer and die. Early Christians traversed this Dantesque hell straining to hear the feeble cries of the little ones. Given the treacherous terrain and poisonous air, it is likely that only one baby could be rescued on each foray. One can imagine a group of men and women standing outside the dump taking turns reentering hell, while others stayed behind giving sponge baths and nursing the nearly dead infants. A few years later in the *agora* (marketplace) of Ephesus, a Christian woman with three or four children tugging at her hemline, moves about shopping. She no longer pays attention to the prolonged gazes of some Ephesian mothers who try to detect a daughter who might have been. Perhaps, nothing else illustrated to the local pagan population the changed ethic of the new, but outlawed, religion. For babies picked up by slavers or Christians, the respective outcomes could not contrast more--a life of slavery or freedom.[a]

Another resonating fact about the thousand-year Roman Empire is the recent discovery of the earliest known letter written in Latin by a woman to another woman (100 AD); this was excavated from Vindolanda, England.[4] Made of birch bark, the tablet letter is an invitation to the prefect [commander] Cerialus' wife, Sulpicia Lepidina, to attend a birthday party. It translates:

"Claudia Severa to her Lepidina greetings.
On 11 September, sister, for the day of the
celebration of my birthday, I give you a warm
invitation to make sure that you come to us, to
make the day more enjoyable for me by your
arrival, if you are present (?), Give my
greetings to your Cerialis. My Aelius and my
little son send him (?) their greetings. (2nd
hand) I shall expect you, sister. Farewell,
sister, my dearest soul, as I hope to prosper,
and hail. (Back, 1st hand) To Sulpicia
Lepidina, wife of Cerialis, from Severa."[5]

---

[a] This historical story has been given by Dr Stowall, President of Cornerstone University. (Trash Heap of Ephesus. In: Stowell J, ed. The Dawning: Christianity in the Roman Empire DVD series. Grand Rapids, Michigan: RBC Ministries; 2011). Harris provides plausibility (Harris WV. Child-Exposure in the Roman Empire. The Journal of Roman Studies 1994;84; p. 1-22). "In many instances Christians rescued exposed infants, baptized them, and brought them up." Will Durant – a secular historian (Christ and Caesar, 1943, p. 598).

Roman men wrote thousands of letters in the first 500 years of the Empire that still exist. Even after the Vindolanda period, there are only a few Latin letters extant from Roman women.[6] Histories speak of the rarely seen status of aristocratic women. It is one thing to state that upper class Roman women lived secluded lives, but the paucity of surviving correspondence by Empire women helps us feel that isolation.

In this fort in the hinterland of northern Britain, we can quantity male versus female correspondence. The Vindolanda tablets represent a cross sectional analysis that is possible because a denominator can be ascertained. Women wrote on four tablets. The total number of tablets recovered so far at Vindolanda is 456; thus, 4/456 (less than 1 in a 100) of the tablets are written by women, or at least have their signature affixed in their own cursive style. Isolation indeed.

One might ask, what was the literacy rate of Roman men and women? Determining the literacy rate of ancient populations is difficult. Even the definition of literacy is a challenge. Illiteracy is easier to define. Harris uses the UNESCO definition of "someone who cannot with understanding both read and write a short simple statement on his everyday life."[7] Even so, in the most literate city in the late Empire, Teos, only 30-40% of freeborn men could read and write. The understanding of the literacy of freeborn women is even sketchier, but Harris estimates that fewer than 5% (or 1 in 20) of women could read or write. Western provinces were even lower with 15%, or 1 in 6, men literate and far fewer women.[8] The latter figures are reinforced by the fact that no journals or personal diaries of Roman women have survived.

Lower class women, of course, had to enter society to earn a living. But they, like the slaves discussed below, are invisible in written records; moreover, in archeological sites we have only basic physical findings about women in the Roman Empire.

The sociologist Rodney Stark[b] concludes,
> "Although some classical writers claimed that
> women were easy prey for any 'foreign
> superstition,' most recognized that
> Christianity was unusually appealing because
> within the Christian subculture women
> enjoyed far higher status than did women in
> the Greco-Roman world at large."[9]

SLAVERY IN THE ROMAN EMPIRE

Slaves are invisible in the archeological record because they did not own anything. Some ancient sources assert slaves outnumbered free citizens in many cities.[10] Overall, most demographers think that about one in four inhabitants of the Roman Empire were slaves; but even the free population is in dispute.

According to Strabo, ancient Greek geographer and historian, the appetite of the Roman Empire for slaves was enormous. A large slave market on Delos (a Greek island) sold 10,000 slaves per day (circa 100 BC). The staggering number has caused some to question Strabo's statement on *a priori* basis as hyperbole.[c]

However, these skeptical authors supply no rational reasons to discredit Strabo's assertion. On the other hand,

---

[b] At the time Stark wrote this paragraph in 1996, he referred to himself as an "agnostic." However, in an interview with Massimo Introvigne in 2007, he said he had [recently] become an "independent [i.e., nondenominational] Christian." A Christmas Conversation with Rodney Stark (http://www.cesnur.org/2007/mi_stark.htm) (Accessed 6-8-2016).

[c] see for example, Scheidel W. The Roman Slave Supply. In: Bradley K, ed. Cambridge World History of Slavery, The Ancient Mediterranean World Cambridge University Press; 2007) In searching for possible scientific plausibility, the current author notes that Delos had a very large infrastructure during the time in question that makes the large trade in slaves entirely plausible. (http://whc.unesco.org/en/list/530 Delos-World Heritage Site accessed May 14, 2016)

Professor Greg Woolf, in his 2012 book, *Rome: An Empire's Story*, upon thoughtful evaluation of the ancient slave market of Delos, asserts "Strabo got it right."[11] The importance of Delos as a slave market faded after it was sacked in 69 BC. Rome and Ephesus became the largest slave market thereafter.[8]

Slavery in the Roman Empire could be pleasant or painful. An example of the first would be working as a Greek tutor in aristocratic households; an apex of slave experience that was rare.

A painful experience was much more common. The Roman Empire consumed huge amounts of metals such as silver, gold, and lead. Davies has elegantly mapped out 1,005 of the "important" mining sites of the Roman Empire that range from the British Isles to Macedonia.[12] [d] An estimate of the number of slaves needed to work these 1,005 mines cannot be calculated; the possibilities are staggering.

Pliny (23 to 79 AD) tells us that 20,000 slaves worked in the Rio Tinto mines or nearby towns of southern Spain. The Rio Tinto mines were among the largest mines in the Empire. While women slaves did not enter the narrow tunnels, on the surface of the mine they unceasingly chipped ore with hammers to increase the concentration of metal before it was smelted. Exploration for lead, copper, and silver involved pick and shovel creation of vertical shafts 30 inches wide that were sunk up to 150 feet deep. If the shaft found a vein of rich metal ore, internal galleries were cut horizontally that were 24 inches x 40 inches wide; these tunnels branched out hundreds of feet. Men crawled into these narrow shafts to chip ore while boys retrieved the ore with grass baskets. Water seepage into the tunnels and drowning of the miner was a constant threat. Water wheels, 16 feet in diameter,

---

[d] The number of mining sites on each of six maps was tallied by the current author. This list is incomplete: it does not include the Middle East or Africa!

contained a central cubicle in which slaves trudged all day like a rat in a cage. The multiple wheels in vertical sequence extracted the water seeping into the mine back up 114 feet onto the surface. Ventilation was problematic with damp air reacting with sulfide deposits creating sulfur dioxide and other poisonous gases.[13] Given the huge production of lead ore by manual methods, the reader can easily calculate scores of slaves who died every day from poisonous gas fumes or collapsing tunnels.[e]

An 1896 survey tallied 18 million tons of slag ore around the mines. Slag is the residual rock waste after the ore has been removed from the smelter. Human bones have been found in the slag heaps indicating the corpses of slaves were thrown out on the slag and not even buried.[14]

The introduction of Christianity made a difference. The Pauline letter to the slave owner Philemon leaves no doubt about the uneasiness early Christians felt about slavery. The logic is obvious. Paul asks Philemon for the release of the Christian slave Onesimus by telling him to treat Onesimus- "No longer as a slave, but better than a slave, as a dear brother" (Philemon 16).

The secular historian, Phillip Daileader, tells us that women and slaves were attracted to Christianity because of its egalitarian nature,

> "In the first three centuries of Christianity's existence, it appealed more strongly to some groups in Roman society than others. Christianity appealed to people alienated in various ways from Roman civilization and unable to participate fully in it. A

---

[e] The production of lead was so great in Rio Tinto that it contaminated upper level atmospheric clouds. In the 1990s, a three-kilometer-long ice core drilled in Greenland revealed that 70% of the lead in the core dated between 150 BC and 50 AD had the chemical signature of Rio Tinto, more than 2,500 miles away. (Yeoman B. The Mines that Built Empires. Archaeology 2010;63; p. 20-5).

> disproportionate number of women, slaves,
> freedmen and freedwomen, and immigrants
> could be found among the early Christians"[15]

The classless nature of early Christianity led increasingly to the question: how can one person own another? The core of the matter was that Christianity recognized the personhood of the slave and not the tool status of the human.

The apostle Paul laid the early foundation for the abolition of slavery in Galatians 3:28, where he states, "there is neither slave nor free." Following the exhortation of Paul, numerous wealthy Christians freed slaves.

> "Some examples: St. Melania emancipated
> 8,000 slaves; St. Ovidius, in Gaul, released
> 5,000; Chromatius, a Roman prefect under
> Diocletian, freed 1,400; and Hermes set 1,200
> free. Many of the Christian clergy at Hippo,
> under the rule of St. Augustine (5th century),
> along with many lay people, freed their slaves
> as an act of piety…and in the 6th century
> Emperor Justinian (527-567) abolished all
> laws that prevented the freeing of slaves."[16]

INTRODUCTION TO THE MIDDLE AGES

The so-called Dark Ages, known here as the Middle Ages, consist of the one thousand years of Western history between 500 and 1500 AD; this period witnessed the abolition of slavery, the liberation of women, artistic achievements of medieval cathedrals, inventions of the printing press, the musical scale, and the mechanical clock.[17]

The whole construct of the Middle Ages is an arbitrary division created during the Italian Renaissance of the 14th century. The historian, Petrarch (1303-1374) perceived a long separation of time that separated his time from the classical period. It was necessary for the Roman Empire to "fall" in order to create a starting point. Petrarch, while he did not use the actual term, referred to an intervening period that later authors denoted as the Middle Ages: "a time of decline into darkness from which the Renaissance thinkers could [then] emerge [triumphantly]."[18] [f] Only the classical period of the Roman or Greek Empires was deemed worthy of study. Anything subsequent would be uncouth. The beauty of the gothic became passé, but only by the subjective hubris of the Renaissance.

Many popular historians use the pejorative term "the Dark Ages" as a label for the millennium of the Middle Ages. The usage of the term "Dark Ages" occurs two ways; one, it has come to mean a lack of written information. This usage is no longer credible since there are abundant archives still untouched and archeology of the period has barely scratched the surface. Worse, many popular historians would have us believe that it was a time of cultural darkness. This is wrong on at least two counts. One, it shows an incredible narrowness of outlook to ignore the Byzantium Empire which carries on Roman Civilization in Eastern Europe.[19] The far bigger and wealthier eastern Roman Empire (after all this is what the Byzantine Empire was) lasts until Constantinople was sacked by the Turks in 1453. Contemporary occupants living in the eastern Empire that survived after Rome was sacked in 455 AD considered themselves "Roman citizens" not "Byzantines". Two, it ignores the unique development of universities in Western Europe which have as their purpose the development of new knowledge.[20] Finally, it ignores the rich documentation that Regine Pernoud has brought alive from the French National Archives concerning the Middle Ages; and for which, there remains a huge depository yet to be examined.

---

[f] Hale is speaking in sarcastic tones here.

REGINE PERNOUD, FRENCH WOMEN'S HISTORIAN

The current author is indebted to Regine Pernoud for her descriptions of women, slavery and serfdom during the Middle Ages in France. Curiously, American historians seem completely unaware of Pernoud's careful historical works.[g]

Regine Pernoud (1909-1998) received a Doctorate in Literature from the prestigious École du Louvre. She became curator at the Museum of the History of France in 1949, and then at the National Archives of France. She was a pioneer women's historian, archivist/paleographer and medievalist.

France serves as an ideal subject for longitudinal study of the Middles Ages as it is the only political entity in Europe to exist roughly the same over 1300 years (Charlemagne 800 AD to now) and for which records have been collected and stored.

A summary of Pernoud's position[21] is that as the Roman Empire dissolved over three centuries (from the fifth to the eighth centuries AD); the associated political entities that succeeded Rome replaced classical law with feudal law; the switch to feudal law progressively became more favorable to women and culminated in the disappearance of slavery in Europe by the High Middle Ages (1000 AD to 1300 AD). For example, in the High Middle Ages, there are numerous original archival papers showing the practice of voting throughout France by women. The language used in the documents indicate suffrage was an ordinary practice and not sensational.

Slaves were gradually replaced by serfs or their positions disappeared entirely. Contrary to popular belief,

---

[g] Google Scholar has only 18 citations of her translated English book: Those Terrible Middle Ages: Debunking the Myths, accessed on 5-12-2016)

serfdom, while not as high of a status as a freedman, was nevertheless a substantial step up from slavery.

French society in the 15th to 17th centuries formed a strong central government under Roman law. Over time, the revived approach led to the elimination of most privileges for women in France; such as, the right to vote and own a business or property. When educational efforts began again in earnest after the 14th century, girls no longer went to primary school and French Universities allowed only men. The irony is that French women would not enjoy the privileges they had in the 11th to the 13th centuries again until the 20th century.

Similarly, reasoning contained within Roman law allowed the re-institution of slavery in the 16th century. This was a form of slavery that was particularly virulent. Or, put in another way, one that is in total discordance with the popular triumphal view of the Renaissance, (i.e., the revival of Roman culture and law-which is what the "renaissance" or "revival" was bringing back). The period of the Renaissance resulted in a marked degeneration of the status of women and Africans becoming ensnarled by slavery. This is hardly a crescendo of cultural progress as portrayed by popular histories of the Renaissance.

The foregoing then is the summary of Pernoud's viewpoint. Now the particulars will be cited.

SLAVERY IN THE MIDDLE AGES

"Slavery is probably the one thing about civilization that most profoundly marks ancient societies. Now it is curious, when one glances through history textbooks, to note the discretion with which this is brought up; whether it is a question of the disappearance of slavery at the very beginning of the High Middle Ages or its abrupt reappearance at the beginning of the sixteenth century, one witnesses a rare restraint on this subject. If

one amuses oneself, as I have done, by going
through school textbooks for high school
classes, one observes that none of them points
out the progressive disappearance of slavery
from the fourth century on. They mention
medieval serfdom in very severe terms but
pass over in silence the rather paradoxical
return of slavery in the sixteenth century. For
a simple mind, there is something surprising
about that; it seems difficult to deny that
ancient society considered slavery to be
natural and necessary."[22][h]

What we find in the early Middle Ages is the
replacement of slavery by serfdom. Agricultural work still
needed to be done.

"The substitution of serfdom for slavery is
without a doubt the social fact that best
emphasizes the disappearance of the influence
of Roman law, and of Roman mentality, in
Western societies from the fifth and sixth
centuries on"[22]

Serfs were different from slaves,

"Serfdom was a state, tied to an essentially
rural and land-based mode of life; it obeyed
agricultural imperatives and, above all, that
necessary stability that a land-based culture
implies. In the society we see come into being
during the sixth and seventh centuries, life
was organized around the soil that nourishes,
and the serf was the one of whom stability
was demanded: he had to remain on the
domain; he was obliged to cultivate, to dig,
rake, sow, and also harvest; for if he was
forbidden to leave this land, he knew that he

---

[h] I have chosen to quote Regine Pernoud extensively rather than
summarize. The Pernoudian sentences are a work of art, even when
translated into English.

would have his part of its harvest. In other
words, the lord of the domain could not expel
him any more than the serf could 'clear out.'
It was this intimate connection between man
and the soil on which he lived that constituted
serfdom, for, in all other respects, the serf had
all the rights of the free man: he could marry,
establish a family, his land, as well as the
goods he was able to acquire, would pass to
his children after his death. The lord, let us
note, had, although obviously on a totally
different scale, the same obligations as the
serf, for he could neither sell nor give up his
land nor desert it. The situation of the serf, as
we see, was radically different and in no way
comparable to that of the slave, who did not
have the right to marry or establish a family
or to avail himself in any way of the dignity
of the human person: he was an object that
could be bought and sold and over which the
power of another man, his master, was
unlimited."[22]

Nonetheless, in a hierarchical society like that of the
Middle Ages, it was better to be a freedman than a serf.
For a free man, especially a noble, to marry a serf was to
demean oneself. As a result, one sought hard to extricate
oneself from serfdom, often by purchasing one's
independence. The Church used money to purchase
freedom for many and otherwise encouraged the
emancipation of serfs.

"Whatever might have been the advantages
and the drawbacks, there was a great distance
between medieval serfdom and the
renaissance of slavery that was abruptly
produced in the sixteenth century in the
colonies of America. Now, that was a matter
of real slavery, of persons considered and
treated as things, sold and shipped as cargo of

> ordinary merchandise. It was this very return
> to slavery determined by colonial expansion
> that characterized the classical period. And as
> in antiquity, the humanism esteemed during
> that period [i.e., Renaissance] does not seem
> to have brought any attention to that portion
> of humanity that was enslaved…Yet it seems
> unquestionable that the renewed influence of
> antiquity played a part in justifying this
> unjustifiable commerce. When, in the first
> half of the sixteenth century, controversies set
> the Dominicans like Bartolome de Las Casas
> or Vitoria against the lawyers of Salamanca,
> these latter took as their authority the example
> of the *Pax Romana* to combat the arguments
> of the religious that denounced before the
> king of Spain the iniquity of the wars of
> conquest and of proslavery politics. Their
> efforts [i.e., the Dominicans] were not going
> to stop the peoples of Europe from
> subjugating those of America, Africa, and
> then in part of Asia to reap economic and
> political profits from them."[23]

During the 1430s, the Spanish were responsible for
reintroducing slavery in the West by bringing it to the
Canary Islands. When word reached Pope Eugene IV
(1431-1447), he threatened to excommunicate any
complicit person, and directed those involved,

> "to restore to their earlier liberty all and each
> person of either sex who were once residents
> of said Canary Islands…These people are to
> be totally and perpetually free and are to be
> let go without the exaction or reception of any
> money."[24]

Over the next two hundred years, the Catholic Church
repeatedly condemned slavery. The problem was that the
church had lost its political power and was left with only

moral persuasion. "Few heard [the church] and most of them did not listen."[24]

The current author could not find any official pronouncements of the Church of England against slavery.[i] Nonetheless, some Anglican priests, notably, John Newton, became opponents. Before becoming an Anglican priest, he captained numerous slave ships plying the Atlantic in the 18th century. He is best known for his lyrics of "Amazing Grace" written after his conversion to Christianity. Newton became a staunch opponent of slavery. Upon hearing falsehoods asserted in the British Parliament describing how pleasant the passage was for African slaves crossing the Atlantic to the New World, he published his slave trade memoirs, *Thoughts upon the African Slave Trade*, to help offset the disinformation campaign in Parliament.

John Fox and the Quakers in England began protesting slavery in the 17th century. John Wesley along with other evangelicals added opposition in the 18th century. However, these groups were part of the "dissenters" classification (i.e., not Church of England) and were outside the main political power structure.

WOMEN IN THE MIDDLE AGES

But what were the activities of the more ordinary woman?

"We have yet to speak of women who were neither great ladies nor abbesses nor even nuns: peasants and townswomen, mothers of families and women practicing a trade. It goes without saying that, to be treated correctly, such questions would demand several volumes and would also require preliminary works that have not been written. It would be indispensable to explore not only collections

[i] That does not mean there are none. More work needs to be done.

of customs and town statutes but also the enormous mass of notarial acts, in the south especially, cartularies, legal documents… we find there, taken from everyday life, thousands of small details, gleaned by chance and without any preconceived order, which show us men and women through the small facts of existence: here the complaint of a woman hairdresser, there of a woman salt merchant (trading in salt), of a woman miller, of the widow of a farmer…It is through documents of this kind that one can, piece by piece, reconstruct, as in a mosaic, the real story…The picture that comes into focus from the whole of these [official governmental archival] documents presents for us more than one surprising trait, since one sees, for example, women voting like men in urban assemblies or those of rural parishes. The vote of women was not expressly mentioned everywhere, but that may be because the necessity for doing so was not obvious. When texts allow us to differentiate the origin of the votes, we see that, in regions as different as the Bearn parishes, certain villages of Champagne, and certain eastern cities like Pont-a-Mousson, or even in Touraine at the time of the Estate-General of 1308, women are explicitly named among the voters, without anything being said to imply it was usage particular to the locality…In notarial acts, it is very common to see a married woman act by herself, in opening, for example, a shop or a trade, and she did so without being obliged to produce her husband's authorization. Finally, the tax rolls, when they have been preserved for us, as in the case of Paris at the end of the thirteenth century, show a host of women plying trades: schoolmistress, doctor, apothecary, plasterer, dyer, copyist, miniaturist, binder, and so on"[29]

What about the idea that the church was hostile to women? Pernoud responds,

"We will not pause here to take up the whole of a question that would necessitate a volume by itself; neither will we go on to discuss the obvious nonsense that has been uttered in this regard. 'It was only in the fifteenth century that the Church admitted that women had a soul.' This statement was candidly affirmed one day on the radio by some writer of fiction who was no doubt motivated by good intentions but whose information showed proof of several lacunae! So, for centuries, soul-less beings were baptized, confessed, and admitted to the Eucharist! How strange that the first martyrs honored as saints were women and not men: Saint Agnes, Saint Cecilia, Saint Agatha, and so many others. How truly sad that Saint Blandine and Saint Genevieve were deprived of immortal souls."[27]

Unfortunately, the church, at times in history when it is less redemptive, reflects the views of the secular society in which it exists.

"It suffices to say that the status of women in the Church is exactly the same as their status in civil society and that gradually, after the Middle Ages, everything that conferred on them any autonomy, any independence, any instruction, was taken away from them. Now, at the very time when the University—which admitted only men—was trying to concentrate knowledge and teaching, convents gradually ceased to be those centers of study that they had been previously…Women thus found themselves excluded from ecclesial life just as from intellectual life."[28]

A fact that speaks volumes on the loss of the personal autonomy of the woman: "It was only in the 17th century that it became obligatory for women to take their husband's name."[25] The "influence [of women] diminished in direct proportion to the rise of Roman law in juridical studies, then in institutions, and finally in customs. It was a progressive obliteration, whose principal stages in France at least, one can follow very easily."[26]

THE BLACK DEATH

Enter the curse of the Black Death. The Black Death was a severe worldwide pandemic that affected Western Europe from 1347-1350 AD. The bubonic plague was caused by fleas infected by the bacterium *Yersinia pestis*; these fleas were carried by rats. In three years, the population of Europe was cut in half from an estimated 150 million to 75 million people! The devastation to society and church has never been equaled before or since.[30]

Priests became so scarce that the Archbishop of Canterbury authorized that dying confessions could be made to any Christian man or woman. This was not far from precedent as midwives had long been authorized to perform baptism rites for babies who would die before a priest could arrive.[31] The best monks and nuns were given to visitation of those dying with the plaque. The Black Death spared no one, including clergy. It is unsurprising that many monasteries and abbeys suffered 100% mortality. Numerous convents and monasteries simply vanished, institutions which had offered universal education of both girls and boys.

The social loss and upheaval was so great that it was as if a reset button had been pushed. The result to the church was that those clergy who kept loving their flock, probably died to a far greater degree than the inauthentic clergy who ran to save their lives. The loss to the church hierarchy of the best and brightest for the same reasons also took place. Unfortunately, the Great Pestilence did not come once; it returned again and again every 10-20 years for the next four centuries. While it only killed 5-10% of the population on later visits, the cumulative effect was to create a low-quality clergy that often was not literate; or, there was not enough time for accepted priests to undergo the trial observation of their moral life.[j] This loss of the best and brightest clergy of the existing ecclesiastical authority was an important development leading to the Protestant Reformation in the 16th century.

Similarly, the faithful government officials who stayed to perform their functions during plague outbreaks also suffered a higher mortality. Craven officials ran. In either case, many local town councils ceased to exist. The result led to a concentration of the few remaining competent officials into strong central governments. For lack of any other models of administration, centralized regimes reintroduced Roman law.

CONCLUSION

In this brief sampling of the history of Rome and the Middle Ages, nothing better illustrates the low esteem the patriarchal Roman Empire society had for women than the practice of infanticide; the victims of which were mostly female. Renaissance and Enlightenment writers praise the humanism of the classical period but fail to note the viciousness of slavery and denigration of women.

---

[j] In Winchester, England in 1349, 27 new members of the clergy were ordained sub-deacons, deacons, and then priests all in the space of a few days—rather than the years normally required for this advancement. They were then sent out to their parishes and church offices with virtually no experience.[31]

In contrast, Christianity in Western Europe began to progressively eliminate slavery from 500 to 1000 AD; it then was absent until the 15th century. Slavery was otherwise universal worldwide during the same time.[32] Improvement in the treatment of women also takes place during the same millennium. However, the zenith of privileges for women, such as voting or autonomy in business, reaches a peak in the High Middle ages and begins to erode.

The Black Death was a disease so devastating that it pushed a reset button between the High Middle Ages (1000 to 1350 AD) and the Late Middle Ages (1350-1500 AD). One response was the redevelopment of strong central governments utilizing Roman jurisprudence.

The decline in women's rights correlates with the reinstatement of Roman law. Unfortunately, the church, for reasons that need much more research, also absorbed the prevailing secular attitudes towards women in the 14th through 17th centuries. Nevertheless, Christian women were still better off than their non-Christian counterparts.[k]

Fortunately, a clarion call to return to early Christian practices revived staunch opposition to slavery and reignited fire for the civil and ecclesiastical rights of women.

---

[k] Hindu priests complained to General Sir Charles Napier, commander-in-chief of India, (circa 1848) about the prohibition of "sati" by British authorities. Sati was the custom of burning a widow alive on the funeral pyre of her husband. When confronted, Napier replied, "It is your custom to burn widows. Very well. We also have a custom: when men burn a woman alive, we tie a rope around their necks and hang them. Build your funeral pyre and beside it my carpenters will build gallows. You may follow your national custom - then we shall follow ours." The ritual of sati was suppressed. It seems few widows still wished to "volunteer." (Paxman J. Empire: Penguin UK; 2012, p. 85) See also: (*Life in India: The Practice of Sati or Widow Burning;* http://www.kashgar.com.au/articles/life-in-india-the-practice-of-sati-or-widow-burning).

Chapter Two
References

1. Harris WV. Towards a Study of the Roman Slave Trade. In: John H, Kopff EC, eds. The seaborne commerce of ancient Rome: studies in archaeology and history. American Academy in Rome: American Academy in Rome; 1980, p. 123.
2. Parkin TG. Demography and Roman Society: Cambridge Univ Press; 1992, p. 95
3. Harris WV. Demography, Geography and the Sources of Roman Slaves. The Journal of Roman Studies 1999; 89; pp. 62-75.
4. Birley R. Vindolanda: A Roman Frontier Fort on Hadrian's Wall. Amberley Publishing Limited; 2012, location 31%.
5. Vindolanda Tablet 291. In: (http://vindolanda.csad.ox.ac.uk/4DLink2/4DACTION/WebRequestQuery?searchTerm=291&searchType=number&searchField=TVII) 2003 (Accessed January 14, 2018).
6. Knapp R. Invisible Romans: Harvard University Press; 2011.
7. Harris WV. Ancient literacy: Harvard University Press; 1991, p. 3
8. Ibid, p. 65-115, 329.
9. Stark R. The Rise of Christianity: How the Obscure, Marginal Jesus Movement Became the Dominant Religious Force in the Western World in a few Centuries: Harper Collins; 1997, p. 95
10. Hale J. Lecture Thirty-One. Slaves-A Silent Majority? Chantilly, VA: The Great Courses; 2006, p. 200
11. Woolf G. Rome: An Empire's Story. New York: Oxford University Press; 2012, p. 92
12. Davies O. Roman Mines in Europe: Clarendon Press; 1935, (maps at back of book).

13. Rio Tinto History: Romans. In: http://www.andalucia.com/province/huelva/riotinto/history-romans.htm (Accessed January 15, 2018).

14. Yeoman B. The Mines that Built Empires. Archaeology 2010;63; pp. 20-5.

15. Daileader P. Constantine the Great-Christian Emperor. Early Middle Ages. Chantilly, VA: The Great Courses; 2004: p. 11.

16. Schmidt AJ. Slavery, Abolition of. The Encyclopedia of Christian Civilization: Blackwell Publishing Ltd; 2012: p. 1.

17. Buckley C. Foreward. Those Terrible Middle Ages! Debunking the Myths. San Francisco: Ignatius; 197, p. 7.

18. Hale J. Lecture Thirty-Five. The End of the World-a Coroner's Report. The Great Courses; 2006, pp. 224-230

19. Januszczak W. The Dark Ages: An Age of Light: ZCZ Films, BBC; 2013.

20. Stark R. How the West Won: The Neglected Story of the Triumph of Modernity: Open Road Media; 2014, pp. 163-169

21. Pernoud R. Those Terrible Middle Ages: Debunking the Myths. San Francisco: Ignatius Press; 2000.

22. Ibid, pp. 85-88.

23. Ibid, p. 95

24. Stark R. For the Glory of God: How Monotheism led to Reformations, Science, Witch-hunts, and the End of Slavery: Princeton University Press; 2015, p. 332

25. Tournier P. The Gift of Feeling: Westminster John Knox Press; 1981, p. 20

26. Pernoud, p. 100.

27 Pernoud, p. 104.

28. Pernoud, pp. 108-109.

29. Pernoud, p. 111.

30. Armstrong D. The Black Death: The World's Most Devastating Plague. Great Courses; 2016, p. 1.

31. Armstrong D. Lecture 16. Plague's Effect on the Medieval Church.. The Great Courses; 2016, p. 115

32. Stark, How the West Won…, location 26%.

Chapter Three Wesley and Women

John Wesley (1703-1791) founded the spiritual renewal movement within the Church of England, known as Methodism, during the 18th century. "Methodist" was a negative tag to mock early adherents; however, the term stuck as it aptly described their approach to Christian living. Remaining an Anglican priest until his death, Wesley did not intend to start a new denomination. The renewal movement within the Anglican Church, and the outside revivals springing from it, gave birth to the Methodist family of churches worldwide. Modern Wesleyans look to John Wesley as a reformer and spiritual forefather.

For an Englishman of the 18th century, Wesley was of an average height and weight at five feet six inches and 120 pounds. In all his portraits, he has shoulder length hair, a keen eye and clear complexion. In 1738, Wesley dated his spiritual awakening to a church service in Aldersgate Street in London where he felt his heart "strangely warmed." As an Oxford Fellow, he spoke with a large vocabulary, though he strove to make himself understandable to the masses to whom he preached Christianity. He taught logic and Greek at Oxford for six years and his writings reflect mastery of both.[a]

His critics charged him with being a "rabble-rouser" and his followers as "enthusiasts."[b] Wesley defended his followers as having a "heart-felt" religion, and not fanaticism.

Our focus here is his interest in social reform as one way for Christians to demonstrate their love for God and neighbor. Wesley's theological and practical impact was to emphasize the doctrines of "free will" (e.g. John 3:16)

---

[a] The reader should obtain a book on the interesting life of John Wesley as more than 40 biographies exist.

[b] "Enthusiast" had an 18th century usage connoting "crackpot."

and the assurance of personal salvation. He also asserted that a Christian could lose their salvation through persistent and willful sinful behavior. These ideas originated with Jacobus Arminius (1560-1609), a Dutch Reformed theologian. However, Wesley went beyond Arminius on holiness and sanctification,

> "Wesley understands entire sanctification as 'love excluding sin.' Scriptural holiness is perfect love; it is a new disposition, a new harmony of spirit, a new mind-set, as it were, displacing the old.' To love God with all the heart and soul and mind, is to leave no place for contrary dispositions . . . His stress on the universal love and grace of God saved him from Calvinism."[1]

Mildred Wynkoop (chapter 20) a 20th century Nazarene theologian and Wesley specialist in the Church of the Nazarene, elaborates further,

> "After any substantial research into John Wesley's writing one becomes aware of the high importance of love to his theology and preaching concerns. No matter which door one enters into his thinking—holiness, sanctification, perfection, cleansing, faith, man, God, salvation, or any other-not only does each of these begin to flow together and intertwine with the others, but the whole channels inevitably into love. Rather than Wesley representing a theology of holiness it would be more faithful to his major emphasis to call it a theology of love."[2]

These ideas stood in opposition to the prevailing theology of John Calvin (1509-1564). The disagreement between Wesleyanism and Calvinism centered around the terms "predestination" and "irresistible grace." Predestination meant that God picked who was going to be saved (i.e., the elect); and as such, one could not resist, or fail to respond to, that grace. Salvation was unobtainable if you were not in the elect. That is, atonement was limited only to the elect. Moreover, one was never certain whether he or she was one of the elect. In early America, strict Calvinists were logical as to their unwillingness to join evangelistic efforts through revival meetings. If one's future had already been determined, why bother?[3]

The pragmatic and unintended effects of strict Calvinism were to reinforce a worldview of a caste-like society; for example, a man was poor because he was destined to be so. Women were fated to have fewer ecclesiastical and social privileges. The practical effects of Wesleyanism were liberating. Free will changed it all. Men or women who repented could help to choose their salvation and future. This idea, combined with knowing the status of one's salvation, fueled the great American revivals of the 19th century. Wesleyanism appealed to the new democratic ideals in ways that Calvinism could not.

THE DEVELOPMENT OF LAYWOMEN PREACHERS

Early in his ministry, John Wesley opposed laymen or laywomen preaching the good news of salvation. Church of England priests needed a college education and evidence of good morals before being ordained as a minister. Ordination typically involves full ministerial rights, including the right to deliver the sacraments (e.g. Lord's Supper) of the Church. The Wesleyan revival in the 1740s swept so many men and women into the "Methodist Connection" that the few Church of England ministers allied with Wesley were overwhelmed in taking care of the new flock. Ever practical, Wesley started to apply a training plan he had learned from the Moravians.[4] His strategy was to subdivide new converts into small same sex groups of 5-6 members or "bands" who would meet weekly to examine their spiritual lives. These groups required leaders. Demographically, women were streaming into the movement at a far greater ratio of 2:1 or more compared to men.

Allowing women to teach women did not violate any conceivable biblical precept. The problem arose when the next division level, the combination of bands into the Methodist "class," a 12-20-member group that contained both men and women. So many classes formed that reliable and experienced male Methodist class leaders were lacking. Wesley installed women class leaders as soon as the need arose. In 1742, the London Society listed 66 class leaders, 49 of whom were women.[5] Wesley reasoned that the encouragement and teaching the class leaders were doing did not constitute preaching in the pulpit.

According to Chilcote, by the middle of the 1740s,

> "The leadership of the movement by this time had evolved into three rather well-defined sections. At the top was John Wesley, surrounded by a small group of Anglican clergy or 'ministers,' including his brother Charles. Directly beneath them, and under their vigilant surveillance was a group of lay preachers, 'helpers' or his 'assistants,' who devoted their full time and energy to the supervision of the societies and the continued expansion of Methodism into previously unevangelized areas. The third and largest group of leaders included the local or non-itinerating preachers, leaders of small groups, sick visitors, stewards, and housekeepers. It was within this sphere that women found the widest range of opportunity and exerted their greatest influence upon the nascent revival. Those areas of leadership and participation which proved to be most significant as a

training ground for the later women preachers were the offices of band and class leader, and sick visitor."[6]

Wesley and the top leadership wrestled with the rationale and development of using laymen preachers, let alone women. The Methodist Conference of 1746 considered the issue and developed three important criteria regarding, "those who believe they are moved by the Holy Spirit and called of God to preach."

1. Do they know whom they have believed? Have they the love of God in their hearts? Do they desire and seek nothing but God? And are they holy in all manner of conversation?

2. Have they *Gifts* (as well as *Grace*) for the work? Have they (in some tolerable degree) a clear [and] sound understanding? Have they a right judgment in the things of God? Have they a just conception of salvation by faith? And has God given them any degree of utterance? Do they speak justly, readily, clearly?

3. Have they success? Do they not only so speak as generally either to convince or affect the hearts? But have any received remission of sins by their preaching? A clear and lasting sense of the love of God? As long as these three marks undeniably occur in any, we allow him to be called of God to preach. These we receive as sufficient reasonable evidence that he is moved thereunto by the Holy Spirit."[7]

Those having these three characteristics of conversion (or grace, gifts and fruit) were placed 'on trial' for one year; at which time, they were further examined by the conference, before being admitted into the "full connection."

Wesley showed continuous change in his lifetime towards the role of women in ministry. Early on, he was opposed to the idea, but circumstances of growing need caused him to experiment by the 1760s. He matured in his thinking and became a strong defender of women ministers in the last three decades of his life. Women who responded to their call from God to minister helped to change Wesley's thinking.

Mary Bosanquet

Mary Bosanquet (1739-1815) became one of the prominent women in Methodism. She was the daughter of wealthy Catholic parents, and it was from a Methodist maid that Mary first heard of the peace that comes with believing. Before she was 20, her father drove her from home because she would not promise to refrain from trying to convert her brothers. She took seriously Wesley's admonition to "give all you can" by using her own money and time to provide for the needy. She opened a shelter in London for the destitute. It grew into a school, orphanage, hospital and halfway house all in one.

Mary Bosanquet became a class leader and then began speaking to groups of even 2,000 to 3,000. Concerned as to whether her activities were proper, she wrote John Wesley on June 13, 1771. He replied,

> "My dear sister, I think the strength of the cause rests there, on your having an extraordinary call. So, I am persuaded as every one of our lay preachers: otherwise, I could not countenance [their] preaching at all. It is plain to me that the whole work of God termed Methodism is an extraordinary dispensation of His providence".[8]

Later, Wesley described Mary's preaching as "fire, conveying both light and heat to all that heard her. . . Her manner of speaking smooth, easy and natural, even when the sense is deep and strong."[9]

Mary withstood much mockery of her preaching. When accused of immodesty in her public speaking, she replied,

> "I do not apprehend Mary could be in the
> least accused of immodesty when she carried
> the joyful news of her Lord's resurrection,
> and in this sense taught the teachers of
> mankind. Neither was the woman of Samaria
> to be accused of immodesty when she invited
> the city to come to Christ."[9]

Sarah Mallet

Sarah Mallet (1764-1846) was born to lower class parents in Loddon (near Norwich) England. Her whole family appears to have been involved with the trade of tailoring. Sarah as a young woman had a variety of physical ailments such as seizures and trouble walking from a foot drop (inability to flex the ankle). Sarah also had "consumption," an 18th century term for tuberculosis. Her biographer, David East, consulted 21st century physicians who suggested she had epilepsy, and/or a stroke, or even hysteria.[10]

Tuberculosis chronically infected more than one-quarter of England's inhabitants in the 18th century. The current author, a physician and medical historian, thinks it more likely she had the protean manifestations of her known tuberculosis (a condition seldom seen by modern physicians). Tuberculosis is an infection that was historically labeled the "great mimicker" from its ability to cause a host of confusing symptoms. Tuberculosis often seeds the bloodstream and as a result can afflict any organ system. Her physical ailments waxed and waned over her long life, observations that are also consistent with the chronic infection of tuberculosis.

During one severe bout of illness in 1786, she recorded, "if He [God] should restore me, I would spend

my last breath in declaring his dying love to sinners."[11]
She regained her strength and began preaching: "Fear and
shame caused me to tremble at first. But the Lord gave me
strength and loosed my tongue." Wesley met her a few
months later on December 4th of that year. He had heard
of a young woman with uncommon fits and one that had
lately preached but was not aware it was the same person.
He talked with her a long time and found her to be "much
devoted to God" and having a "strong understanding."

On October 27, 1787, Wesley instructed the
Conference (Manchester) to write,

> "we give the right hand of fellowship to Sarah
> Mallet, and have no objection to her being a
> preacher in our connection, so long as she
> preaches the Methodist doctrines, and attends
> to our discipline."[12]

Sarah Mallet clearly influenced Wesley's thinking on
women in ministry as evidenced by their extensive
correspondence. Nine letters exist from Wesley to Sarah
in the final four years of Wesley's life. Unfortunately,
there are no surviving letters from Sarah to Wesley, but
his answers infer her questions. He worried over her
limited finances, "I know that neither your father nor
uncle is rich; and in traveling up and down [to preach]
you will want a little money."[13] We know she requested
books in her pursuit of learning, as she appears to have
reminded him that she had not received one. In lending
theological books, he was offering the same support as he
had for other lay preachers.

His fatherly advice continued,

> "You are in far greater danger from applause
> than from censure, and it is well for you that
> one balances the other. However, I trust you
> will never be weary in well doing. In due time
> you will reap, if you faint not. Whoever
> praises or dispraises, it is your part to go
> steadily on, speaking the truth in love."[13]

Despite her physical handicaps, and frequent opposition by others, Sarah Mallet continued to preach hundreds of sermons for more than 50 years and died at age 82.

Five years before his death, Wesley made a radical declaration about the working equality of women in the life of the church and in their secular lives as well,

> "But may not women, as well as men, bear a part in this honorable service?" Undoubtedly, they may; nay, they ought to; it is meet, right, and their bounden duty. Herein there is no difference; 'there is neither male nor female in Christ Jesus.' Indeed, it has long passed for a maxim with many that 'women are only to be seen, not heard.' Accordingly, many of them are brought up in such a manner as if they were only designed for agreeable playthings! But is this doing honor to the sex? Or is it a real kindness to them? No; it is the deepest unkindness; it is horrid cruelty; it is mere Turkish barbarity. Moreover, I know not how any woman of sense and spirit can submit to it. Let all you that have it in your power assert the right that God of nature gives. Yield not to that vile bondage any longer! You, as well as men, are rational creatures. You, like them, are in the image of God; you are equally candidates for immortality; called of God you too have time, to 'do good to all men.' Be 'not disobedient to the heavenly calling.' Whenever you have opportunity, do all the good you can, particularly to your poor, sick neighbor. Moreover, every one of you likewise 'shall receive your own reward, according to your own labor."[14]

What were the number of laywomen preachers in Methodism? Chilcote records more than 40 women Methodist preachers for which he can find substantive biographical information.[15] However, he goes on to state that the 40 listed represent only a "small number" of the actual total of the anonymous women preachers and workers during Wesley's time. There are many women ministers cited in personal letters of the time for which we have no biographical information at all.[16]

> "Far from being a history of exceptional or
> even deviant women, the phenomenon of
> women preachers in the religious revival of
> the Wesley's represented a natural progression
> within the context of the Methodist societies.
> It was a logical extension as well of the
> Wesleyan theology of religious experience."[17]

John Wesley died in 1791. Apart from the Quakers, Methodists were the only religious groups to allow and even promote women as full lay preachers in the 18th century anywhere in the Christian world. It was not new in Christianity, but for the times it was revolutionary.

References
Chapter Three

1. Herbert M. Arminius and Wesley on Original Sin. didache.nazarene.org/pdfs/Eu2000-
07_McGonigle_Arminius.pdf. 2007.
 (Accessed January 18, 2016).
2. Wynkoop MB. A Theology of Love. Beacon Hill Press. 2007, location 4%.
3. Smith TL. Revivalism and Social Reform. Baltimore: John Hopkins University Press; 2004, p. 22.
4. Henderson DM. John Wesley's Class Meeting: a Model for Making Disciples: Evangel Publishing House; 1997, p. 60.

5. East D. My Dear Sally the Life and Times of Sarah Mallet, one of John Wesley's Preachers. Amazon Digital; 2014, location 62%.
6. Chilcote PW. John Wesley and the Women Preachers of Early Methodism. Lanham, Maryland: Scarecrow Press; 1991, p. 243.
7. Ibid, p. 79.
8. Ibid, p. 143.
9. Dayton L, Dayton D. Your Daughters Shall Prophesy": Feminism in the Holiness Movement. Methodist History 1976; January 1, 1976,
p. 69.
10.   East, location 20%.
11.   East, location 17%.
12.   Chilcote, p.195.
13.   Chilcote, p.196.
14.   Wesley J. On Visiting the Sick (Sermon 98) from Works; Volume 7. 1786, p. 125-6.
15.   Chilcote, pp. 253-287.
16.   Chilcote, p. 201.
17.   Chilcote, p. 3.

Chapter Four Women Preachers

Between the death of John Wesley in 1791 and the 1848 Women's Rights Convention, Methodism mushroomed in America. In 1855, when reliable numbers are available, there were more than 1.5 million members of Methodist churches; Baptists counted 1.2 million adherents. Together, these two denominations accounted for 70 percent of Protestants. Wesley's followers alone formed 38 percent of the whole. The two groups differed in that Baptists were predominantly rural and Southern while mid-century Methodism had grown in the cities and Eastern states.[1]

While Roman Catholics would begin immigrating in large numbers to the United States over the next 50 years, in 1850 they formed only 1/20th of the number of Protestants.[a]

How important socially was Methodism?

"Some non-Methodists, e.g., Winthrop Hudson, Philip Schaff and, and others, [refer] to the last half of the 19th century and the first half of the 20th century as the 'Methodist age' in American history. The Methodists were not only the largest denomination numerically, they convinced half of the rest of the Protestants (and some Roman Catholics) to act like Methodists; thus, becoming the country's most culturally influential religious tradition…One of the ironies of the American religious historiography is that, despite these facts, Methodism has hardly ever, and then only recently, been used as a lens

---

[a] Irish fleeing from the potato famine in the late 1840s formed the first great wave of Roman Catholic immigration. Prior to this, the Catholics in the United States were a small minority. They were mostly English and a "tight-knit group of landowning, educated aristocrats."
http://nationalhumanitiescenter.org/tserve/nineteen/nkeyinfo/nromcath.htm

through which to view the larger religious experience. American religion has been classically read through the New England Puritan tradition."[2]

Timothy Smith directs us into a scholarly approach to American religion,

> "Preoccupation with the learned and sophisticated minority is as misleading as over attention to the crackpot fringe. Neither course will disclose the part which religion really played in our country's development. Especially we must go beyond the solemn quarterlies published for clergymen and sift the literature with which their parishioners read. Vast collections of devotional biographical tracks, popular histories of revival and reform movements, and files of weekly denominational newspapers remain almost unexplored… [There was never] a typical Protestant point of view on religious and social matters nor even, in most cases, one which was common to the great body of believers within it in a major denomination. Every sermon, newspaper article, and essay must be studied in the light of its author's relation to the contending groups in his sect."[3]

Nor can mid-19th century American clergymen be divided simply into the two categories of "orthodox" and "liberal." Smith describes four significant strains of thought and feeling which flowed freely across denominational lines. *Traditionalism* is a term which best describes the mood common to High Church Episcopal and Old Lutheran leaders. *Orthodox Calvinism*, the bogeyman of social historians, was a dying dogma. *Revivalistic Calvinism* was, paradoxically enough, almost Arminian on the matters of election and free will and leaned as well toward 'new measures' and interfaith fellowship. *Evangelical Arminianism* claimed the legions of a vast army of Methodists of all sorts, the German Wesleyan sects, the Friends, many New Lutherans, the Cumberland Presbyterians, and the Freewill Baptists.[4]

WOMEN PREACHERS AFTER JOHN WESLEY

What happened to the status of women lay preachers in Methodism after John Wesley's death? Twelve years after the death of the original leader of Methodism, the 1803 Conference Minutes of the MEC in Britain recorded in a question and answer section:

"Q. 20. Should women be permitted to preach among us?

A. We are of opinion that, in general, they ought not. 1. Because a vast majority of our people are opposed to it. 2. Because their preaching does not at all seem necessary, there being a sufficiency of Preachers, whom God has accredited, to supply all the places in our Connexion with regular preaching. But if any woman among us thinks she has an extraordinary call from God to speak in public, (and we are sure it must be an *extraordinary* call that can authorize it), we are of opinion she should, in general, address her *own sex*, and *those only*. And upon this condition alone should any woman be permitted to preach in any part of our Connexion; and, when so permitted, it should be under the following regulation: 1. They shall not preach in the Circuit where they reside, until they have obtained the approbation of the Superintendent [at] a Quarterly Meeting. 2. Before they go into any other Circuit to preach, they shall have a *written* invitation from the Superintendent of

such Circuit, and a recommendatory note
from the Superintendent of their own Circuit."[b]

Some authors have referred to this 1803 conference text as a "ban" on women preaching within Methodism all over the world.[5,6] It was nothing of the sort. The statement was merely a question and answer item in British Methodist Conference minutes responding to a written question as to how that leader would handle the appointment of women preachers. This statement did not rise to the level of ecclesiastical law of the Methodist Episcopal Church. Those rules were contained in the *Methodist Discipline*. A modern British Methodist author, East, questions the content of this statement as to how the "majority of our people" were ascertained as to their objections to the practice. He also notes that a year later (i.e.1804) British Conference elders were complaining that there were not enough preachers to serve the denomination.[7]

Who would read the 20th question and its answer buried in a retrospective report? Timothy Smith would warn us not to pay attention to the 1803 statement. It was a technical discussion in obscure conference minutes.[c]

The 1803 question and answer was never enforced in Britain. In any case, it appears that "grand-mothering" of existing lay women preachers was allowed. The *Dictionary of Methodism* states that the conference statement

> "did not deter some 25 women already
> preaching from continuing to do so…we have
> evidence that Sarah [Mallet] preached in at
> least nine different [British] Circuits in the
> period 1828-1841, which means that her
> preaching was at least accepted, if not
> encouraged, by nine superintendents."

------

[b] Italics are in original document
[c] As far as the author could determine, this statement was not repeated in American Methodist Episcopal Church statements.

There is no evidence that Sarah restricted her preaching to only women. She was not required to have a note of recommendation from her own Superintendent or written invitations to other circuits.[8]

Women preachers were employed to large degree in the expansion of early 19th century offshoots of mainline British Methodists, such as the Primitive Methodist and Arminian Methodists.[d] At least two authors, Chilcote and Tabraham cite the desire to continue using women ministers as one of the principal reasons for these groups breaking away from the British Methodist Episcopal Church.[9,10]

DR ADAM CLARKE: FAMED COMMENTATOR SUPPORTING WOMEN

The current author doubts that many American Methodists read, or even were aware of, the 1803 British Methodist Q and A session about women preachers. On the other hand, many read the writings of Dr Adam Clarke. Four women's rights reformers in the Wesleyan-Holiness tradition, Luther Lee, Phoebe Palmer, Catherine Booth and Francis Willard (all discussed later in this book) cited Adam Clarke liberally.

Dr Clarke (1760-1832) was a celebrated Methodist minister in Britain who wrote a six-volume commentary on the Bible first published in 1811. In John Wesley's letters to Clarke, Wesley referred to Clarke as his "affectionate friend and brother." (Letter, November 21, 1787).

Clarke was strongly supportive of women in the church and society. Part of Paul's letter to the Galatians (3:28) states,

---

[d] "Primitive" in a Wesleyan context means following the practices of the early church as shown in the New Testament and first two centuries AD.

> "There is neither Jew nor Gentile, neither
> slave nor free, nor is there male and female,
> for you are all one in Christ Jesus." Clarke
> commented: "Under the blessed Spirit of
> Christianity, they [women] have equal *rights*,
> equal *privileges*, and equal *blessings*; and let
> me add, they are equally *useful*." (Italics by
> Dr Clarke).[11]

Concerning the outpouring of the Holy Spirit at
Pentecost (the official beginning of Christianity) "both the
daughters and sons prophesied." Clarke insisted that "the
gifts shall not be restricted to any one class or order of
people."

Clarke relates a humorous incident in his
autobiography,

> "I strongly recommended that females should
> be employed; and, in doing this, mentioned
> the case where many men had been sent into a
> particular district, of which they could make
> little or nothing [of raising money]; and when
> after several trials, it was still unproductive, at
> the suggestion of a friend, a number of
> women were sent to the same ground, who
> labored faithfully and to good effect: and,
> when an inquiry was made and a balance
> struck, it was found that one woman was
> equal to seven and a half men! Here the
> emotion was intense, and the effect general.
> The Marquis laughed downright, and the
> Bishop smiled aloud, and the Earl joined as
> heartily as the rest. The eyes of the ladies
> sparkled like diamonds…and cheers
> proceeded from all quarters."[12]

Personal observations about Dr Adam Clarke help to
authenticate his position towards women. One observer,
Rev George Pegler, in a prolonged stay in London in the
late 1820's, became personally acquainted with Dr

Clarke. Pegler considered the older minister to be a "model preacher."[e] Pegler describes Clarke as,

> "A robust man, and somewhat inclined to corpulence. He was very tidy in appearance, and neat and plain in his dress. His countenance was always beaming with kindness and good humor; ever solemn and serious, but never gloomy or morose; and in every case of doubt or slavish fear he was ever ready to apply some precious promise or relate some suitable anecdote that invariably brought a smile of delight and joy from many a down-cast countenance. In the pulpit, he was quite graceful and attractive. He was always natural, impressive, and instructive, and there was no attempt at display or oratory, or forced eloquence. None could hear him without profit, and a deep conviction that he was a man of God and master in Israel. He was greatly in favor of employing women whenever and wherever it could be done with the prospect of usefulness and success, especially as class-leaders and in financial matters."[13]

Nor was this only a public persona. Pegler's wife-to-be, Miss Morris, worked in decorating the Clarke home for six months. She told her future husband many anecdotes and summarized with, "The kindness and love of Dr Clarke to his family and domestics could not be surpassed."[14]

WOMEN PREACHERS IN AMERICA

After the American Revolution, Wesley appointed Dr. Thomas Coke and Francis Asbury as co-superintendents

---

[e] Rev Pegler re-enters our narrative in chapter six as the first pastor of the Wesleyan Chapel in Seneca Falls, New York

of Methodism in America in 1784. With the United States' new political independence from Great Britain, Wesley felt it necessary to allow the Americans religious independence as well. Coke's and Asbury's mission was to oversee the American Methodist movement autonomously from the English Methodist Connection.

What was the reality of women preachers in America in the first decades of the 19th century? One author was able to discover more than 80 women who were preaching in the United States between 1800 and 1845 among the Methodists, African Methodists, Freewill Baptists, and Christian Connection.[15] Short stories about two black Methodist women in the 19th century illustrate the activity of women ministers in early America.[f]

Jarena Lee

Jarena Lee was the first black female preacher in the American Methodist Episcopal Church (AMEC) for

---

[f] A brief history of black involvement in the AMEC is in order to help the reader to properly place the setting of Jarena Lee's ministry. In 1758, John Wesley baptized two "Negro slaves," which set the pattern for receiving black members into the British Methodist connection. In 1784, Richard Allen and Absalom Jones were the first black men to be granted licenses to preach in the AMEC. Drawn by the AMEC anti-slavery stand, blacks (slave and free) made up 20 percent of the 57,631 American Methodists in 1790. However, there were troubles in some areas. In November 1787, white elders attempted to relegate black parishioners to a newly built gallery at St. George's Methodist Church in Philadelphia. This led to local black members forming a church under their control in Philadelphia. called Bethel Church. In 1816, the Bethel Church became the "mother church" of a new denomination, the African Methodist Episcopal Church (AME). The AME incorporated several churches in the mid-Atlantic area with a total of 4400 members at its inception. Rev. Richard Allen was elected the first bishop. Rev Allen was instrumental in using Methodist Episcopal doctrine and government as the model for the AME. It appears, though, that around 16,000 blacks remained in the mainline AMEC church, so it should not be construed that all blacks deserted the AMEC.

which we have a significant amount of information. Her autobiography, *The Life and Religious Experience of Jarena Lee*, was published in 1836. Born in 1783 to free but impoverished parents, she was placed in domestic service at age seven. She was converted at age 21 under the preaching of Rev. Richard Allen, a black Methodist Episcopal minister in Philadelphia. On that day in church where hundreds were present, she felt a great amount of malice against one individual and the sin of her hate. She then felt enabled to forgive that individual.

> "I did leap to my feet, and declare that God,
> for Christ's sake, had pardoned the sins of my
> soul. Great was my ecstasy of my mind, for I
> felt that not only the sin of malice was
> pardoned, but all the other sins were swept
> away together."[16]

Four months later she sought the experience of sanctification and received assurance from God in prayer that she had received the complete blessing of God. Five years after these events, she felt called of God to preach and sought the advice of Rev. Richard Allen. He encouraged me to do good. "But as to women preaching, he said our *Discipline* knew nothing at all about it--that it did not call for women preachers." She felt relieved, but then struggled with her call to preach over the next eight years; in 1815, she was again in the Bethel Church listening to Rev. Richard Williams preach upon the text of Jonah 2:9, "Salvation is of the Lord." As the sermon progressed, Jarena sensed he began to lose his way. She jumped to her feet "as by an altogether supernatural impulse," and told them she was, "like Jonah; for it had been nearly eight years since the Lord had called me to preach his gospel to the fallen sons and daughters of Adam's race, but that I had lingered like him, and delayed doing the bidding of the Lord." Fearing she "might be expelled from the church," she sat down. Instead, Bishop Allen rose up in the assembly and related,

"that [Jarena Lee] had called upon him eight
years before, asking to be permitted to preach,
and that he had put me off; but that he now as
much believed that I was called to the work,
as any of the preacher's present."[17]

Jarena Lee first started to preach in homes. This
allowed her to develop confidence in speaking and still
care for her young "sickly" son. Receiving a call to
preach for a week among the Methodists 30 miles away,
she accepted the request despite her son's illness. Friends
took care of her son while she was gone. Lee returned
home to find no harm had come to him. As she recalls, "I
now began to think seriously of breaking up
housekeeping, and forsaking all to preach the everlasting
Gospel."[18]

Jarena Lee's itinerant preaching career began and
reached from upper New York State to Maryland and then
as far west as the wilds of Ohio. In one year in the 1820s,
she traveled more than two thousand miles, often by foot,
and preached more than one hundred seventy-five
sermons. She spoke to large congregations, both black
and white. When possible, she traveled with another
woman evangelist. While away from home, she left her
child with Bishop Allen and his family.

In Maryland, she was invited to address churches of
the "old Methodist Connection." She felt "thankful that
the middle wall of partition had, thus far, been broken
down." On another occasion, "I preached in the Old
Methodist Church to an immense congregation of both the
slaves and the holders and felt liberty in word and
doctrine; the power of God seemed without intermission."
At a camp meeting of the AME Church, she preached to
slaves, some of which who had walked up to 70 miles to
worship God. It is extraordinary how widely she traveled
in the South as a free black woman during slavery.[18]

Never officially licensed or ordained, Jarena Lee was
an effective and prodigious female preacher for the

Methodists. Women in the AME Church were first approved for local preacher licenses by the 1884 AME General Conference.

Julia Foote

Julia Foote (1823-1901) was born in Schenectady, New York to parents who were former slaves. At age 15, she received salvation in a Methodist church by praying, "Lord, have mercy on me a sinner." She then saw a "ray of light [flash] across my eyes, accompanied by a sound of far off singing." She responded by singing, "Redeemed! Redeemed! Glory! Glory! Such joy and peace as filled my heart." Six months later, a couple visited her and explained sanctification. Receiving the experience, Foote felt she was,

> "plucked as a brand from the burning and [was] sealed unto eternal life. . . I no longer hoped for glory, but I had the full assurance of it. . .my constant prayer was answered, that I might be strengthened in the inner man; that being rooted and grounded in love, I might be able to comprehend with all the saints what is the length, and breadth, and height and depth, and to know the love of Christ which passes knowledge and be filled with all the fullness of God."[19]

The phrase "brand plucked from the fire" (Zechariah 3:2) was a favorite theme of Foote and was undoubtedly adopted from John Wesley. Wesley repeatedly referred to his rescue from a house fire at age five where many thought he should have perished. Wesley felt it was an indication he had been saved to minister to others.

Moving to Boston with her husband, Foote could not escape her feeling that she was called to preach. Her bias distressed her,

"I had always been opposed to the preaching
of women, and had spoken against it, though,
I acknowledge, without foundation. This rose
before me like a mountain, and when I
thought of the difficulties they had to
encounter, both from professors and non-
professors, I shrank back and cried, 'Lord, I
cannot go."

Accepting her call as a member of her local church, the African Methodist Episcopal Zion (AMEZ)[g], she began preaching in homes. This alarmed the church minister, Jemial Beman. He forbade her to preach because she should not "preach her holiness stuff here." It was clear though that being a woman was the principal problem. He threatened excommunication for her and anyone in the congregation who went to listen to her anywhere in Boston!

She began an extensive itinerant evangelistic ministry that crossed many denominations: Wesleyan Methodist, MEC, AMEZ, Free Methodist, Mennonite, Church of God, and Presbyterian.

In addition to opposition to her preaching as a woman, she faced racial prejudice both within and without the church. To paraphrase from her autobiography: In 1849, I was traveling from Oxford to Utica, New York on a canal (i.e., the Chenango, a branch of the Erie Canal) boat. The hour was late, and I took an empty berth in the ladies' cabin. Soon a man burst into the cabin saying that all the berths in the gentlemen's cabin were occupied and that he was going to sleep in the ladies' cabin. He pointed to me and said, "That nigger has no business here." The captain was called, and he asked me to get up, but I remained still. Finally, the abusive man and the captain left. The

---

[g] African Methodist Episcopal Zion (AMEZ) should not be confused with the designation AME or the African Methodist Episcopal Church

next night the captain found lodging for me at an inn. "Thus, I escaped further abuse from the ungodly man."[19]

In Chillicothe, Ohio, the white Methodists (presumably from the AMEC) invited Foote to speak for them, but they did not want the "colored people" to attend. She refused to speak at their church.

It was a different story in Zanesville, Ohio where a white Methodist church agreed to open their doors for the first time to both races, if she would come speak for an extended number of meetings. Foote agreed. She felt the hand of God when, "hundreds were turned away at each meeting, unable to get in; and although the house was so crowded, perfect order prevailed."[19]

Thomas Doty interacted with Foote on a regular basis. Doty was a leading Holiness evangelist, Wesleyan Methodist clergyman, and editor of the monthly *Christian Harvester* newspaper. Eccentric in his mannerisms, "Slight in form, with his black cap, a shawl under his arm and a bundle of *Christian Harvesters*, [he] was a loved and familiar figure for many years" at Holiness gatherings.[20]

Doty expressed his admiration for Foote's speaking when he recounted that "those of us who heard her preach last year . . . where she held the almost breathless attention of five thousand people, by the eloquence of the Holy Spirit, know well where the hiding of her power is."[20] Doty wrote the introduction for Julia Foote's autobiography and published it. He was on the same speaking program with her many times. Doty strongly defended women's preaching—because, as he said, "Today is a Pentecostal day."[20] [h]

Julia Foote stressed the problem of prejudice and the need for inclusion among Christians. Foote wrote

----

[h] This refers to the fact of women receiving the power of the Holy Spirit on the first day of the Christian church in Acts 2. (See current book chapter 21). This is one of many Biblical supports for preaching by women.

passionately about the bigotry that she had experienced firsthand and her belief that only God's holiness could overcome such discrimination.

> "O Prejudice! Thou cruel monster! Wilt thou
> ever cease to exist? ... Not until all shall know
> the Lord, and holiness shall be written... upon
> all things in earth as well as in heaven. Those
> who are fully in the truth cannot possess a
> prejudiced spirit. They cannot reject those
> whom Christ has received."[20]

Thomas Doty agreed. "Holiness takes the prejudice of color out of both the white and the black," Doty penned in his introduction to Foote's autobiography.[20]

John Wesley would have agreed. He believed the practical outcome of sanctification was to follow the royal law of love: "Love the Lord your God with all your heart, soul, and mind, and your neighbor as yourself."[21] [i]

While "not all were so clearheaded about the rampant racism and sexism of the day, Doty, Foote and a few other late nineteenth century Holiness advocates spoke out against the generally accepted social norms that were characteristic of affluent mainline congregations."[20]

Many historians have used Foote's life story to postulate their theories of black women's self-actualized drive to overcome sexism and racism,

> "She possessed an inordinate faith in herself"
> (Bettye Collier-Thomas); she participated in
> 'religious self-recovery' (Yvonne Chireau);
> and she 'reformulated her identity through
> self-recovery' (Delores Williams). In contrast
> to these characterizations of the self's quest
> for personal power, when we read Foote's
> own description of the source of her spiritual
> confidence, she unfailingly credited her

[i] Wesley was so dedicated to this concept that the royal law is painted in large letters on the wall behind the pulpit in his London chapel for all to meditate on during sermons. (This can still be viewed today).

success to the empowerment of the Holy
Spirit. According to Foote's account, the
cause of her authority and identity change was
not internal, but an external intervention of
the divine—what Susie Stanley, Cheryl
Sanders, and Estrelda Alexander refer to as
the 'sanctified self' or a liberating ethic of
empowerment. Gregory Schneider has stated
well that such women had a "confidence in a
self that was no longer a woman's own self,
but God's, and that, nevertheless, felt freer
and more authentic than she had ever felt
simply on her own."[20]

Phoebe Worrall Palmer

Phoebe Worrall Palmer (1807-1874), was a central
catalyst in the revival of Wesleyan-Holiness in the 19th
century.[22,23] She was a lay theologian, writer, revival
speaker, reformer, and an advocate of women's
empowerment by the Holy Spirit for the ministry.

Palmer was born in New York City to parents
committed to Methodism (AMEC). Her spirituality
developed at an early age and showed unusual maturity in
her comprehension of theology and in piety of life.
Despite only an eighth-grade education, her eventual
writings show intricate insights into Scripture and
holiness theology.

In 1826, Phoebe met Walter Clarke Palmer, who
(according to Charles White), embarked on three projects
as a young man, "establishing a medical practice,
superintending the Sunday school at the Allen Street
Methodist Episcopal Church, and wooing Phoebe
Worrall."[24] Walter and Phoebe married on September 28,
1827.

The Palmers were well suited both in interest and
personality. Their marriage was happy but affected by

tragedy. They lost three of their four children to early deaths. The deaths of her children influenced her to seek sanctification. She reached that "day of days" on July 26, 1837. Palmer attributed the delay to her lack of realization of the "depth" and gravity of truly surrendering her "idols." From that day forward, she developed the famous "Altar Covenant" that aided persons seeking sanctification; it consisted of three steps: consecration, faith, and testimony."[24] To Palmer, the outcome need not be confirmed with great emotion. She wrote at one point "I felt no emotion, except a sacred stillness."[25]

She fervently believed that holiness was not for a few but was rather a "state of grace in which every one of the Lord's redeemed should live." Sanctification wasn't the culmination of the Christian life, but the beginning of it."[23]

She and her husband achieved international fame as a speaking team. Phoebe became better known than Walter from her prolific authorship. Space is too limited here to explore her ideas on holiness and social reform. Our focus is her effect on the lives of women.

It was the last step in Palmer's three step formula that affected women most directly,

> "Her emphasis on public testimony usually took the form of varying degrees of insistence that testimony was not only essential to the promulgation of Christian holiness, but even more essential to the personal retention of that grace. One had to give public testimony to be "clear in his or her experience."[26]

Palmer describes her own experience,

> "The Spirit then suggested: If it is a gift from God, you will be required to declare it as his gift, through our Lord Jesus Christ, ready for the acceptance of all; and this, if you would retain the blessing, will not be left to your

own choice. You will be called on to profess
this blessing before thousands!"[26]

Palmer recommended that women should testify to God's sanctifying power in public. Even if it was considered "undignified" for a woman to speak. She must be willing to do what God asked of her, even if it went against social norms.

Palmer's interest in women's rights focused on the freedom of women to preach. She felt ordination was an unnecessary step for men or women since the rite was not in the New Testament. She advocated that all Christians should be preaching the good news. To this end, her book, *The Promise of the Father*, contained her reasoning as to the need for women to preach the gospel.

> Beyond agitating in behalf of sanctified women to publicly say so, Phoebe did not engage in the broader women's rights movement. The most she would state was, "We believe woman has her legitimate sphere of action, which differs in most cases material from that of man and in this legitimate sphere she is both happy and useful. Yet we don't doubt that some reforms contemplated in recent movements may in various respects, be decidedly advantageous."[27]

Palmer also thought it would not be improper for women to play a prominent part in legislative halls or church conventions.[28]

"At the very least, Palmer is recognized now for her advancement of the cause for women. Palmer has been cited as a key contributor to the nineteenth-century debate concerning the role of women in the church. Donald Dayton writes,

> "It was ... the denominations produced by the mid-nineteenth century 'holiness revival' that most consistently raised feminism to a central principle of church life. This movement

largely emerged from the work of Phoebe Palmer."[29]

The Wesleyan tradition produced many women public speakers before the 1848 Seneca Falls Convention. They testified of God's grace and their call to preach the good news by the Spirit of God.

References
Chapter Four

1. Smith TL. Revivalism and Social Reform. Baltimore: John Hopkins University Press; 2004, p. 22.
2. Donald D. The Global Impact of the Wesleyan Traditions and their Related Movements. In: Charles Yrigoyen ed. The Global Impact of the Wesleyan Traditions and their Related Movements. Lanham, Maryland: Scarecrow Press, Inc.; 2002: p. 6-7.
3. Smith, p. 9.
4. Smith, pp. 32-33.
5. Westerkamp M. Women in Early American Religion 1600-1850: the Puritan and Evangelical Traditions. New York City: Routledge; 1999, p. 113.
6. Smith O. Romantic Women Writers, Revolution, and Prophecy: Rebellious Daughters, 1786-1826: Cambridge University Press; 2013, p. 51
7. East D. My Dear Sally the Life and Times of Sarah Mallet, One of John Wesley's Preachers. Amazon Digital; 2014; location 62%.
8. Ibid, location 63%.
9. Chilcote PW. John Wesley and the Women Preachers of Early Methodism. Lanham, Maryland: Scarecrow Press; 1991, p. 243
10. Tabraham B. The Making of Methodism. Peterborough, United Kingdom: Epworth Press; 1995, p. 60
11. Clarke A. Holy Bible...: With a Commentary and Critical Notes1834. Galatians 3:28.

12. Clarke A. The Life and Labours of Adam Clarke. To which is Added an Historical Sketch of the Controversy Concerning the Sonship of Christ 1834, p. 358

13. Pegler G. Autobiography of the Life and Times of George Pegler. https://archive.org/details/autobiographyofl00pegl; 1875, location 38%.

14. Ibid, location 48%

15. Brekus, cited by Miller SJ. Grace Sufficient: A History of Women in Methodism 1760-1939. Nashville: Abingdon Press; 1999, p. 99.

16. Andrews WL. Sisters of the Spirit: Three Black Women's Autobiographies of the Nineteenth Century: Indiana University Press; 1986, p. 29.

17. Ibid pp. 35-45.

18. Miller, pp. 100-104.

19. Foote J. A Brand Pucked from the Fire. Sisters of the Spirit: Indiana University Press; 1879: p. 161-245.

20. Knight HH. From Aldersgate to Azusa Street: Wesleyan, Holiness, and Pentecostal Visions of the New Creation: Wipf and Stock Publishers; 2010, location 36-37%.

21. Wesley, J. A Plain Account of Christian Perfection. Kansas City, MO: Beacon Hill Press; 1966; pp. 12-21.

22. Knight, location 24%.

23. Laird R. Ordained Women in the Church of the Nazarene: The First Generation. Kansas City, MO: Nazarene Publishing House; 1993, location 11-15%

24. White, cited by Knight, location 25%.

25. Palmer P. The Promise of the Father (Salem, OR. Schmul Publishers; 1859, location 33%.

26. Knight, location 27%.

27. Palmer, location 3%.

28. Dayton D, Strong D. Rediscovering an Evangelical Heritage: a Tradition and Trajectory of Integrating Piety

and Justice. Second ed. Grand Rapids, Michigan: Baker Academic; 2014, p. 73.
29. Dayton D. Discovering an evangelical heritage: HarperCollins Publishers; 1976, p. 96.

Chapter Five Wesleyans and Slavery

Slavery has been a universal practice in world history until recently. Wesley was among the first in 18th century England to oppose the slave trade. He denounced it as "the sum of all villainies."[1] In a circulated essay, *Thoughts on Slavery*, Wesley was disturbed that slavery reappeared in the 15th century after its thousand-year disappearance from Western Civilization.[a]

On his deathbed in 1791, Wesley encouraged William Wilberforce, another evangelical, to keep up his long-standing effort to abolish slavery through bills introduced into Parliament,

> "Unless the divine power has raised you up....
> I see not how you can go through your
> glorious enterprise in opposing that
> [abominable practice of slavery], which is the
> scandal of religion, of England, and of human
> nature. Unless God has raised you up for this
> very thing, you will be worn out by the
> opposition of men and devils. But if God be
> for you, who can be against you? Are all of
> them together stronger than God? Go on in
> the name of God, and in the power of His
> might." (Letter, Feb. 24, 1791)

Harking back to the founder of Methodists, the Wesleyan Methodists took a strong stance against slavery. In 1843, the issue was so important that a large group of churches in nine states stretching from New England to Ohio, severed themselves from the main Methodist movement, the American Methodist Episcopal Church (AMEC).

The older denomination was not pro-slavery. But, with a large membership in the North and South, the bishops of

---

[a] The disappearance was under the influence of Christianity.

the Methodist Episcopal Church attempted neutrality in the years 1836-1844. The new policy would avoid pronouncements about the evils of slavery.

Contemporary events likely influenced the AMEC leadership. The U.S. House of Representatives instituted the "gag rule" on March 16, 1836, forbidding the House from considering anti-slavery petitions. Representative John Quincy Adams of Massachusetts raised the most impassioned objection to the procedure. Adams shouted during the roll call vote, "I hold the resolution to be a direct violation of the Constitution of the United States." Adams continued to fight against the gag rule, declaring it a restriction on free speech.

In May 1836, the AMEC General Conference in Cincinnati was the setting of a fierce debate about "modern abolitionism." A 110-page document recording the dispute is available.[2] Briefly, the bishops were not pro-slavery, but feared more the "dismemberment" of the church from a southern schism. The bishops struggled to maintain ecclesiastical nonalignment. This neutrality was in stark contrast to the "vigorous opposition to slavery" of the American Methodist Episcopal Church's *Discipline* in 1786.[3]

Fifty years earlier, the AMEC not only denounced slavery but set forth practical guidelines for their members to dissociate themselves from the scandal,

> "We view it as contrary to the golden law of
> God, on which hang all the law and the
> prophets, and the inalienable rights of
> mankind, as well as every principle of the
> Revolution, to hold in the deepest
> debasement, in a more abject slavery than is
> perhaps to be found in any part of the world
> except America, so many souls that are all
> capable of the image of God. We therefore
> think it our most bounden duty to take
> immediately some effectual method to

extirpate this abomination from among us.'
They then required every Methodist to
'execute and record within twelve months
after notice from the assistant' a legal
instrument emancipating all slaves, in his
possession, at specified ages. Any person
concerned who should not concur in this
requirement had liberty to leave the Church
within one year, otherwise the preacher was
to exclude him."[4]

Siebert states that the AMEC rules requiring divesture of slaves emancipated many.[5] Records are sparse, though. It should be noted that ex-slaveholders were harassed by their peers, and the practice of manumission increasingly became illegal in southern states. Moreover, the identification of the freed slave (full name, lack of a birth certificate, etc.) was often sketchy.

Kenneth Carroll illustrates the impact of the Methodist rules requiring emancipation of slaves. The legal records of three counties, Dorchester, Caroline, and Talbot, in Maryland from 1780 until the Civil War were studied.[6] These districts were predominantly Methodist. The lists of manumitted slaves from Wesleyans in this period total 3,711. The deeds of manumission often cite religious ideas for setting the slave free such as [the] "practice of slavery is repugnant to the pure precepts of the gospel of Jesus Christ."[7] Further work needs to be done, but the numbers in these three counties suggest a very large impact if extrapolated.[b]

LUTHER LEE, WESLEYAN ABOLITIONIST

Reverend Luther Lee (1800-1889) a 36-year-old AMEC minister and prolific writer, had not paid attention to topic of abolition. When listening to the debates at the

---

[b] Indeed, in 1860, from Carroll's tabulation, there were more free blacks in these counties than slave (10,434 versus 8587).

1836 AMEC General Conference in Cincinnati his awareness began. He was troubled that the southern delegates demanded silence about slavery on part of the Conference; and, that they called upon the church to "put their foot upon the abolition viper and crush it out." In contrast, he was impressed when the 36-year-old Reverend Orange Scott, a presiding elder (district superintendent) of the New England Conference, stood up alone on the other side, and made an "able argument against slavery, both dignified and calm."[8] Scott's opponents responded by charging him with either being a "reckless incendiary" or *non-compos mentis* ["not of sound mind"].[9]

The abolitionists were supported by their British Methodist counterparts who attended from overseas. The fraternal English delegate, William Lord, expressed his hope that the American Conference could devise plans for the termination of slavery as soon as possible. The English urged the AMEC to lead public

opinion towards a "unanimous rejection" of it and its "social mischiefs."[10]

The AMEC national leadership would have to choose between purity and popularity. In the end, the clergy leaders waffled on purity and choose popularity. The upshot was that the AMEC started eight-years of wandering in the wilderness. To appease Southern Methodists, the leadership attempted to distinguish between slavery, which they labeled wrong, and slaveholders which could still be church members. The illogic failed to please Northern or Southern Methodists.

The drawback to walking the fence is that both sides are seldom satisfied. One can sympathize with the bishops, given that the all-consuming issue was blocking other conference issues; and how it was diverting the church from more important concerns such as evangelism. Nevertheless, in the words of a Methodist historian, "the bishops had decided to be soft on slavery and hard on abolitionists."[11] [c]

The final step in transforming Lee's thought came in November 1837, when Elijah Lovejoy, a Presbyterian clergyman and journalist, was murdered by a pro-slavery mob in Alton, Illinois. In newspaper columns, Elijah Lovejoy had forcefully spoken out against slavery. Deeply moved, Lee "judged it wrong to remain silent any longer." He condemned the mob violence and announced his support for the principles of abolition that Mr Lovejoy stood for. At the same time, Illinois officials remained silent, except for a young state representative named Abraham Lincoln, who spoke out against the crime.[12]

Shortly thereafter, Lee wrote in *Zion's Watchman*, an independent antislavery paper, that he,

> "did not deny that the persistence of the anti-slavery men might end in the dismemberment of the church, but. . .the [fault and] fall would be on the part of the opposers of abolition. . . If the church could not be purified from slavery without dismemberment it would be infinitely preferable to being held together by the bonds of human slavery and being submitted by the blood of enslaved millions."[13]

In 1838, a church elder charged Lee with violating the neutrality rule on slavery. He was scheduled to be tried in a church conference. In the interests of unity, the minister who made the allegations stood up the next morning and

---

[c] It was not the finest hour for American Christianity. New England Congregational ministers and representative Baptist bodies rejected abolitionism outright. The Roman Catholic Clergy opposed abolitionism. Quakers avoided the subject and abolitionists since the latter had a "motive we do not understand." Episcopalians remained silent as did the Presbyterian Assembly at meeting in Pittsburgh. An abolitionist minority in the Presbyterian Assembly described slavery as a moral paradox and a sin, but they were suppressed like their Methodist brethren. (Matthews p 144).

withdrew all charges. All was to be forgotten.
Nonetheless, Lee found himself appointed to a very
undesirable location for his next pastoral charge. Before
accepting the position, he requested and was granted a
sabbatical. He then became a lecturer for the New York
State Antislavery Society for one year.

There was little support for abolition at the time.
Siebert states: "The truth is, the mass of the people of the
free states were by no means abolitionists; they cherished
an intense prejudice against the Negro and permitted it to
extend to all anti-slavery advocates."[5] The support for
abolition did not improve greatly until the decade of the
1850s.

In an 1839 book, *Abolition a Sedition, by a Northern
Man*, the secular author fears that the abolitionists were
anarchists because they advocated the leveling of all
"distinctions in society, of rank, color, caste, and *sex*."
(italicized word in original manuscript)[14] [d]

Apologists for slavery consistently maintained that
churches should not interfere in secular politics.[e]

During his speeches for the Antislavery Society,
Luther Lee described on different occasions being pelted
with rotten eggs or liquid boot black. He heard booing
and even gunfire. Lee received a death threat in Albany,

> "I would advise you as a friend to leave the
> city as soon as possible, or you will lose your
> life. Such conduct as you are pursuing will
> not do; you must not try to blind people's eyes
> with false stories. You had not better deliver
> another lecture in this city; if you do you will
> surely you lose your life. It may not be in the
> church, but the remedy is sure. A Friend."[15]

Despite concerns of associates, Luther Lee gave the
speech in Albany anyway. Never intimidated, Reverend
Lee observed that more people signed up for the

---

[d] This, of course, is what vital Christianity does. (Luke 14: 7-14).
[e] Sound familiar on any reform measure?

Antislavery Society on the occasions when he was persecuted than when he was politely received.

Meanwhile, after the 1836 Conference, Rev. Orange Scott was quietly removed, because of his abolitionist expressions, from being a presiding elder in the New England Conference. Like Lee, he was appointed to an undesirable pastorate in Lowell, Massachusetts where there were only 30 members. Undaunted, Scott helped the church swell to 120 members within a year. He was elected by local pastors as a general delegate to the AMEC National Conference in 1840 to be held in Baltimore, Maryland. Unfortunately, the Baltimore conference was a replay of the Cincinnati conference; but even worse since the abolitionists were completely shut out of debate. Scott left disillusioned.

LAROY SUNDERLAND, WESLEYAN, WANTED DEAD OR ALIVE

LaRoy Sunderland (1802-1885) was the blunt speaking editor of *Zion's Watchman*. Begun in 1836, the newspaper's circulation soon eclipsed all other Methodist publications. The AMEC Bishops sought to muzzle the abolitionist views of the paper. From 1836 to 1840, Sunderland's writings were charged in five trials with violation of church doctrine. There were multiple counts each time. In first four trials, Sunderland's fellow ministers in the New England Conference came to his rescue and acquitted him of all charges.[16]

In the 5th and final trial, counts had been drawn up by Bishop Soule, the presiding judge. Emotions ran high. The Bishop permitted an article critical of Sunderland to be read out loud at the trial by the prosecutor, C.A. Davis. Sunderland rebutted by reading a letter from the New York Weekly Messenger in which Davis, had called Sunderland "an unprincipled man" and "ecclesiastically dead." Sunderland contended that if his own language constituted libel, so did that of Davis. Bishop Soule interrupted and ordered Sunderland to stop reading the article.

Sunderland then turned to Soule and said, "I will read the Davis letter despite all the bishops in the land." Bishop Soule replied, "In all my experience and in all my intercourse with my fellowmen, I have this to say that LaRoy Sunderland is the first man that ever dared to speak to me in that manner." An exasperated Sunderland shouted back, "I thank God, sir, that you have lived long enough to find one man who will tell you to your face what many others say of you behind your back."[16]

His fellow ministers acquitted Sunderland on all charges but one, a minor one of "conduct unbecoming a minister." He was required to sign a paper humbly acknowledging that he had behaved inconsistently with the character of a Christian minister. He also had to publish the repudiation without comment in the *Zion's Watchman*. He did so on August 1, 1840 but surrounded the retraction by dark black lines.

Feelings ran high against Sunderland in the South. A reward of $150,000 was offered in New Orleans for him dead or alive. Officials in Montgomery, Alabama offered $50,000 for his capture.

Similarly, in the North, in a civil trial in 1837, Sunderland was indicted for "contempt of the laws of New York State" and offending "the peace" by libeling David Miller, a postmaster in Western New York. Sunderland had published a letter from George Storrs, an abolitionist minister, who gave an account of George Miller inciting a mob to blow up the meeting house where an abolition lecture was to be given. Sunderland spoke in his own defense for almost an hour, climaxing with a plea for freedom of the press. The jury acquitted him.

THE WESLEYAN METHODIST CHURCH IS BORN

LaRoy Sunderland, Orange Scott and Jotham Horton announced on November 8, 1842 that they were withdrawing from the AMEC. Within weeks, Luther Lee and Lucius Matlack joined them. They agreed "that it would be a sin to remain in a church that seemed so intent on betraying its antislavery heritage." Horton was an active abolitionist writer and had been in the minority of Methodist ministers that supported Scott in the 1836 Conference. Matlack was denied ordination twice because of his abolitionist views. In Orange Scott, he found a friend who brought him on church staff in Lowell, Massachusetts and who saw to it that his ordination was approved.[17]

A new church, the Wesleyan Methodist Church, was begun at a convention in Utica, New York. Here many Wesleyan-tradition congregations holding abolitionist beliefs met on the last day of May 1843. Orange Scott was elected President. During the convention, Reverend Scott asked Reverend George Pegler to become the first pastor of the Wesleyan Chapel in Seneca Falls. Reverend Pegler and Luther Lee were among five people charged with developing an original *Discipline,* or operating manual of the new denomination. The banner of the new denomination's newspaper, *The True Wesleyan*, became "First Purity, then Peace."[16]

After the Wesleyan Methodist Church severed ties, the American Methodist Episcopal Church met for their quadrennial Conference in New York City on May 1, 1844. This time the bishops either would not or could not enforce the gag rule. A complicated case of a southern AMEC bishop who had inherited one non-working slave was tried. A twelve-day debate ensued. An effort at compromise failed. More churches from New England threatened to secede. Finally, a motion asking the southern leader to desist from serving as a bishop ultimately passed, 111-69. The lot was cast. The Southerners left.

Attempts at reconciliation with the Southern Methodists failed. What was merely a legislative motion to Northerners was schism to the Southerners. The AMEC (northern residual) then unequivocally readopted the historical anti-slavery stance of Methodism. This time the Methodists preceded Congress. John Quincy Adams from Massachusetts finally mustered enough votes in the House of Representatives to defeat the gag rule on December 3, 1844.

The Baptists proceeded to split in the same north-south manner a year later.[f] Thus, the two largest denominations, comprising 70% of all church members in the United States, became alienated. Before the country divided its political institutions, its churches did. In 1844, Luther Lee foresaw ominous "thunderbolts" on the national horizon.

The man who embodied Methodist abolitionism, Orange Scott, died at age 47 from tuberculosis. At Scott's funeral in 1847, Luther Lee preached with clear foresight,

> "If it be insisted that he [Scott] was ultra and rash, it was because he lived in advance of his age. He advocated no sentiments, and resorted to no measures, which are not destined, very soon, to become the moderate sober views of the world."[18]

---

[f] Local Baptist churches were nearly congregational in polity and a weak confederation at the national level. The split came when the confederated national Baptist missionary society refused to give credentials to a southern slave holder. Baptist Churches began lining up behind a newly created southern mission board versus the traditional one. Thus, there were no clergy otherwise affected. This crisis was not nearly as wrenching for the Baptists as the Methodists where the episcopal polity required an organic sundering of the church denomination.

References
Chapter Five

1. Wesley J. Thoughts upon slavery. Google book; 1774.
2. Ohio Anti-Slavery Society. Debate on "Modern Abolitionism," in the General Conference of the Methodist   Episcopal Church, held in Cincinnati, May, 1836. With notes. (Accessed November 6, 2015). (https://archive.org/details/debateonmodernab00meth1836).
3. Dayton D, Strong D. Rediscovering an Evangelical Heritage: a Tradition and Trajectory of Integrating Piety and Justice. Second ed. Grand Rapids, Michigan: Baker Academic; 2014; p. 73.
4. History of the Methodist Episcopal Church. In: (http://wesley.nnu.edu/holiness-classics-library/history-of-the-methodist-episcopal-church/volume-2-book-iii-chapter-4) (Accessed January 19, 2018).
5. Siebert WH. The Underground Railroad from Slavery to Freedom: Reprint Services Corporation; 1898, p. 94.
6. Carroll KL. Religious Influences on the Manumission of Slaves in Carolina, Dorchester, and Talbot Counties. Maryland Historical Magazine 1966; 56, p. 176-97.
7. Ibid, p. 192.
8. Lee L. Autobiography of the Rev. Luther Lee New York: Phillips & Hunt 1882, p. 134.
9. Matlack LC. The History of American Slavery and Methodism, from 1780-1849, p. 240.
10. Mathews DG. Slavery and Methodism: A Chapter in American Morality, 1780-1845: Princeton University Press; 2015, p. 140.
11. Black R, Drury K. The Story of the Wesleyan Church. Indianapolis: Wesleyan Publishing House; 2012, p. 54.
12. Smith TL. Revivalism and Social Reform. Baltimore: John Hopkins University Press; 2004, p. 22.

13. Lee, p. 140.
14. Colton C, 1789-1857. Abolition a Sedition. By a Northern Man Philadelphia: George Donohue; 1839, p. 73.
15. Lee, p. 176.
16. Jervey ED. LaRoy Sunderland: Zion's Watchman. Methodist History; 1968; (http://archives.gcah.org/handle/10516/1504?show=full) (Accessed March 22, 2018) p. 16-32.
17. Black, pp. 29-35.
18. Dayton, location 59%.

Chapter Six Seneca Falls, New York

Backsliding over slavery was the main reason Wesleyan Methodists left the AMEC. But there were other motives. A second was the autocratic rule of the bishops. The new denomination was far more democratic. Elected lay members could vote on every level. Third, while there was some confusion in the formative year of 1843, by 1844 Wesleyan Methodist women were voting in church assemblies.[1] Perhaps the Wesleyan women were the reason for the exception clause contained in the thirteenth *Sentiment*, "and, *with some exceptions*, [women are excluded] from any public participation in the affairs of the Church."[a]

FIRST PASTOR, REV. GEORGE PEGLER

The first pastor of Seneca Falls Wesleyan Chapel from 1843-1845, Reverend George Pegler, set the tone for social change. Rev. Pegler persistently uses the inclusive phrase "men and women" throughout his autobiography; this is unusual for male authors of the time. Moreover, he repeatedly asks his wife for counsel, spiritual and otherwise, and takes the advice to heart.[2]

In 1827, Pegler filled in for a missionary who worked among the Chippewa Indians. He continued the absent missionary's efforts at insisting upon the equality of the women with the men. The status of Chippewa women seemed worse to Pegler than slavery. In the frequent moves typical of the tribe, the wife bore all the burdens of the travel. She pitched the wigwam, cut the wood, and prepared the meals. This was while his "lordship stretched himself full length on the ground, and stoically watched the proceedings and preparations made for his comfort."

---

[a] See chapter one for the *Sentiments*. See also Appendix A for an essay comparing Quakers and Wesleyan Methodists

Even worse, to Pegler, was that if there were not enough food to go around, the wife was the one who had to go to bed supperless. The latter practice, by Indians who had not been converted to Christianity, was felt by Pegler to be "inhumane." Hence "no Indian could partake of food at the public table on the missionary premises, however hungry he might be, without the company of the wife."[3]

Pegler's terminology when describing Seneca Falls is of interest. Born in London, Pegler sailed to China, South America, and the Caribbean among other world destinations for 12 years as a young merchant marine. As such, few people of the time would have had his perspective of geography. Yet, when called to Seneca Falls, he refers to it as a "large manufacturing village in central New York." His viewpoint of the 4,000-person township is reasonable; for comparison, the 1840 US Census lists New York City as the largest city in the United States with only 330,000 persons. Albany, New York had a population of only 33,000, yet it formed the 10th largest US city. One often reads from modern authors about the first women's rights convention taking place in a backwater place, Seneca Falls. Pegler tells us that this was not the perception of a world traveler of the time.[4]

When Rev. and Mrs. Pegler arrived in the summer of 1843, the 70-member congregation was meeting in the Seneca Falls Academy.[4] As many attenders at church do not join the official membership, the number of people at worship services of the Wesleyan Chapel would have likely been much greater. The free college prep school, originated in 1832, was supported by contributions from the town.[5]

Construction of the new sanctuary was completed in October 1843. Pegler adds to the knowledge of the early furnishings of the chapel by mentioning the last two items completed. These were the "pulpit slips" and the "altar."[6] The pulpit slips, now called "pews", would likely have been backed benches for seating near the pulpit podium.

The altar, in the time of early American revivals, would probably be the "mourner's bench," a long unbacked bench stretching across much of the front of the sanctuary. When finally completed, the Wesleyan Chapel was dedicated to the worship of God with a sermon by the President of the New York Conference, Rev. Luther Lee.[4]

The Underground Railroad was a system of cooperation among antislavery people in the United States by which fugitive slaves were secretly helped to reach Canada. Pegler was known to be an activist for the Railroad. In 1844, he described a fugitive slave named Peter Bannister who came to his house in Seneca Falls to rest and to obtain assistance for his journey to Canada. Pegler gave Bannister an entire church service, so the visitor could give an "inside view of the institution [of slavery]" and "place some heavy thrusts at the morals of slaveholders."[7][b]

With his openness to fugitive slaves and his descriptions of women, Reverend George Pegler set an excellent example as the inaugural minister of the Wesleyan Chapel.

SECOND PASTOR, REV. SAMUEL SALISBURY

The Wesleyan Methodists retained the practice of the AMEC for all ministers to be moved to different locations every 2-3 years. From 1845-1847, the second pastor of the Wesleyan Chapel was Samuel Salisbury. The *Portrait and Biographical Record of Seneca and Schuyler Counties of New York* says of Rev. Salisbury,

> "He was one of the early agitators for the
> abolition of slavery; in fact, so strong was his
> opposition to this institution that he incurred
> the enmity of many Southern sympathizers,

---

[b] For the archeological study of the runaway slave hideout under the Syracuse Wesleyan Methodist Church, see pictures in chapter seven and reference 13 this chapter.

and his life was at times in great danger. He was actively connected with the 'underground railroad,' and assisted slaves who were fleeing to Canada."[8]

A fugitive slave law had been enacted in 1793 by Congress. However, the US Supreme Court in 1842 held that states were not obligated to enforce it, but neither could they make laws abridging it.

As a result, a much stronger fugitive slave act was enacted in 1850. It was part of a package of laws known as the Missouri Compromise of 1850. (Even though it brought California in as a free state and banned slaveholding in the District of Columbia, slaveholders were helped in Texas). Abolitionists were rankled. The law read in part (edited):

"Any person who shall knowingly and willingly obstruct any person from arresting a fugitive from service or labor, or shall rescue, or attempt to rescue, such fugitive from service or labor, from the custody of [the slaveholder]; or shall conceal such fugitive, so as to prevent the arrest of such person; for either of said offences, be subject to a fine not exceeding one thousand dollars, and imprisonment not exceeding six months. He shall also pay, by way of civil damages to the party injured by such illegal conduct, the sum of one thousand dollars for each fugitive so lost."[c]

After leaving Seneca Falls, Rev. Salisbury published a clear statement of opposition to the fugitive slave law. It appeared in 1855 in Frederick Douglass' paper under the heading of "Is the Fugitive Slave Bill a Law? Should It Be Obeyed?" Salisbury stated the bill was "unreasonable,

---

[c] The sum of $1,000 was enormous and far exceeded most worker's annual salary at the time.

inhuman, unmerciful and ungodly. . .[and] we say, unhesitantly, that it should not be obeyed."[9]

We do not have specific comments about women from Rev. Salisbury. The arrival of Rhonda Bement, the excommunicated woman from the Presbyterian Church (chapter one), shortly before his appointment and her ongoing attendance at the Chapel would infer his open attitude towards her and her supporters.

THIRD PASTOR, REV. SAMUEL PHILLIPS

Rev. Samuel Phillips was the third pastor of the Wesleyan Chapel from 1847 to 1849. The printer's minutes of the July 1848 women rights convention lists the Wesleyan Chapel pastor as "Saron Phillips." This is surely an error in transcription as we no longer have the written minutes. His name was listed as "Samuel Phillips" in the Rochester Conference of the Wesleyan Methodist Church records.[9] Since the Wesleyan Methodist Conference was responsible for giving Rev Phillips each of his three-year church rotation assignments, the District Superintendent would certainly have his name correct. Moreover, "Samuel" was a favorite name given by Methodist mothers to their sons since John Wesley's father and eldest brother were both named Samuel. "Saron" is a name the author cannot find in any listing of the 19th century.

Since the doors of the Chapel were locked upon the arrival of the leadership team on July 19, 1848, some have speculated Rev. Phillips perhaps changed his mind about the women's rights convention locating at his church. The reader can judge for themselves from the original source,

> "When those having charge of the
> Declaration, the resolutions, and several
> volumes of the Statutes of New York arrived
> on the scene, lo! the door was locked.
> However, an embryo Professor of Yale

College was lifted through an open window to
unbar the door; that done, the church was
quickly filled."[10]

The latter statement does not infer ill-intent, rather a
hint of humor. The delegates clearly understood the pastor
was favorably inclined as he attended the conference and
was one of only 32 men to sign the *Declaration of
Sentiments*. (chapter one).

Concerning Samuel Phillips, Frederick Douglass on a
visit to the Chapel in April 1849 commented,

"I found Mr Phillips, the minister, as usual on
hand, warmly interested, and ardently
laboring to promote the cause [i.e. abolition] .
. .the house was crowded with a very
respectable audience, all apparently anxious
to hear, and to be instructed. With such an
audience, and such a subject, it was
impossible to be cold and lifeless. The
meeting continued for more than two hours.
At the close I obtained eight subscribers to
the North Star."[9,11]

"S. Phillips," likely the Rev. Samuel Phillips,
Wesleyan Methodist minister, sent a letter to the *Free-
Soil Union*, transmitting the resolution,

"That this meeting, without regard to sect,
name, or parties, recommend Henry Bibb to
the confidence and hospitality of the Christian
public in every State in which he may travel.
And we bid him God speed in the cause of
suffering humanity, and in his noble effort to
induce the Christian public to send the Bible
to the slave."[9]

The current author could discover little more about the
first three pastors of the Wesleyan Chapel. In terms of its
members, there are more interesting facts.

The Wesleyan Methodists forbid slave owners from
joining the denomination but welcomed blacks both into

membership and leadership. Joshua Wright had joined the Seneca Falls Wesleyan Church by 1848. He became a trustee (lay board member or supervisor). He was still active in the congregation in 1868. Samantha Wright, his first wife, and Mary Jackson, his second wife were both active members of the church.[9]

Thomas James was an early African American member who also became a trustee of the Chapel in 1850.[9] In 1850, James refused to tell the census taker where he had been born. His 13-year-old daughter listed Canada as her birthplace, so it seems logical that the James' had moved to Seneca Falls sometime after 1830. Both Joshua Wright and Thomas James were self-emancipated slaves.[12]

Finally, The New York State Men's Temperance Conference took place in nearby Syracuse New York, on June 17, 1852. However, Susan B. Anthony of Rochester was not allowed to address the floor. After the refusal, Rev. May, announced that Elizabeth Cady Stanton would speak that evening at the Wesleyan Methodist Church in Syracuse. (The church was undoubtedly made available by the pastor, Rev. Luther Lee). A reporter attending the Wesleyan Methodist gathering noted "a large number of ladies were in attendance among whom we noticed Miss Susan B. Anthony of Rochester and Mrs. Stanton and Mrs. Bloomer of Seneca Falls." The reporter also observed that considerable dissatisfaction was expressed at the unceremonious way the lady delegates to the morning convention had been treated.[13]

It seems clear that the rebuff at Syracuse lead to the planning of a statewide women's temperance convention. Four months later, on October 14, 1852, the friendly confines of the Seneca Falls Wesleyan Methodist Chapel hosted the conclave. Susan B Anthony was one of the secretaries, and Lucy Stone, among others, served on the business committee. Delegates debated issues of divorce, religion, and women's suffrage before agreeing to petition the legislature on behalf of the recently enacted Maine law abolishing liquor sales. There was also a presentation on abolition of slavery. Many participants had signed the *Declaration of Sentiments* from the first women's rights convention. This meeting at the Wesleyan Chapel illustrates how the effort for women's rights intersected with movements for both abolitionism and temperance.

To conclude, in the first decade of the Wesleyan Chapel in Seneca Falls, the Wesleyan Methodists demonstrated their commitment to the abolition of slavery, promoting women's rights and temperance by hosting large groups wanting to advance these controversial reform issues. Again, it was not by accident that the first women's rights convention was held in the Wesleyan Chapel.

References
Chapter Six

1. Black R, Drury K. The Story of the Wesleyan Church. Indianapolis: Wesleyan Publishing House; 2012, p. 54.
2. Pegler G. Autobiography of the Life and Times of George Pegler.
https://archive.org/details/autobiographyofl00pegl; 1875.
3. Ibid, p. 150.
4. Ibid p. 408.
5. History of Seneca County [New York]: Google books; 1876, p. 56-57
6. Pegler, p. 414.
7. Pegler, p. 389.
8. Portrait and Biographical Record of Seneca and Schulyer Counties, New York: Containing Portraits and Biographical Sketches of Prominent and Representative Citizens of the Counties. Goggle books: Chapman Publishing Company; 1895, p. 487
9. Gable W. Stories from Discovering the Underground Railroad, Abolitionism, and African American Life in Seneca County, 1820-1880. 2006: 47-51.

10. Stanton EC, Anthony SB, Gage MJ, Harper IH. History of Woman Suffrage, volume one: Susan B. Anthony; 1889, p. 69.
11. Gable, p. 47.
12. Judith W. The Road to Seneca Falls: Elizabeth Cady Stanton and the First Women's Rights Convention. Chicago: University of Illinois Press; 2004; location 40%.
13. Armstrong DV, Wurst L. Clay Faces in an Abolitionist Church: The Wesleyan Methodist Church in Syracuse, New York. Historical Archaeology 2003; 37; p. 19-37.

Chapter Seven The "Jerry" Rescue

THE LIBERTY PARTY

The major political parties in the 1840s, the Whigs and Democrats, refused to denounce slavery. Unable to make progress, many abolitionists came to be disenchanted with politics. As one contemporary put it, the parties were entrenched with "servility to slavery."[1]

Seeking a new approach, Orange Scott and Luther Lee, gave their support for an uncompromising party. One editor declared "both politics and religion will gain by it. Politics will be ennobled, and religion will be humanized."[2] Of the nine key early leaders in the Liberty Party, two, Lee and Scott, would become founders of the Wesleyan Methodist Church three years later.[3]

On the other hand, many were unsure of the morality of the direct political approach. Orange Scott urged, "Are the politics of a Christian country so diverse from religion, that the moral and political bearings of the great question of human rights cannot both be kept before the community at the same time?"[4]

In Albany, New York, in May 1839, during a meeting to consider a new party, a contemporary noted that Luther Lee "made the conclusive argument that decided the action of the convention [i.e., in a favorable manner]."[3]

Thus, in April 1840, the Liberty Party was born. With little time to field candidates for the 1840 general election, Birney, the presidential candidate, received less than one percent of the total votes cast. Wesleyan Lucius Matlack was one of the few who supported Birney, saying that he counted it a privilege to be "one of that seven thousand who repudiated Baal worship of America." Moreover, Matlack estimated that members of the AMEC were "more numerous than any other class in [the] band of political pioneers [voting in 1840]."[3]

The True Wesleyan, the Wesleyan Methodist's newspaper inaugurated in 1843, gave strong support to the new party. References to the Liberty Party appear in *The True Wesleyan* newspaper in early every issue. Luther Lee referred to the Liberty Party as "our party." The number of Liberty votes in elections were reported. Even party and church meetings were held concurrently in the same cities. Nonetheless, the Liberty Party was not a religious organization and the Wesleyan Methodist Church was not a political party. The two entities differed in function. Moreover, Wesleyans did not comprise a majority of Liberty party members.

Gerrit Smith (1797-1874), a wealthy businessman and philanthropist, was one of the founding nine members of the Liberty Party. While not a Methodist (AMEC) until late in life, he was a key supporter of the Liberty Party. He was also intimately involved in the day to day working of the party's effort in abolition politics.

In the first five years of its existence, the Liberty Party emerged as the first real political venue for women. Reinhard Johnson reviews the enormous effort made by women. Women spearheaded petition drives. Men looked for women to join them at Liberty Party functions. The 1843 national nominating convention in Buffalo, New York, had over 2,000 attendees, "of whom a considerable portion were female."[4] There were three female writers on major newspapers who wrote articles favoring the Liberty Party. Abby Kelley (chapter one) gave a long speech at the 1843 national nominating convention in Buffalo.

In June 1848, one month before the Women's Rights Convention in Seneca Falls, the Liberty Party convention met in Buffalo. Two noteworthy items occurred. First, Lucretia Mott was nominated as one of several for Vice-President of the United States. She received five votes or five percent of the total delegate total. Second, Gerrit Smith complained about the lack of universal suffrage for women in the United States in his nominating speech at the Liberty Party Convention.[6][a]

The clearest expression for the equality of women is contained in the last platform of the Liberty Party in 1852. The first statement in this document reads:

> "Resolved, that the Liberty Party cannot consent to fall below, nor, in any degree, to qualify, its great central principle, that all persons - black and white, male and female - have equal political rights, and are equally entitled to the protection and advantages of Civil Government.[6][b]

In the period of 1844 to 1852, one wishes there was more documentation surviving for the Liberty Party's call for equality and suffrage. These ideas were astonishingly ahead of their time compared to any other party platform in U.S. history.

What follows is an extraordinary story of a struggle between Liberty Party men and women in Syracuse, New York, on one side, and the Federal government on the opposite side, over enforcement of the Fugitive Slave Act.

---

[a] These events provide background for the Seneca Falls Convention a few weeks later. Lucretia Mott has been widely seen as the principal organizer of the Seneca Falls Women's Rights Convention; yet, the author can find no credit for the Liberty Party influence on her activities.

[b] Johnson asserts that historians have ignored the Liberty Party. He cites the Party's success, especially in winning local elections. Moreover, Reinhard lists party members who would be eventually elected, though not necessarily under the banner of the Liberty Party. In this group, there would be 10 U.S. Senators, 25 U.S. Congressmen, 10 governors, 17 who founded colleges, and 16 who were college presidents. This was no ragtag group. Unfortunately, the Liberty Party kept poor records of their membership and meetings. Reinhard believes the list of achievements will grow as more people will be discovered to have been part of this political group. Unfortunately, the rights of women were dropped as the Liberty Party merged into the Free Soil Party for the fall 1852 national elections. The Free Soil Party then merged into the Republican Party in 1854.

THE JERRY RESCUE IN SYRACUSE, NEW YORK

Syracuse, New York is 33 miles from Seneca Falls. The new Erie Canal made the journey faster and smoother than the rutted dirt roads between the towns. Luther Lee founded the Wesleyan Methodist Church in Syracuse in 1843 and pastored until the fall of 1844. He was then elected President of the national Wesleyan Methodist Church. Lee's church in Syracuse was the only one in the city that did not segregate blacks who came to worship; and, where "all people were welcomed as equals."[7] In 1850, Lee penned his opposition in the *True Wesleyan* to the Fugitive Slave Law,

> "The law is unconstitutional because it
> deprives persons of liberty, without due
> process of law, and seeks to secure the results
> of a solemn adjudication, without the
> intervention of a court, or the action of a
> judge"[8]

In Syracuse, Lee wrote details about what he called "the largest work of my life on the Underground Railroad." If refugees made it to Syracuse, they were travel-weary, often hungry, fearful, and uncertain of their future. The runaway slave was insecure. Arrival in Syracuse meant liberty was close, yet not final. Those trying to help were subject to legal prosecution. These then were the components of the abolition movement in Syracuse.

"Freedom seekers" (another term for "fugitive slaves") could get on a railroad car and travel all the way to Canada, without charge. Luther Lee wrote,

> "I had friends, or the slave had, connected
> with the railroad at Syracuse, of whom I never
> failed to get a free pass in this form, 'Pass this
> poor colored man,' 'or poor colored woman,"
> or 'poor colored family,' as the case might be.

The conductors on the route understood these
passes and they were never challenged."

After escorting the fugitives into a railroad car, Lee
would warn them to "keep their seats until they crossed
the suspension bridge, and then they would be [safe] in
Canada."[9] [c]

The defiance represented by the Underground Railroad
did not go unchallenged. In May 1851, Secretary of State
Daniel Webster, a supporter of the Fugitive Slave Act,
came to Syracuse. In his speech he strongly condemned
any violation of the pro-slavery edict. Webster
characterized resistance to it as "treason."[10] He threatened
that violators,

> "bring upon themselves the penalty of the law
> … Depend upon it, the law will be executed
> in its spirit and to its letter. It will be executed
> in all the great cities—here in Syracuse—
> amid the next anti-slavery convention, if the
> occasion shall arise"[11]

The "next anti-slavery convention" mentioned by
Daniel Webster was a direct reference to the Liberty
Party. It seems that the federal authorities planned at least
a month ahead of time to arrest a fugitive slave in
Syracuse, New York named William "Jerry" Henry. Jerry
was a 40-year-old refugee from slavery in Missouri who
had lived in Syracuse for more than a year. He was a
"large and muscular" man, with unusual reddish hair.
Jerry earned his living as a collier (maker of wooden
staves for barrels). The townspeople thought well of Jerry.[d]

---

[c] There are sources beyond Lee for the number of freedom seekers
passing through Lee's Church and for the no charge nature of the
local railroad transport to Canada. See Wesleyan Chapel, Syracuse.
http://pacny.net/freedom_trail/WesleyanChpl.htm (accessed 11-17-
2015).

[d] There are multiple accounts of the rescue of William Henry. The
following is a selection from different accounts that seem most
probable to the author. The latest and most complete recent account is
Angela Murphy's book, The Jerry Rescue.[10]

The federal intervention of October 1, 1851, was poorly timed. Syracuse was packed with thousands of visitors to the Onondaga County Fair and with attendees at the county Liberty Party convention. For his part, however, Jerry was planning to have a quiet day and go about his carpentry.

Around Noon, five Federal Marshals burst into his shop to capture Jerry. He was accused of theft. Only later would Jerry be told the real charge was that of a fugitive slave. The Marshals hoped the lesser charge would enable them to take Jerry peacefully. They were wrong. He vigorously resisted. He was subdued. He was shackled with heavy manacles used for runaway slaves. Bloody and battered, Jerry was thrown into a pushcart. Four men sat on him. He was dragged through town with blood dripping from the handcart. The spectacle sparked anger from the few observers, but word-of-mouth reports worked their way through Syracuse fanning outrage and indignation.

Taken to the federal building Jerry was to be arraigned in front of the Federal Commissioner, Joseph Sabine. Earlier in September, Sabine had shown his abolitionist sympathies by frustrating the Marshals and slave hunters by demanding a deed of sale and proof of Jerry's identity. This documentation from Missouri took days to arrive. When it did, Sabine, reluctantly issued the warrant for the arrest of Jerry.

After Jerry arrived at the federal building, the wife of the commissioner, Margaret Sabine, leaked the news of Henry's arrest to the Liberty Party convention. The meeting adjourned. Gerrit Smith and Lawrence Gibbs, an attorney, ran to the hearing room.

The hearing began at 2:00 PM. Lawrence Gibbs and Gerrit Smith acted as defense attorneys. The defense immediately asked for a postponement to better prepare their case. Sabine denied the motion but stopped the proceedings for half an hour to find a larger room. In the transition, Jerry made a break for it. With the help of a sympathetic spectator, Charles Merrick, Jerry was shoved out the door. Others hurled him tumbling down the stairway. Still in handcuffs, he staggered down the street.[11] He was soon re-captured a few blocks away.

The hearing started again. But meanwhile, the atmosphere around the federal building had changed. Church bells were ringing in a pattern warning the city that a fugitive slave had been captured. This was a signal for inhabitants to assemble at the federal building. A disgruntled abolitionist throng of both men and women, black and white, numbered more than 2,000. They crowded the hallways, spilled onto the porch and surrounded the building. There was standing room only inside the courtroom. The proceedings were packed with citizens and U.S. Marshalls.

One disgusting feature of the Fugitive Slave Act was the short legal review required; the intent of the law was the immediate return of slaves. Incredibly, only the sworn affidavit of the bounty hunter capturing the suspected slave was needed. The alleged slave's statement counted for nothing.

The proceedings went slowly. The defense raised strenuous objections and tried to prolong the hearing. The crowd outside grew restive. Shouts demanded the release of Jerry. Inside, it became difficult to hear. Commissioner Sabine wished to postpone the hearing. But Federal Marshal Allen wanted to conclude the issue. Rocks and other objects began crashing through the windows. One projectile nearly hit Commissioner Sabine's head. He emphatically postponed the hearing until the next morning.

Federal Marshalls took Jerry to the back room of the police office and turned on gas lamps to keep an eye on Jerry. Marshal Allen had to leave the building in a disguise to make his way safely through the crowd. Later Allen recalled that he had assumed Jerry had been taken to the nearby federal penitentiary. Had he known Jerry was to remain in the police office, he [Allen] would have remained within the besieged building.

The Syracuse Vigilance Committee, a biracial 12-member group formed in case of such an emergency, met within two hours to devise an escape. Four of the participants, Charles and Montgomery Merrick, George Carter, and Edward K. Hunt were Wesleyan Methodists. Gerrit Smith was a fifth member.

At 8:00 PM, a pre-arranged time, the members of the Vigilance Committee joined the crowd outside the federal building. Soon, someone shouted, "Now!" At the signal a group of men attacked the building with axes and clubs. One of group of men showed up with a ten-foot-long wooden beam. The battering ram soon broke the front door down. Hoping to circumvent a hail of gunfire from the room where Jerry was held, the assault group went to the adjoining room and began battering the wall. The intent being the wall should fall in on the Marshals and prevent gunfire.

During the beating of the wall, Federal Marshal Henry Fitch emerged from the captive's room. He fired two warning shots. While he did so, someone struck his pistol arm and knocked his weapon away. Fitch thought better of his plan to face down the crowd and jumped from the nearest second floor window. The other men guarding Jerry released the captive by pushing him through the doorway. The guards then assumed defensive postures.[e]

Shackled at the wrists and ankles, Jerry emerged. Two black men carried him out of the building. A carriage whisked him away. It drove in circles to confuse pursuers. At one point, the carriage stopped at a blacksmith to get the shackles removed.

It is possible that the Vigilance committee considered hiding Henry in the basement of the Syracuse Wesleyan Methodist Church. The cellar contains evidence that it

---

[e] One account has them hiding in the closet.

was a hide-out for fugitive slaves in transit. The clay soil has a tunnel dug out with a right-angle turn. This would likely fool anyone who might look in from the doorway. (Figure 7.1).

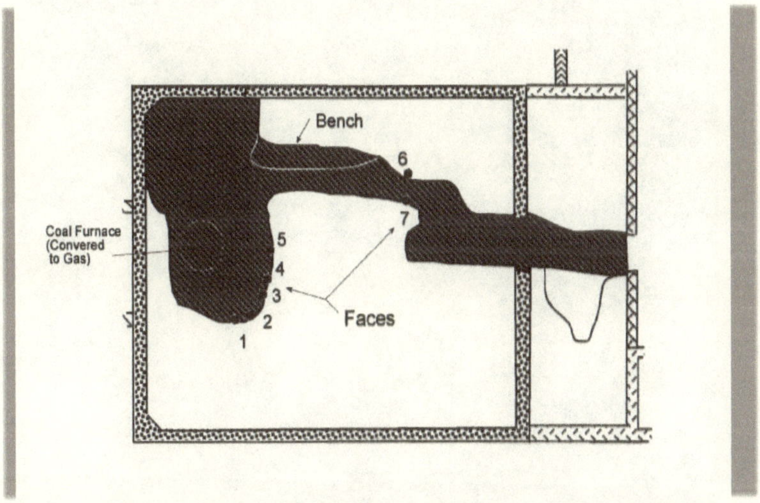

Figure 7.1 Diagram of tunnel in Syracuse Wesleyan Methodist basement. The sharp turn to the right near the number seven was supposed to hide the main waiting room for refugees. The numbers refer to clay faces sculpted in the walls. Reproduced with permission, Historical Archeology.[8]

A large earthen bench was present beyond the turn. Most fascinating is the presence of seven sculpted faces on the walls. These have the characteristic appearance of African Americans. The best-preserved clay face is shown in figure 7.2.

Figure 7.2 Sculpted clay face number one in tunnel of figure 7.1. The face is 14 cm wide and 18 cm high. It has the date "1817" carved beneath it, but this is of uncertain significance. Reproduced with permission, Historical Archeology.[8]

Historical and archeological research supports their antebellum dating. Three of the faces are now preserved in the nearby Onondaga County Museum.[8]

It is likely that federal forces during their four-day search combed the church building of the well-known abolitionist congregation. Unfortunately, police records in Syracuse prior to 1870 were destroyed in a fire. Details from the law enforcement side about the Jerry rescue are sketchy.

In an earlier incident in 1839, a woman slave named Harriet Powell, was brought to Syracuse with her owners, the Davenport family, who were visiting the city. Her escape was arranged by Gerrit Smith and others. In that incident, Angela Murphy says that all the homes of abolitionists in Syracuse were searched.12 Undoubtedly, the 1851 Vigilance committee would have remembered this pursuit pattern and sought to avoid it.

Instead, Jerry was concealed at the home of a Democrat and supporter of Daniel Webster, Caleb Davis, a butcher. While Davis may have been an opponent of abolition, he deeply resented the invasion of federal forces into his local community. The strategy of the Vigilance Committee was brilliant. Who would ever think to search the home of an anti-abolitionist? During the four days Henry was hiding in his home, Davis took to the streets to disingenuously denounce the abolitionists and rescuers.[13]

Law enforcement watched the exits to town for days after the escape. However, Davis had a good excuse with his meat deliveries to visit outlying districts. On the next delivery day, Davis covered Jerry and hid him under his wagon. Searchers were evidently reluctant to disturb packages of bloody meat. In any case, Davis got Jerry across the bridge and out of town; but not before he had the foresight to bribe the toll keeper to delay pursuers. Indeed, Davis was found out and chasers followed sometime later. The pursuers were stymied by a toll man that seemed unusually difficult to wake up. Jerry reached Kingston, Ontario, Canada by boarding a schooner departing from Oswego.

In Syracuse, the atmosphere remained tense for fugitive slaves who had previously felt safe. Nineteen days after Henry was rescued, several black couples of the Wesleyan Methodist Church in Syracuse resigned their membership. Next to their names in the membership rolls is the notation: "Removed to Canada to escape slave catchers!"[14]

For weeks, the atmosphere was anxiety ridden for rescue participants. Federal officials thundered possible indictments for "treason," a capital offense. The *Syracuse Standard* dismissed such talk as "political bravado" and correctly emphasized that the offenses were not treasonous in nature. It cited Article 3 of the U.S. Constitution where treason is defined as "levying war against the [United States] or giving aid and comfort to its enemies." Opposing a federal law was hardly treason.

Nonetheless, to intimidate locals (and other cities), Federal indictments were handed down within weeks for more than a score of men. One was Montgomery Merrick, a Wesleyan Methodist, and 12 were black. After numerous postponements (e.g., when the prosecution objected to Gerrit Smith – a non-lawyer – appearing on behalf of the defense, the Court of Appeals immediately issued an order admitting Smith to the bar), the trials began in January 1853. The court cases dragged on for two years. Only four cases (all black men) were heard and only one, Enoch Reed, was found guilty on petty larceny. Reed died while waiting the appeal of his case, though his arrest was "obtained by false pretenses."[15]

Luther Lee was not in Syracuse when the Jerry rescue occurred but was living in New York City as editor of the *True Wesleyan*. He would return six months after the Jerry rescue to pastor the Wesleyan Methodist church a second time.

In 1855, one thousand citizens of Syracuse rallied to support two persons who had been arrested in Milwaukee for assisting the escape of slaves. Lee was called upon for the last speech. "It was getting late," Lee recalled, "the people were weary, and I must strike boldly or fail." He stood and orated,

> "I had never obeyed it [i.e., the fugitive slave law] – I never would obey it. I had assisted 30 slaves to escape to Canada during the last month. If the United States authorities wanted anything of me, my residence was at 3909 Onondaga Street. I would admit that they could take me and lock me up in the penitentiary on the Hill; but if they did such a foolish thing as that, I had friends enough in Onondaga County to level it with the ground before the next morning.' The immense throng rose upon their feet and shouted, 'We will do it! We will do it!' And I have no doubt at that moment they thought they would."[9]

References
Chapter Seven

1. Willey A. The History of the Antislavery Cause in State and Nation. New York: Greenwood Press; 1860; reprinted 1969, p. 149

2. Strong DM. Partners in Political Abolitionism: The Liberty Party and the Wesleyan Methodist Connection. Methodist History. Lake Junaluska, NC 1985; 23; p. 99-115.

3. Matlack LC, Whedon DD. The Antislavery Struggle and Triumph in the Methodist Episcopal Church. New York: Phillips & Hunt; 1881, p. 202-204.

4. Scott O. An Appeal to the Methodist Episcopal Church: D. H. Ela, publisher; 1838, p. 118.

5. Johnson RO. The Liberty Party, 1840-1848: Antislavery Third-Party Politics in the United States: LSU Press; 2009, location 7%.

6. Smith G. Proceedings of the National Liberty Convention, held at Buffalo, N.Y., June 14,15, 1848. Syracuse University: http://library.syr.edu/digital/collections/g/GerritSmith/453.htm 1848.

7. Dayton D, Strong D. Rediscovering an Evangelical Heritage: a Tradition and Trajectory of Integrating Piety and Justice. Second ed. Grand Rapids, Michigan: Baker Academic; 2014; p. 130.

8. Douglas A, LouAnn W. Clay Faces in an Abolitionist Wesleyan Methodist Church in Syracuse, New York. Historical Archeology 2003; 37; p. 19-37.

9. Lee L. Autobiography of the Rev. Luther Lee: Phillips & Hunt; 1882, p. 320-336

10. Murphy A. The Jerry Rescue: the Fugitive Slave Law, Northern Rights, and the American Sectional Crisis. New York: Oxford University Press; 2016, p. 107

11. Sokolow JA. The Jerry McHenry Rescue and the Growth of Northern Antislavery Sentiment during the 1850s. Journal of American Studies 1982; 16; p. 427-45.

12. Murphy, p. 38.

13. Murphy p. 121.

14. Murphy p. 126.

15. Roach MP. The Rescue of William "Jerry" Henry: Antislavery and Racism in the Burned-over District. New York History 2001; 82; p. 135-54.

Chapter Eight Ordination of Women

The ordination of the first woman minister, Antoinette Brown Blackwell, by Rev Luther Lee was a momentous time in American history. Blackwell was one of the first women to graduate from Oberlin College in Ohio, where she had studied theology.[a] Lacking a call to preach from a local church, Antoinette Blackwell accepted the offer of her classmate Lucy Stone to join the circuit of women's rights speakers. Stone had also graduated from Oberlin College in 1847.

Founded in 1833, Oberlin was the first coeducational college in America. Its beginnings were made against resistance, "This amalgamation of sexes will not do. If you live in Powder House, you blow up once in a while."[1]

Charles Finney, a famous evangelist of the 19th century, joined the faculty in 1835. He helped to guide the Arminian and pietistic theology of the institution. Together, Finney and Oberlin College formed the "New School of Presbyterianism" versus the "Old School of Presbyterianism" based in Princeton Theological School. The older school maintained a type of conservative Calvinism (chapter three).

Blackwell was also a committed abolitionist and temperance reformer. On one of her speaking tours, she visited South Butler, Wayne County, New York. After hearing her speak, the local Congregational church asked her to become their pastor. In the spring of 1853, Blackwell took up her pastoral duties of preaching two

---

[a] Antoinette Brown (1825-1921) married Samuel C. Blackwell at age 31 (1856). We will use her married name throughout this book to prevent confusion since she had a long list of accomplishments before and while married. Her husband died in 1901. Samuel C. Blackwell was the brother of Henry B. Blackwell who married her famous friend, Lucy Stone.

sermons each Sunday. An observer noted, "Her voice is silvery, and her manner pleasing."[2]

By that summer, the church's governing board decided to proceed with her ordination. Briefly, in this context, ordination means the official recognition of a minister's credentials and character that allows the recipient to add the appellation of "Reverend." Ordination requires advanced theological education. The authority of a congregational church is vested entirely in the local parishioners. The church board recognized,

> "the ceremony would not change her role; she already performed all the functions of a minister, including administering the sacraments. But it would be a public statement about a woman's right to preach, and a confirmation of the rather risky step the church had taken."[2]

A conservative deacon told Blackwell that neither he nor anyone else was opposed to the plan. However, it would be reassuring to all local church members if Gerrit Smith, whose family's money had built the church, came and spoke in favor of the service.

Gerrit Smith wrote back to Blackwell indicating he did not think an ordination service necessary. Blackwell replied,

> "We do not care whether the ceremony is performed in the usual way or not. We only want something done to show the world that we believe in a woman's being initiated into the ministry and something which will answer without questioning as a legal ordination in the eyes of the Law & Public Opinion. . . Every person present may express himself opposed to all ordinations & welcome, if he will only be willing in addition to put woman upon the same platform with man, and recognize me as much a minister as others. . .

> It will do them good, and me good, & good to
> the cause of woman."[2]

Blackwell asked Charles Finney from Oberlin to perform the ordination service. She reported to Lucy Stone,

> "Finney wrote a long fatherly letter, called me
> his dear child, daughter, dearest sister and
> expressed a world of sympathy but said he
> could not at present act-his wife would if she
> were a man-but he would examine the subject
> pray over [it] and if he could assist, he
> would."[2]

In any case, the 60-year-old Finney did not make the 800-mile round trip that would have required at the time about one week of uncomfortable travel.

Cazden relates that when Blackwell's ordained Congregational colleagues refused to officiate at the ordination service, Blackwell turned to someone she knew through the temperance movement, Rev Luther Lee. However, Cazden does not tell us exactly where and when her acquaintance with Lee began.[2] Blackwell must have known Rev Lee from his high profile with the Liberty Party. She had worked in Gerrit Smith's congressional campaign of 1852, which Smith won. The Brown family were known to be active in the Liberty Party.[3] We may never know where they formed their acquaintance. In any case, Luther Lee was not one to shrink from controversy.

The dedication service of Antoinette Brown Blackwell by Rev Luther Lee took place in the Congregational church in South Butler, Wayne County, New York on September 15, 1853. Interesting excerpts[4] [b] from his sermon are,

> "The ordination of a female, or the setting
> apart of a female to the work of the Christian
> ministry, is, to say the least, a novel
> transaction, in this land and age. It cannot fail

---

[b] https://www.loc.gov/item/tmp83029911)

to call forth many remarks, and will, no
doubt, like many censures."

Reverend Lee took for his principal text the Pauline
passage from Galatians 3:28,

"There is neither Jew nor Greek, there is
neither slave or free man, there is neither male
nor female; for you are all one in Christ
Jesus." Lee asked, "What does this text mean?
– I cannot see how the text can be explained
so as to exclude females from any right,
office, work, privilege, or immunity which
males enjoy, or perform. If the text means
anything, it means males and females are
equal in rights, privileges and responsibilities
upon the Christian platform."

Lee then cited the venerated Methodist Bible
commentator, Dr. Adam Clarke, "Under the blessed Spirit
of Christianity, they [women] have equal *rights*, equal
privileges, and equal *blessings*; and let me add, they are
equally *useful*."

Lee noted it was not new for women to lead in the
Christian church and cited numerous examples from the
Old Testament and New Testament. In terms of
qualifications,

"We are not here to make a minister. It is not
to confer on this our sister, a right to preach
the gospel. If she has not that right already,
we have no power to communicate it to her.
Nor have we met to qualify her for the work
of the ministry. If God and mental and moral
culture have not already qualified her, we
cannot, by anything we may do by way of
ordaining or setting her apart."

Lee concluded, "[It is] our belief, our sister in Christ,
Antoinette Brown Blackwell, is one of the ministers of the
new covenant, authorized, qualified, and called of God to
preach the gospel of his Son Jesus Christ."

For Blackwell it was a weighty occasion,
> "It seemed to me a very solemn thing when
> our three deacons and these clergymen all
> stood around me each placing a hand upon
> my head or shoulder [praying for me] and
> gravely admitting me into the ranks of the
> ministry."

The "great wall of custom," as she had once described it to Lucy Stone, had been breached at last.[2]

One observer, Dr. Harriot Hunt, felt the service was,
> "monumental to the cause of woman. There
> was something grand and elevating in the idea
> of a female presiding over a congregation and
> breaking to them the bread of life. It was a
> new position for woman and gave promise of
> her exaltation to that moral and intellectual
> rank which she was designed to fill."[2]

Gerrit Smith reassured the church: "I congratulate you upon your selection of a pastor. You have chosen one who is wise and strong, and good, and faithful, and trusting, and full of love."[2]

Lee's ordination message, *Woman's Right to Preach the Gospel*, was immediately published as a thirty-page booklet. The Wesleyan Methodist paper quickly announced its sale. Editor Lucius Matlack followed up with a strong editorial,
> "Woman is our equal in all respects. Her
> rights, as ours, are to be known by her ability
> and opportunity to act. She may appear,
> fittingly in the highest professional positions,
> as in the common pursuits of life. We concede
> her right to free thought, free speech, freedom
> of the platform, forum, pulpit, bar, and ballot
> box."[5]

Matlack went on to cite Lee's sermon and gave a lengthy quote from Edward Smith's *Christian Statesman*. Smith expressed his delight over the oration and added:

"We are much encouraged to hope that the day is not far distant when woman will take her proper place in the church of God. That day must come before the world can be saved."[5]

The ordination did not change Blackwell's routine.
"My work through the following winter after
my ordination proceeded in the usual way.
We had good audiences for the conditions of
the surrounding country, and no friction
occurred anywhere in the church or the
congregation. I did a good deal of lecturing
and of attendance on other meetings."[2]

Antoinette Brown Blackwell vigorously asserted the Bible supported equal rights for women. Some feminists disagreed.[c]

Blackwell was concerned that the anti-Christian views of some feminists would be assumed to be the official stance of the woman's rights movement; thus, prejudicing public opinion against the push for equality. When hearing Elizabeth Cady Stanton refer to Paul's epistles as "human parchments," Blackwell wrote a strong dissent,
"I am very sensitive about fastening
theological questions upon the woman
movement. It is not that I am horrified at your
calling St. Paul's writings 'human
parchments,' but because I think when it is
done officially that it is unjust to the cause. It
is compelling it [the woman's rights
movement] to endorse something which does

------

[c] However, later in the century, a search was made by Elizabeth Cady Stanton to find feminist women who could join her editorial board. These women needed to assert that the Bible advocated an inferior position for woman. Susan Anthony cautioned Stanton to recruit at least a few editorial board members "who have read the Bible once through, consecutively, in their lives." (Kern K. Mrs. Stanton's Bible: Cornell University Press; 2002, p. 137.) That even one panel member had ever done so was never clear. Not a high bar for a critic, one would think.

> not belong to it. When you write for yourself
> say exactly what you please. But if you write
> as Chairwoman of the [recent Cleveland]
> Woman's Rights Convention do not compel
> us to endorse anything foreign to the
> movement."[2]

Towards the end of her first year of ministry, Rev Blackwell began to suffer physically and mentally from uncertain causes. What she called "brain fever" may have been a combination of mental confusion, nightmares, and the like. Or, she may have had an episode of mild viral meningitis.[d] In any case, in July 1854, Blackwell left South Butler and went home to her parents' farm to rest.[2] She eventually became a Unitarian minister (for a few years) and ardently worked for women's suffrage for the remainder of her life.

Her Christian life continued to promote peacemaking. Alice Rossi, in a sociometrical chart of American women suffrage leaders, determined that "Nettie" (her nickname) had the most amical relationship with the other first-generation suffrage leaders. She frequently soothed ruffled feathers between sparring suffragettes.[6]

The next evidence we have for a woman preacher being ordained was through the Wesleyan Methodist Church. In 1861, the Illinois conference of the Wesleyan Methodist Church made Mrs. Mary A. Will an elder of the church. The ordination set off controversy at the 1864 General Conference. However, by a vote of 38 to 8, the 1864 Conference upheld the decision for the ordination of Mary Will. Further, the Conference refused to pass a motion to disapprove future ordinations of women on the astute basis that "Scriptures were not sufficiently clear" for women to be denied such status.[5]

A century later it would be claimed by some that Olympia Brown, a Unitarian minister, was the first woman in America (1863) to be ordained, with "full

---

[d] Author's medical opinion.

denominational authority."[7] The author believes the latter-day claimants misunderstand Congregational polity since the entire authority for making ecclesiastical decisions lies with the local congregation. However, even if one disagrees with the precedence of the Antoinette Brown Blackwell ordination, Mary Will, in the Wesleyan Methodist Church, was confirmed with full denominational authority in 1861. The latter sanction would still precede the action for Olympia Brown.

Why not the first for the Quakers? The Quakers did not formally recognize or ordain any minister, whether male or female. There was, however, an informal recognition of lay ministers for each local Friends group. The predominantly rural Quakers discouraged both their male and female members from obtaining a college education or advanced theological training. It was thought these actions would interfere with a life lived simply. While different Quaker groups would begin to alter their attitude towards advanced education later in the 19th century, these changes would not come in time for Quakers to be the first group to ordain a woman in America.

In summary, the first woman ordained in modern times was Antoinette Brown Blackwell. A Wesleyan Methodist, Luther Lee, boldly stepped forward to perform the ceremony. As noted previously, it was not a new custom in Christianity, but a return to earlier equivalent practices. In the 19th century, women were becoming more visible and active in many Christian denominations. These activities even included leadership positions; but they rarely rose to the level of ordination. Nonetheless, in the parlance of a 20th century metaphor, it still matters that the glass ceiling was broken with the rite of ordination since it is the clearest example of equality in the church.

References
Chapter Eight

1. Dayton D, Strong D. Rediscovering an Evangelical Heritage: a Tradition and Trajectory of Integrating Piety and Justice. Second ed. Grand Rapids, Michigan: Baker Academic; 2014, p. 92.
2. Elizabeth C. Antoinette Brown Blackwell: a Biography. Old Westbury, New York: The Feminist Press; 1983, p. 73-90
3. Johnson RO. The Liberty Party, 1840-1848: Antislavery Third-Party Politics in the United States: LSU Press; 2009, location 53%.
4. Lee L. Women's Right to Preach the Gospel: a Sermon, Preached at the Ordination of the Rev Miss Antoinette L. Brown, at South Butler, Wayne county, N.Y., Sept. 15, 1853. https://www.loc.gov/item/tmp83029911/ , Syracuse, New York; 1853.
5. Caldwell Wayne ed. Reformers and Revivalists: History of the Wesleyan Church. Indianapolis, Indiana: Wesley Press; 1992, p. 58-59.
6. Rossi AS, ed. The Feminist papers: From Adams to de Beauvoir: Columbia University Press; 1988, p. 276.
7. Olympia Brown-Dictionary of Unitarian & Universalist Biography. http://uudb.org/articles/olympiabrown.html (accessed 1-30-2018).

Chapter Nine The Salvation Army

The Salvation Army is one of the most remarkable organizations for women's rights in the Wesleyan Holiness tradition.[a] The focus of this chapter is on William Booth and his "equal partner" wife, Catherine Mumford Booth. It is a story of their egalitarian attitude for women in the Salvation Army. A particular interest is how suffragists picked up on the methods used by the Salvation Army women officers to spread the gospel.

William Booth was born in 1829 to a family that is best described as near poverty. At age 13, he was apprenticed to a pawnbroker. Two years later, Booth was saved at the Methodist Chapel in Nottingham. At age 21, he was appointed a Methodist lay preacher. Booth worked as minister in the Methodist Episcopal Church and the Methodist New Connection until 1862.[b]

Booth stayed with the Methodist New Connection for more than seven years. His desire to hold revivals and engage in full-time evangelism did not match what the denomination wanted him to do. The disagreement was over methodology, not Wesleyan doctrine. Booth abandoned the conventional concept of a church and a pulpit and traveled throughout England holding revivals.

William met his future wife, Catherine Mumford, in 1852. Catherine Mumford Booth was the same age as William. However, her childhood reflected challenges of scoliosis (curvature of the spine) and tuberculosis; both of

---

[a] Many books exist on the social reform and practice of Christian mercies of the Salvation Army. The author recommends the reader obtain one.

[b] The Methodist New Connection separated from the main Methodist body in Britain in 1797, five years after John Wesley's death. William was ordained in the Connection in 1858 and is probably its most famous member. It eventually merged with other Wesleyan groups in 1932 to form the "Methodist Church" in Britain.

which restricted her to bed for long periods. Reflecting her lifelong love of learning and self-control, she was said to have read the Bible through eight times before age 12. Self-educated, she preferred non-fiction and read many theological books. The only novel she reported reading was Uncle Tom's Cabin, one that she frequently referenced in her letters. William and Catherine were married in 1855.

Catherine was heavily influenced by the American Methodist (AMEC) holiness writer, Phoebe Palmer. Phoebe, and her husband, Walter, came to England on a four-year speaking tour from 1859-1863. Shortly after Phoebe Palmer started preaching in churches, Rev. Arthur Ross, wrote a pamphlet critical of women preachers. This diatribe awakened the resentment of Catherine Booth. She wrote her mother, "I am determined that this fellow not go unthrashed." Catherine then (1859) penned a pamphlet: *Female Ministry; Or a Women's Right to Preach the Gospel*. The opening lines state,

> "The first and most common objection urged
> against the public exercises of women, is that
> they are unnatural and unfeminine. Many
> labor under a very great but common mistake,
> viz. that of confounding nature with
> custom. . . Why should woman be confined
> exclusively to the kitchen and the distaff, any
> more than man to the field and workshop?"

After rebutting common misconceptions, she then reviews Christian history and meaning of Biblical passages about women in a well-reasoned essay.[c]

However, Catherine had not yet preached a sermon. In 1860, Catherine was listening to William preach. When he finished, she stood up and walked to the pulpit and asked him if she could say a word. She gave her testimony:

[c] Woman's Right to Preach the Gospel. Booth, Catherine Mumford, http://purl.dlib.indiana.edu/iudl/vwwp.

"I daresay many of you have been looking upon me as a very devoted woman, and one who has been living faithfully to God, but I have come to know that I have been living in disobedience, and to that extent 1 have brought darkness and leanness into my soul; but I promised the Lord three or four months ago [to start preaching], and I dare not disobey. I have come to tell you this and to promise the Lord that I will be obedient to the Heavenly vision."[1]

After she was done, William whispered a question to Catherine. After she nodded yes, William turned to the audience and said, 'my wife, Catherine, will preach tonight.' Thus, an extensive career in preaching was begun by Catherine.[d]

Both Catherine and William were proponents of Wesleyan Holiness. Later, William Booth would endorse a plain statement of Christian Holiness written by Salvation Army Officer Samuel Brengle,

"There are people who fail to get the blessing, because they are seeking something altogether distinct from Holiness. They want a vision of Heaven, of balls of fire, of some angel. Or, they want an experience that will save them from all trials and temptations, and from all possible mistakes and infirmities. Or, they want a power that will make sinners fall like dead men when they speak. They overlook the verse which declares that 'the end of the commandment is love out of a pure heart, and of a good conscience, and of faith unfeigned;'

---

[d] Sixty-two of her sermons are transcribed on audio: http://www.sermonindex.net/modules/articles/index.php?view=article &aid=29772 (Accessed February 4, 2018)

which teaches us that Holiness is nothing
more than a pure heart, filled with perfect
love, a clear conscience toward God and man,
which comes from a faithful discharge of duty
and simple faith without hypocrisy."[2]

Catherine spoke to well to do congregations; whereas William preached to the middle and lower classes. Her efforts became increasingly important for fundraising for their ministry and later the Salvation Army.

Nonetheless, she was still criticized. Regarding Adam Clarke, the venerated Methodist commentator who interpreted scriptures positively for women to preach, Catherine Booth said,

"Oh, for a few more Adam Clarkes to dispel
the ignorance of the church. Then we should
not hear the very pigmies in Christianity
reasoning against holy and intelligent women
opening their mouths for the Lord in the
presence of the church."[3]

William and Catherine Booth were eventually invited to hold a series of evangelistic meetings in the East End of London in 1865. A tent with seating for 200 was provided in a Quaker graveyard, and their services became an instant success. Here they planted roots. His renown spread throughout London. For American readers, the East End of London was the poorest section of the City.

"The physical needs of the masses were
overwhelming. Four years of civil war in the
United States had upset trade across the
Atlantic, resulting in rising unemployment
and poverty in England. Unemployment
forced greater numbers of working-class
families into the slums of East London each
year. Children as young as five were
compelled to work for up to fourteen hours a
day in factories, earning no more than a

pittance. People frequently starved to death,
their lifeless bodies discovered among the
refuse and waste in the dirty alleyways.
Sickness and disease were rampant among the
deprived of Victorian England. The open
sewers and poor water supply further
enhanced the spread of disease."[4]

Thieves, prostitutes, and drunkards were among the Booth's first converts to Christianity in the East End. To the desperately poor, he preached hope and salvation. Catherine was also deeply influenced by the poverty she encountered in the East End of London. She recalled,

"I remember in one case finding a poor
woman lying on a heap of rags. She had just
given birth to twins, and there was nobody of
any sort to look after her. I can never forget
the desolation of that room. I was soon busy
trying to make her a little more comfortable.
The babies I washed in a broken pie
dish…Since coming more in contact with
them [the very poor], I have found their
condition to be so much worse than anything I
had previously conceived. I have often felt
confounded, disheartened, and almost
paralyzed. I have seen many hundreds of
thousands of the lower classes gathered
together during the last two or three years,
and have often said to myself, 'Is it possible
that these are our fellow-countrymen in this
end of the nineteenth century, in this so-called
Christian country?"[4,5]

Catherine Booth inspired salvationist women. Many women attributed their joining the Army from her example. The Hallelujah Lasses, as Salvationist women were known transformed the practice of female ministry.[6]

Salvationist women stood in the streets, claiming spiritual authority and called upon others to repent. They did not preach as other evangelicals had done but took their inventive style from the urban culture around them. The Hallelujah Lasses used the broad gestures of popular entertainment to dramatize their spiritual vision.

In 1880, Eliza Haynes paraded the streets of Marylebone with a sign around her neck that read, "I am Happy Eliza." Her hair was loose and flowing in a manner that was usually reserved for inside the home. She played the fiddle and handed out announcements of where she would preach.[6]

> "Like the celebrated women of the music hall, Salvationist women used costume, song, and gesture to capture their audience. Many women played musical instruments, composed songs, or wrote new words to popular music hall tunes. These young women were aware of the enormous appeal of commercial entertainment, and they eagerly capitalized on it. As soon as a woman succeeded with a new technique, others picked it up and often added their own innovations. Crowds gathered for Army meetings, and everyone realized the Lasses were an important draw."[6]

Predictably, "the Lasses horrified many observers." Crowds pelted them with rotting vegetables and told them to go home; and, they were subjected to a particularly sexualized form of abuse and ridicule. Salvationist women reported that "the language used by the men . . . has been of the vilest character."[6]

The Army men and women were attacked physically in the streets in England. In 1882 alone, 699 officers and soldiers, 251 women and 23 under age 15 were brutally assaulted generally while marching through the streets singing hymns. The strange idea of the authorities was that the Salvationists were the cause of their own trouble. However, it was thought by many that the authorities were paid to look the other way. Early on, it was the Salvationists who were arrested for "disturbing the peace." In the same year of 1882, 86 Army personnel were imprisoned, 15 of whom were women.[7]

THE SALVATION ARMY IN AMERICA

The Salvation Army invaded the United States on March 10, 1880. Salvation Army Commissioner George Scott Raiton and seven women officers from England knelt on the dockside at Battery Park in New York City to give thanks for their safe arrival. These pioneers met opposition on their first official street meeting. They were ridiculed, arrested, and attacked. Over time, several officers and soldiers even gave their lives.

For example, Captain Dixon's testimony started with her farmer daughter's origin in Pennsylvania. At age 18, she lost her husband and mother. Feeling willful and selfish, she sought forgiveness for her sins. She found salvation and joined the army. She served in a corps and was promoted to local commander. She was attacked, imprisoned and sentenced for the crime of marching in the streets. She spent 60 days toiling at "arduous" labor and survived "loathsome" conditions. Despite the prison soap taking the skin off her hands, and the food revolting, "the peace of God filled our hearts and we found recompense of reward talking to the poor, sinful, despairing creatures."[8]

Persecution did not stop the army. In many cases, it won them sympathy. By 1883, the Salvation Army had expanded into California, Connecticut, Indiana, Maryland, Massachusetts, Michigan, Missouri, New York, Ohio, and Pennsylvania.

From the very beginning, the Salvation Army welcomed the equality of women. Clause 14 of the Foundation Deed submitted in 1875 specified that,

"Nothing shall authorize the conference to take any course whereby the right of females to be employed as evangelists or class leaders shall be impeded or destroyed or which shall render females ineligible for any office or deny to them the right to speak and vote at all or any official meetings of which they may be members."[9]

In 1878, only three years after Clause 14 was formulated, forty-one of the total ninety-one Salvation Army officers in the field were women.[9] Officers in the Salvation Army are equivalent to trained clergy in other denominations. Officers are considered corps commanders in charge of the local station; this would be the same as the senior clergy-person leading a local church.

Salvation Army women achieved parity with men in the areas of privation, positions, and pay. Privation or hardship was the lot of most officers whether men or women. This is important since Army women were not delicate flowers to be placed on the shelf. They were in the thick of Army battles with street marching, singing and preaching. After the decade of the 1880s, public harassment of the Army significantly diminished in large cities but persisted in smaller towns. However, by the turn of the 20th century, the uniform of the Army woman became so recognized for helping the disadvantaged that the woman officer could walk with immunity through saloons and brothels on her mission to help the poor.

While Salvation Army in the United States would start out in 1880 with seven women officers to one male officer, the ratio would more nearly equalize in the late 19th and 20th centuries. Women officers have tended to outnumber their male cohorts by as much as 33%.

Administrative staff officers, either working in headquarters or in supervisory positions, have had a ratio of men to women of two to one. Around one or two per one hundred officers held administrative positions, representing a tiny fraction of the Army's officer contingent. One difference may be that college educated officers entering the Army have been much more likely to be moved into an administrative position. Until recent times, men have graduated from college in a larger ratio than women.

On the front line throughout the organization's history, women officers could do everything their male counterparts did: a woman, whether single or married, could lead public worship, conduct weddings, dedicate (christen) a child, visit the sick and bury the dead.[3]

Unmarried male and female Army officers have had parity in pay. However, it must be pointed out that the pay has always been subsistence pay. A late 20th century officer put the recompense in perspective by saying one could not support the use of a private automobile on such a salary.[5] Marriage is not required of any officer. However, Salvation Army rules require that officers must be married to another army officer. The payment rules are more complex for married couples as they are treated as a single entity for pay purposes with a family allowance.

Women's rights go far beyond bringing home the vote for women. It includes a safe and comfortable environment. The Salvation Army was a key player in attacking the "white slavery" problem in the late 19th and 20th centuries. At the time, "white slavery" was a euphemistic term for young females who were forced into prostitution under age 16. Prosecution was difficult in cases where the child was over the age of consent of 13 years.

William and Catherine Booth prepared a petition to raise the age of consent for boy and girls to 16 years of age. Also, the procurement of young people for immoral purposes was advanced as a criminal act. Protests over the issue lasted 17 days during which the Salvation Army collected 393,000 signatures; pasted line by line, the signatures stretched more than two and one-half miles. The petition was carried with fanfare from Salvation

Army bands, and a group of mothers, through crowded streets to the House of Commons. On August 14, 1885, the Criminal Law Amendment was passed by the House of Commons. As the news spread, Australia and some parts of the United States followed suit.

A safe and comfortable environment for women also meant restoration of homes by reclaiming alcoholic men. The stories were multiplied untold times. One woman recounted, "It used to be starvation for my family before they [the Salvation Army] came. Now, [my husband] brings his wages home to me, instead of taking them to the public house."[10]

The annals of women officers are full of bravery. In October 1900, a fire broke out in the Salvation Army Children's shelter in Cincinnati. Two officer-matrons, Staff Captain Selma Erickson and Captain Bertha Anderson, gave up their lives to rescue their five little charges. All seven were buried in a common grave. The city of Cincinnati maintained a Salvation Army flag over the grave for decades.[2]

ARMY WOMEN INFLUENCE BRITISH AND AMERICAN SUFFRAGISTS

In terms of women's suffrage, the Salvation Army inspired the second generation of suffragists to imitate the Army's methods. The women's movement in Britain formed in 1867. But in 1903, it was to receive a boost of energy from the Women's Social and Political Union (WSPU). Led by Emmeline Pankhurst and her daughters, Christabel and Sylvia, the WSPU adopted "militant" tactics and pushed the campaign issue into the nation's streets and squares.

WSPU leaders and members have left a trail of evidence that their inspiration was the Salvation Army,

"In her memoir, *My Own Story*, Emmeline Pankhurst directly attributes the WSPU's revivalist methods to the

Salvation Army. Teresa Billington-Greig commented that the militant suffrage movement had 'become as effective in its methods of revivalism, advertisement, and management as the Salvation Army, to which it bears more than a superficial resemblance.' Christabel Pankhurst instructed local WSPU organizers to adopt the Salvation Army's strategies of holding open air meetings, staging giant processions, and selling newspapers and pamphlets door-to-door. Several former Salvation Army officers brought their ideas and expertise to the WSPU. Jennie Baines, for example, was known for the extraordinary preaching abilities she had developed while serving as a Salvation Army captain. Her preaching skills 'stood her in good stead in suffrage work. She had a magnificent voice, which no opposition could drown."[11]

Suffragettes flooded the streets with parades, pamphlets, and soapbox speakers. At opportune moments, they staged huge rallies, patterned after evangelical revivals, to galvanize suffrage supporters. The WPSU would typically march through the West London streets, with rows upon rows of women carrying brightly colored banners featuring tributes to queens, scientists, and suffrage pioneers.[11]

The Salvation Army did not directly agitate for women's suffrage. But, the radical equality of men and women within the organization, and the methods used by the Army women were barrier breakers. The aggressive tactics of the Salvation Army were borrowed by the second and third generation of suffragists, first in England and then America. These women were not content with the passive activities of lectures and pamphlets.

In conclusion, Catherine Booth died aged 61 in 1890 after a two-year bout with breast cancer. Thousands thronged the streets of London to mourn her passing. Salvationists during her lifetime and afterwards called her the "mother of the Salvation Army." The Army has expressed Christian compassion to many disadvantaged people over the past 150 years. The uniformed officer rendering spiritual aid and comfort to the needy has most often been a woman.

References
Chapter Nine

1. WT Stead. Life of Mrs. Booth, the Founder of the Salvation army. New York: Fleming H. Revell Company; 1900, p. 157.
2. McKinley E. Marching to Glory: The History of the Salvation Army in the United States, 1880-1992. Grand Rapids, MI: WB Eerdmans Publishing Co; 1995, p. 114.
3. Waldron JD. Women of the Salvation Army. Oakdale, Ontario, Canada: Salvation Army; 1983, p. 123.
4. Yaxley T, Vanderwaal C. William and Catherine: The Life and Legacy of the Booths, Founders of the Salvation Army. Minneapolis, MN: Bethany House Publishers; 2003, p. 131.
5. Stead, p. 198.
6. Walker P. A Chaste and Fervid Eloquence: Catherine Booth and the Ministry of Women in the Salvation Army. In: Kienzle B, ed. Women Preachers and Prophets through Two Millenia of Christianity. Los Angeles: University of California Press; 1998. pp. 296-299.
7. Railton G. The Authoritive Life of General Booth: Founder of the Salvation Army. George Doran Company; 1912, p. 72.
8. Winston D. Red-Hot and Righteous: The Urban Religion of The Salvation Army. Cambridge, Massachusetts: Harvard University Press; 1999, location 29%.
9. Tucker R, Liefeld WL. Daughters of the Church: Women and Ministry from New Testament Times to the Present: Zondervan; 1987, p. 265.

10. Baudinette C. Our people: the Remakable Story of William and Catherine Booth and the Salvation Army. [United States]:DVD, 2008.
11. Devries JR. Transforming the Pulpit. Preaching and Prophecy in the British Women's Suffrage Movement. In: Pamela W, ed. Women Preachers and Prophets through Two Millenia of Christianity Los Angeles: University of California 1998, pp. 320-1.

Chapter Ten Two Methodist Leaders

April 11, 1861. Charleston, South Carolina. Dozens of Confederate cannons fire artillery shells onto Fort Sumter. The island fort is flattened. Federal troops hold out for 34 hours and then surrender. The Civil War has begun. A war that would cause as many as 750,000 casualties; more than all other conflicts added together in American history.

Abraham Lincoln was sworn into office on March 4, 1861. The United States of America was in grave danger. On April 15, 1861, the President issued a call for 75,000 volunteer soldiers to report for duty.

Within days Bishop Matthew Simpson, from the Methodist Episcopal Church, came to the President's Office and was welcomed by Lincoln. The two men became acquainted when Simpson was living in Evanston, Illinois. After the 1860 election, Simpson traveled to Springfield to visit the president-elect to discuss support for Northwestern University.

General Clinton B. Fisk[a] recalls the day. During the meeting,

> "several members of the Cabinet dropped in… The bishop expressed the opinion that 75,000 men were but a beginning of the number needed; that the struggle would be long and severe. Mr. Seward [Secretary of War] asked what opportunity a clergyman

---

[a] Clinton Fisk was a Methodist (AMEC) layman who commanded armies in Missouri during the Civil War. He worked for the Freedman's Bureau after the War to start free public schools for black and white children throughout the South. He was a Presidential candidate for the Prohibition Party in 1888 and received 250,000 votes. The Prohibition party platform contained two key pieces for women's rights. It unequivocally supported suffrage for women. Second, "men and women should receive equal wages for equal work."

could have to judge such affairs as these.
Judge Bates [Attorney General] replied that
few men knew so much of the temper of the
people as Bishop Simpson; Montgomery Blair
[Postmaster General] sustained the view of
Judge Bates. A Cabinet meeting followed.
After it was over, Lincoln and Simpson
remained together quite a long time. The
bishop gave him, in detail, his opinion of men
throughout the country whom he knew."[1]

Lincoln had few, if any, confidants who did not have some political conflict-of-interest. The President valued the Bishop's viewpoint because the office of a Methodist bishop was constantly moving between the regional conferences of the AMEC. As such, Simpson brought a non-political assessment of the mood and thinking of the entire nation outside the capital in a way no one else could. The peripatetic movement of a Methodist Bishop contrasted with most church denominations where the titular head of the church stays in one diocese or geographical area.

The two men had much in common. Both experienced a difficult childhood. Lincoln lost his mother at age nine. Simpson lost his Methodist father at an early age. For the era, Lincoln was very tall at six feet four inches, and Simpson was only two inches shorter. Both had jet black hair. Simpson seemed self-conscious about his big ears as many photos portray his hair combed over his ears attempting to hide this fact. Lincoln also thought his own ears too large. Both had a rugged expression befitting a leader. Contemporaries were impressed by the intelligence and kindness of both men. Both were anti-slavery and pro-women's suffrage.

In 1852, Simpson was elected as one of the Bishops of the Methodist Conference. His speaking was described as conversational in manner. Audiences were known to both laugh and weep during the same talk. Simpson preached his precept of equality for all. Yet, despite his stature as a bishop, he was said to always be accessible to the youngest minister or layperson.

At the time of his election as Bishop, he was editor of the *Western Christian Advocate*, an official weekly newspaper of the AMEC based in Cincinnati, Ohio; the editorship required election by the General Conference four years earlier in 1848. Under Simpson's management, the newspaper turned into a strong advocate for temperance and anti-slavery.

Prior to this, Simpson was the President of DePauw University, a Methodist supported institution in Indiana, where he had risen from Professor of Mathematics and Science; all the while being an ordained Methodist minister. From his days as professor and president of DePauw University, Simpson "had urged better educational opportunities for young women [and] had been sympathetic with women's rights. In the manner insisted upon by leaders of the suffrage movement, he had always addressed his own wife as Mrs. Ellen H. Simpson. He [also] subscribed to the Lucy Stone's *Woman's Journal*."[2]

The Independent, a congregational church and abolitionist-oriented journal, published a letter by Simpson in 1869.

> "Bishop Simpson on Woman's Suffrage
> Editor: It is already well known, but we wish to repeat the fact that bishop Simpson of the Methodist church is an advocate of woman's suffrage. His name is a tower of strength to the cause. The Brooklyn people, who are to hold a mass meeting in favor of equal rights on Friday, May 14, invited the bishop to speak on that occasion, and have received from him the following reply:
> 'My dear Sir: your letter inviting me at the meeting in Brooklyn in behalf of women's

enfranchisement, [was reviewed] upon my
return home.
I find, however, that it will be impossible for
me to be present as ecclesiastical duties call
me west at that time. Believing, as I do, that
the ballot in the hands of woman will add
strength to all our moral enterprises, and
especially to eradicate intemperance and city
vices. I have long desired to see her invested
with that power. In an ordinary political
canvass, I do not see that anything would be
gained. The vote would simply be increased,
without any probability of change; but on all
moral questions, and on questions affecting
the right of women to engage in any
honorable calling to gain a livelihood, the
ballot in her hands would be a powerful
element.
With high regards, yours truly, M. Simpson."[3]

In 1871, The *History of Women's Suffrage* recorded
Simpson's speaking at the Pennsylvania Constitutional
Convention: "The earnest and forcible words of the
eloquent speaker, and his solid array of arguments, made
a deep impression on the attentive audience."[4]

Later, Simpson expressed his faith in the ultimate
success of suffrage in a letter to Susan Anthony.
Philadelphia, March 28, 1884
"My Dear Miss Anthony,
Impaired health for several weeks past
prevented my sending you earlier my note
which I had designed. For more than thirty
years I have been in favor of suffrage for
woman. I was led to this position, not by the
consideration of the question of natural rights
or of alleged injustice or of inequality before
the law, but by what I believed would be her
influence on the great moral questions of the

day. Were the ballot in the hands of women, I
am satisfied that the evils of intemperance
would be greatly lessened; and I fear, without
that ballot, we shall not succeed against the
saloons and kindred evils in large cities. You
will doubtless have many obstacles placed in
your way; there will be many conflicts to
sustain; but I have no doubt that the coming
years will see the triumph of your cause, and
that our higher civilization and morality will
rejoice in the work which enlightened women
will accomplish.
Wishing you success, yours truly, Matthew
Simpson"[5]

Simpson's died three months later. The national 1884
NAWSA convention memorialized Simpson and ten
others for their work in suffrage: "the year 1884 has been
one of irreparable losses to our movement."[6]

GILBERT HAVEN

Born to Gilbert "Squire" Haven and Hannah Haven on
September 19, 1821, Gilbert Haven, Jr. came into a
Massachusetts family of rich heritage. Squire was a sixth-
generation Puritan who had turned to Methodism.
Hannah's father was one of the soldiers of the Revolution
who had endured the terrible winter at Valley Forge.
Gilbert remained close to his mother throughout his life
and wrote letters to her frequently.

Haven left home at age 18 to attend the Wesleyan
Academy in Wilbraham in western Massachusetts.
Removed from the constraints of home, he began to learn
to play cards, drink intoxicants and chase women. The
eventual restraint to his unchecked behavior came from
the terminal illness and death of his sister, Bethiah, to
whom he was deeply attached. He began a re-evaluation

of his life that led to his conversion to Christianity during college.

Haven was a genial and popular student at Wesleyan. One of his classmates remembered later that Haven was "apt in the use of sarcasm, loving to prick the bubble of sophistry or vanity;' that he spoke swiftly, loved debate, and engaged in 'prodigious mental activity;' and that he hated 'shams, hypocrisy, and oppression." Haven was a young man of medium frame with broad shoulders and a large head which was covered with "fiery red hair." He had "a keen, flashing eye" and "a rosy, joyous face."[7]

Receiving a call to the Methodist Episcopal ministry, Haven pastored several charges in New England. Then in 1867, he was elected editor of the Boston publication, *Zion's Herald*. Begun in 1823, the Herald was one the oldest and greatest Methodist weekly newspapers.

The first issue under Haven brought forth his reform thesis for the next five years: "No Caste in the Church of God." (This headline also became part of the masthead for the journal). This theme was threefold in nature: the universal brotherhood of mankind and the need for racial equality within society and the church; the need for women's suffrage; and the elevation of the laity to help govern the Methodist Episcopal Church.

Haven zealously continued the abolitionist position of the paper that had begun in 1835. However, many antebellum reformers abandoned the idea of helping black people after the civil war; this was particularly true after the Fifteenth Amendment passed in 1870 giving black men voting rights. Haven continued towards true equality. He wanted the church to become a racially inclusive community. And in doing so, to prod the nation to move towards a racially integrated community and just society. Haven looked upon racial separation in the church as "a scandal and offense, a stench in the nostrils of the Almighty."[8]

He railed at the use of racial categories of black and white in church membership lists and the use of the descriptor in church publications.[b]

Haven urged that the only remedy was to recover the Pauline standard of early Christian equality cited in Galatians 3:28. If the church accepted the challenge of racial integration, Haven believed the nation would follow and racial caste would be destroyed.

Unfortunately, some Methodists balked. While resistors were willing to grant freedom, education and voting rights for black men, they stopped short at the idea of full integration of the church. Since the practice of segregation had gone on in some AMEC churches since 1787, Haven was swimming upstream in a well-established river rather than a recent rivulet.[c]

Haven did not merely theorize these changes but sought to achieve some measure of integration in New England Methodism. He hoped the New England Conference would lead Methodism, as it had in antislavery reform, and denounce the sin of caste and promote Christian brotherhood. In Boston, he worked to develop fraternal relations between white and black clergymen. For example, in 1864, he led the Boston Methodist Preacher's Meeting to a session of the Annual Conference of the African American Episcopal Church.

---

[b] These designations in official AMEC reports and statistics appeared to have disappeared by 1873. Gravely states the General Conference was the source for the ruling that racial categories no longer be reported; but the author could not find the actual statement in any General Conference document. (see Gravely p. 208)

[c] Without specific local numbers, it is difficult in retrospect to judge how widespread racial prejudice was ingrained in the Methodist Episcopal Church (or in any denomination, for that matter). Nor do we know how many churches were segregated (i.e., blacks could only sit in one section). Many local churches were integrated so a generalization about the AMEC simply cannot be made given current data.

Haven also brought black ministers as his guests to the weekly Preachers' Meeting.[8]

One of Haven's close associates was John Mars, a well-known black minister who had served as a chaplain in the Union Army, and as a missionary among the freedman. While Mars had been a popular black preacher as a revivalist and camp meeting speaker in the New England Conference, he had not been permitted to join the clerical membership of the conference. Racial prejudice was too great to allow his regular appointment unless he would serve a black congregation. Mars membership was symbolic at the time and Haven made it a test case for racial integration in northern Methodism.[d]

At a time when few people were thinking about it, Haven's editorial emphasis also extended to women's suffrage, In the first four years of leadership of the *Herald*, he penned 11 editorials advocating the rights of women. In 1868, he had an important role in organizing the New England Woman Suffrage Association; a few years later he served as president of the American Woman Suffrage Association. Haven regularly shared the platform with Lucy Stone, Julia Ward Howe, and Abby Kelly Foster.

At the 1869 convention of the New England Woman Suffrage Association, Haven was recorded as making "a masterly argument from the Bible in favor of the equality of the sexes, using the same texts commonly brought forward in favor of woman's subjection to man."

Haven was met on leaving the meeting, by one who did not know his opinion on the subject.

> "This person expressed surprise on seeing
> him [i.e., Haven] at a Woman's Rights
> meeting, and said, 'What--you here?'

---

[d] Gravely writes at length on Haven's effort at the integration of church and society in his 47-page chapter entitled, "Beyond Emancipation. This chapter is quite interesting (and relevant today), but it is too long to be even summarized for the purposes of this book.

"Yes,' said he, 'I am here! I believe in the
thing, and I'm not going to wait to come in at
the tag end of this reform. I am going to start
in the beginning, and ride with the
procession.'"[9]

Also, in 1868, at a Monday meeting of Methodist
ministers he made a speech in which he warned his
brethren that, whether they wanted it or not, woman
suffrage was sure to come "as soon as a few more of you
old fogies are out of the way."[10]

His quotes made Bostonians sit up and think about the
rambunctious editor of the *Zion's Herald*. He loved to
plague opponents. One listener heard him discomfit a
staid audience by delivering a one-two punchline, "The
time may come when a *woman* will be President of the
United States;" he then paused, and quipped, "A *black
woman*!"[11]

In a discourse on women's suffrage in 1868, he stated,
"She is of the Commonwealth, having equal
rights with every other member. She is bone
of our bone and flesh of our flesh. Surely, all
enforced exclusion of her from her just claims
is the greatest injustice. If we pre-eminently
despise the man who strikes a woman, how
should we feel toward the State which thus
strikes down all its women, and robs them of
all power of defense from its blows? Above
all, we need her help. Christ is seeking to
establish his empire in the earth. It is an
empire of peace, of unity, of righteousness, of
love. It is to be established in good-willing
men, in holy laws, in sacred institutions, in
purified society. How can this be done except
by the cooperation of the best and most
numerous members of that society? Only by
woman's vote can the kingdom of God be
completely established. Only thus can we

save the State from debauchery and utter
demoralization. That work will go forward. It
is advancing everywhere; and when the next
election comes, may we see our sisters sitting
by us, and transforming the dirty, smoky
atmosphere of the voting-rooms into sweet
and quiet parlors, full of pleasure and
peace."[12]

In 1864, when few Methodists, ministerial or lay alike, were interested in the issue, Haven wrote a 40-page pamphlet, *Lay Representation in the Methodist Episcopal Church.* Women and men laypersons in the AMEC could vote on local church matters and were considered equals in local issues of membership. However, while ministers and laity could attend the annual conference and general conference meetings, only ministers, who were men, could vote. Thus, only a few select ministers could be selected as delegates by other ministers at regional annual conferences for representation at the quadrennial General Conference. The *Discipline*, or governing set of rules for the AMEC, could only be amended at the national four-year conference.

The idea of laymen participating in the annual conferences and general conferences preceded the advocacy of Haven and was first broached by the Methodists in 1852. The possible reform was referred by the general conference to a committee that was chaired by the newly elected Bishop Matthew Simpson. And while the committee report returned a negative recommendation, Simpson began to increasingly talk and discuss the matter in a favorable manner as he traveled the national circuit.

The participation of laymen was referred out for a national vote by AMEC local members and ministers by the 1860 General Conference. It lost badly by a 2:1 margin by both ministers and laity (this would have included women voters). With war clouds gathering,

Methodists had other things on their mind than ecclesiastical reform. In 1864, the matter was not even presented for consideration.

The issue of lay representation gained momentum after the war. In 1868 the general conference passed a resolution instructing the national church to conduct voting on the issue by both laity and ministers. The measure was approved to create an Electoral Conference. Laymen were chosen as delegates for the next general conference in 1872. While women voted for members of the Electoral Conference, it was not clear if they could either become a part of the Electoral Conference or whether they were eligible to become delegates to the quadrennial general conference. Were "women" fully included at higher levels of ecclesiastical government beyond the local church? [e] In any case, some annual conferences began choosing women as delegates to the 1880 Electoral Conference; moreover, there were no recorded objections at the time to this practice.

At the 1872 General Conference, Gilbert Haven was elected a Bishop of the AMEC. Many observers felt that the fiery editor of Zion's Herald would have to exchange his radical stances for the reserved demeanor normally expected of a bishop. The African American Methodist editor, Benjamin Tanner, disagreed. Tanner foresaw that the action of the General Conference to restrain Haven by placing a "crown" on the extremist would not sever the new bishop from his lifelong commitments. Indeed, no pullback took place in Haven's life. Even before the month-long General Conference had ended, Haven had published a letter of protest in the *New York Tribune*

---

[e] The Discipline recognized only two classes of Methodist members, "minister" and "laymen;" given the equality of women Methodists at the local level since inception of the AMEC, this language limitation seemed not to restrict women at the time who possessed no different privileges from their male lay counterparts. Since women were full members of the local church and were subject to the same discipline as "laymen," then the term "laymen" included women.

deploring the discriminatory treatment that a black ministerial delegate had received at a "well-known Oyster House on Fulton Street." Haven urged a boycott of the establishment until a public apology was issued for the insult.[13]

Bishop Haven was assigned as residence the city of Atlanta. While he was still responsible for traveling the entire United States, he requested and received permission to concentrate on southern annual conference responsibilities. This was done to reassure AMEC members who were nervous over his stance on race relations.

Haven's first meeting with the east Tennessee conference revealed his approach. He canceled separate services for blacks before arriving and supervised integrated services. The first day of the meeting, Haven called for administering the Lord's supper to both black and white ministers. "The ice was broken at the start," wrote Haven. At the end of the conference, he ordained the ministers by alphabetical order rather from a list of consecutive white ministers or black ministers. He later wrote that east Tennessee "got the idea of black equality, before they knew it."[14]

Other conferences would not be so easy. While the Georgia district did not respond quite as well as the east Tennesseans, they were better than the Alabama conference whose members were "stunned." Haven wrote,

> "The idea of black equality had never got in
> there. They looked on them as pious mules.
> But I had put through my alphabetic
> ordinations and asking black presiding elders
> to assist in ordaining white ministers; and it
> was like an electric shock to an ox—he don't
> know why, or where, or what, except that he
> is immensely stirred up."[14] [f]

---

[f] Haven received opposition for his attempts at integration from some

Haven served as a bishop for almost eight years before becoming seriously ill. A major part of his declining health came from repeated bouts of malaria he had contracted from a three-year assignment in Liberia, Africa. He also developed cancer of the hip and heart problems.

Exhausted, Haven returned to his childhood home in Malden, Massachusetts in November 1879, where his 93-year-old mother helped take care of him. Haven dictated final messages to his friends and kept up his good humor in the sickroom. Nevertheless, he succumbed to his illnesses at age 58 on January 3, 1880. Ever promoting equality, Haven had requested that Rev. John Mars should be on the platform and deliver an oratory at his funeral. This was honored.

Contemporaries described Haven as being strongly radical and conservative at the same time. Radical in that he was outspoken, at the head of a long line of reformers, against injustices within and without the church. He was not an ivory tower writer, but one who practiced his ideas of reform. Conservative in that he held steadfast principles of right and Christian precepts.

> "It was this [latter trait] that gave him security when venturing out where other men have lost themselves; and it was this which rendered his ideas and projects safe, which in the hands of others have either been doubtful or disastrous. He was anchored to the eternal verities."[15]

Women rights advocates took note of his passing. Haven was labeled "the good bishop" and his loss in the procession of suffrage reform was deplored.[9]

Methodist papers in the north and south. Other non-Methodist denominational papers piled on. However, the opposition from these sources was not nearly the vituperation he received from southern secular papers. The author does not care to repeat the wording here by the secular papers. The reader may refer to Gravely where it is likely that only the "milder" forms of abuse are printed.

Methodists took note of his death, but black Methodists especially expressed dismay. The Methodist minister, Marshall Taylor, acknowledged the loss to the nation and church, but to blacks, he claimed, "much more is he our dead." Black Methodist churches throughout the south held solemn memorial services in Haven's honor.[16]

References
Chapter Ten

1. Sweet WW. The Methodist Episcopal Church and the Civil War: Methodist Book Concern Press; 1912, p. 155.
2. Clark R. The Life of Matthew Simpson. New York: Macmillan; 1956, p. 298.
3. Editor. Bishop Simpson on Woman's Suffrage. The Independent 1869; vol 21 (1067).
4. Stanton EC, Anthony SB, Gage MJ, Harper IH. History of Woman Suffrage, Volume 3: 1886, p. 488.
5. National American Woman Suffrage A, Upton HT. Proceedings of the Twenty-sixth Annual Convention of the National American Woman Suffrage Association, held in Washington, D.C., February 15, 16, 17, 18, 19, and 20, 1894. Washington, D.C.: The Association; 1894, p. 123.
6. Stanton EC, Anthony SB, Gage MJ, Harper IH, Association NAWS. History of Woman Suffrage, Volume 4: Susan B. Anthony; 1902, p. 61.
7. Gravely W. Gilbert Haven, Methodist Abolitionist: A Study in Race, Religion, and Reform, 1850-1880: Abingdon Press; 1973, p. 23.
8. Gravely, p. 127-128.
9. Robinson HJH. Massachusetts in the Woman Suffrage Movement: A General, Political, Legal and Legislative History from 1774 to 1881. Boston: Roberts Bros.; 1881, p. 53.

10. Ibid, p.147.
11. Daniels WH. " Graduated with Honor.": Memorials of Gilbert Haven, Bishop of the Methodist Episcopal Church: BB Russell & Company; 1880, p. 78.
12. Ibid, p. 343.
13. Gravely, p. 200.
14. Gravely, p. 207-210.
15. Daniels, p. 133.
16. Gravely, p. 255.

Chapter 11 The WCTU and Frances Willard

Founded in 1874, The Woman's Christian Temperance Union (WCTU) was by far the largest women's suffrage organization of the late 19th century. The numbers speak for themselves. The WCTU dues paying membership was 150,000 in the early 1890s; compared to the next suffrage organization, the National American Woman Suffrage Association (NAWSA), which had 13,000 members at its inception in 1890.[1][a] NAWSA membership numbers include men. The WCTU did not allow men into membership. Exclusion of men as full members by the WCTU broke new ground. Men could become honorary members. No other organization existed over which women possessed complete control.

It is puzzling then why so little is written about the WCTU in the history of women's suffrage in America. Feminist historians "do not so much deny the importance of the temperance movement for women's causes as [they] ignore it."[2]

Worse, there is a popular misidentification of Carrie Nation with the WCTU. Carrie Nation, the hatchet wielding destroyer of saloons, was a member of the Anti-Saloon League. The ASL, started in 1906, had only one purpose. The WCTU determinedly disavowed the aggressive tactics of Carrie Nation.

The first two national leaders of the WCTU, Anne Wittenmyer (1874-1879) and Frances Willard (1879-1898) were active Methodist Episcopal (AMEC) laywomen. Methodist women formed much of the WCTU leadership at all levels. Borden studied a sample of WCTU leaders in depth (n=126) and found 45% were

---

[a]After merger of the National Woman Suffrage Association and American Woman Suffrage Association.

Methodist, far more than any other church denomination or secular category.[3]

Anne Wittenmyer, the first president, worked for the Christian Commission during the civil war overseeing 200 women who provided relief for sick and wounded northern troops. The Civil War was the first event in American history to draw out large numbers of women from home. In 1868, Wittenmyer established a unique evangelizing work by women to help the poor. This was done with the approval of the leadership of the AMEC church. Anne Wittenmyer issued a challenge to church members,

> "What can woman do for Christ and
> humanity? What is 'woman's work for
> Jesus?'...Painting a vivid picture of ladies
> who were martyrs to fashion rather than for
> Christ, she blasted middle-class women's
> idleness, frivolity, and vanity. She insisted
> that the Scriptures warned against such
> sinfulness and that instead, they called women
> to works of charity."[4]

By doing so, Wittenmyer rocked the women's pedestal of virtue. She implied that "women and men shared in a particularly awesome equality before God the Judge."[4]

FRANCES WILLARD

Frances Willard (1839-1898) was born in central New York near Rochester. She was named after the English novelist Frances (Fanny) Burney.[b] Willard's family moved in 1841 to Oberlin, Ohio, where her father, Josiah Willard, wished to prepare for the ministry. Because Josiah's health began to decline after four years in Oberlin, the Willard family moved to southern Wisconsin to engage in farming. There the family moved their

---

[b] Burney (1752-1840) wrote satirical novels about female identity and influenced many writers in the 19th century, including Jane Austen.

membership from the Congregationalists to the
Methodists (AMEC). Then in 1858, the family moved to
Evanston, Illinois so Frances and Mary, her younger
sister, could attend Northwestern Female College.
Following her graduation from the college in 1859,
Frances taught school for a decade in several places, the
farthest away being Lima, New York.

Willard was of medium height with dark red hair. At
age 21, she described herself as not good looking yet not
unpleasant in face or figure. She disliked house chores but
loved to read.[c] Portraits of Willard's face show resolution.
She felt she had a good mind and some facility as a
writer. For much of her life she kept a journal filled with
honest assessments of herself and others.

Unafraid to travel, she toured Europe and the Middle
East with a friend, Kate Jackson, from 1868 to 1870 and
kept a detailed journal. In 1869, five years before the
WCTU existed, Willard expressed her wish that American
women could vote. In one humorous entry, Willard wrote
of neighbors in Paris,

> "Madame & her sister Matilde indulged in a
> tirade against the idea of women 'meddling'
> in what did not concern them & at its climax
> exclaimed 'those people over there [America]
> even dare to propose that women vote!' Kate
> laughed immoderately & said 'Didn't you
> know that Miss Willard & I cherish the hope
> of going to the polls someday & dropping our

---

[c] The Frances Willard Library has a diverse collection of more than a
thousand of Willard's books. She wrote comments on the inside
covers. Willard had a thorough knowledge of the Bible. After reading
Overton's biography on John Wesley, she wrote that Wesley was "the
most interesting figure in the whole gallery of men." Willard read of
all of Shakespeare's plays before age 17. She admired Abraham
Lincoln. Willard received many books on women's rights and was
asked to comment on them. (Rosalita Leonard. The Secret History of
Frances Willard's Library. *The Union Signal*. Volume 53, February
1977, pp. 8-11).

opinions on white paper into the ballot box?'
There was a look of horror on the expressive
French faces & that shrug that utters a whole
quarto volume was pushed toward the
ceiling."[5]
Not all were against women advancing in France.
Willard visited the country's leading women's right's
figure, Julie Victoire Daubie. Daubie was the author of a
book on the status of poor women in France. She told
Willard, "It is from you [Americans] that we got the idea
that woman might dare to be & to do more than she has
yet." The hostess showered Willard and Jackson with
questions about the women's movement in America.
Finally, Mademoiselle Daubie said,
> "The greatest evil for women here [Paris] is
> the seduction of young girls –who work for
> their living-by rich men. Wages are so low
> that the poor things often sell their honor to
> eke out the pittance they [otherwise] could
> *honorably* earn." [Italics by Willard].[5]

Returning to Chicago, Willard accepted the presidency
of the newly founded Evanston College for Ladies. When
the college merged with Northwestern University, Willard
became the Dean of Women. She remained dean until the
spring of 1874, when an intractable dispute developed
with the University President, Charles Fowler, a man with
whom she had been briefly affianced to 13 years earlier.[d]
The disagreement between Fowler and Willard was over
the governance of women. Willard eventually resigned as
Dean of Women.

In the autumn of 1874, Willard attended the Illinois
State WCTU convention in Bloomington, where she was
elected secretary. She attended the first national WCTU
convention in Cleveland, on November 18-20, 1874.
Offered the nomination for the presidency of the WCTU,

---

[d] She had broken the engagement, but in the interim Fowler had
married one of Willard's friends who then died in childbirth.

she promptly declined. However, she accepted the nomination and won the national position of Corresponding Secretary. Willard found the principal duty of the corresponding secretary to be recruiting new members. The WCTU wanted to move into states where state unions did not exist and multiply the number of local unions in states already organized.

At first, organizing was done by mail. Willard wrote prominent clergymen in every state and territory asking for the names of women active in the temperance cause. She wrote 2,000 letters during the summer of 1875 without any secretarial assistance. She also corresponded with local unions. Her years of extensive travel would come later. But as the year moved on, she traveled more and more, begging railroad passes and lodging, depending on free-will offerings for the rest of her expenses. At first her trips were to nearby communities, but her wide correspondence was building her a national constituency. Before the 1875 national convention, she attended state WCTU conventions in Missouri, Minnesota, Rhode Island, and New York, while also addressing sympathetic groups. Her travel and her letter-writing not only facilitated the growth of the Union but enhanced her personal prestige as well.

In the spring of 1876, Willard's autobiography relates, while alone on her knees in prayer, "there was borne in upon my mind, as I believe from loftier regions, the declaration, 'You are to speak for the woman's ballot as a weapon of protection to her home and tempted loved ones from the tyranny of drink." As she put it later, God himself had spoken and approved her open espousal of the suffrage cause."[6]

Susan B. Anthony wrote a firsthand account of Willard's "public committal." Writing to Willard, Anthony was delighted that Willard had overcome "all the timid conservative human counsels. . .I wish I could see you and make you feel my gladness, not only for your sake personally, but the cause's sake—for temperance and virtue's sake and for woman's sake."[6]

Willard decided to use the phrase "home protection ballot." The home-protection slogan became a masterstroke of public relations. Her motto made suffrage palatable to many, both men and women, who might not otherwise have been able to accept it. It convinced the Union to embrace suffrage as a goal, and it provided a fresh way of interpreting and justifying political demands.

The suffrage movement was quick to recognize its usefulness, although suffragists did not make the argument their own until later in the century. Lucy Stone wrote in the Woman's Journal in 1879 that "the one standing objection to Woman Suffrage has been that the home was the province of women and if they attended to it, they would have no time for politics. The women of the Christian Temperance Unions said, 'The home is the special care of women. Home protection shall be our watchword."[6]

The membership of the Union exploded in the 1880s. By its tenth anniversary, the WCTU was organized in every state and territory on the state level. In a few years, the WCTU network of local unions had penetrated everywhere except rural areas. In 1890 over half the counties in the United States were organized, to say nothing of scattered local unions in many others. Willard began this wide-ranging pattern of organizing down to the local level and continued it through her presidency.[7]

Scores of other women on the international, national, and local scene tirelessly pursued new members. The integrated tiers were the dynamic that made the WCTU unique among nineteenth century organizations.

Frances Willard consistently embraced ecumenicism. The Union welcomed Jew, Gentile, Protestant, and Catholic despite its preponderance of Protestant Christian members. Willard warmly greeted fraternal delegates from Catholic temperance societies and enthusiastically sent WCTU representatives to their meetings. She did not apologize when Boston's temperance women rebuked her for welcoming Catholics to the platform of the national convention. She "believed the time for such narrowness was past." The 1895 WCTU convention passed a resolution formally inviting Catholic and Hebrew women to join the WCTU. Willard was supported in this issue by the WCTU national leadership.[7]

The WCTU had several newspapers when Willard became president, but no single national publication reached the entire membership. Many of these papers were financially weak and limited in circulation. Willard began in 1880 to push for consolidation to create a single strong voice. By 1884 the Union Signal was the most popular temperance journal in the country, with 14,000 subscribers. By 1890 it was the largest women's paper in the world, with circulation pushing 100,000.[7]

Frances Willard's "do everything" approach with 37 departments showed the organization's efforts to improve the lot of women in many practical ways; these included such efforts as literacy, job training, day care and refuge houses.

Prison reform was the first non-temperance issue to attract attention from the WCTU. Men, women, and children often occupied squalid prison quarters together in the 1870s.

> "Prostitutes, elderly drunks, felons, and young
> children might all share a single cell.' In
> 1882, the national Superintendent of Prison
> and Police Work commented, 'It is a standing
> rebuke to our civilization that women are
> arrested and given into the hands of men to be
> searched and cared for, tried by men,
> sentenced by men, committed to . . .
> institutions where only men have access to
> them."[8]

In a very few years a WCTU department for prison and jails was petitioning for rehabilitative reformatories and police matrons, establishing halfway houses for released women prisoners, and demanding women appointments to state boards of charities and corrections.[8]

    "Pressure from the WCTU put four police matrons in Philadelphia station houses by 1885, and increased the number employed by Chicago from ten in 1885 to twenty-one in 1890. By that year, through Union efforts, matrons were employed in thirty-six United States cities, the larger cities employing several. By 1894, Willard strongly recommended support for policewomen—not just matrons but women on the beat. Willingness to participate in the work of this WCTU department was almost universal; there were active departments in forty-five states and territories as early as 1889."[8]

One of the WCTU's major social contributions was its enthusiastic promotion of the kindergarten movement. Willard called it the "greatest theme, next to salvation by faith that can engage a woman's heart and brain." San Francisco's Golden Gate Kindergarten Association founded the first free WCTU kindergarten in 1880, and ten years later that center alone had over fifteen hundred children enrolled.[9]

Children of working mothers were enrolled in kindergartens. Enrollees had three meals a day and spent 12 hours, from 7:00 a.m. to 7:00 p.m., at the "crèche." Mothers who could afford to paid 10 cents a day. The San Diego Union, only three years old at the time, established a day nursery in 1887. The nursery lasted well into the twentieth century and is an example of a WCTU social welfare project on the local level that was both meaningful and permanent.[9]

WILLARD'S SPIRITUAL LIFE

Carolyn Gifford transcribed the 45 personal journals of Frances Willard in the 1980s. In doing so, Gifford has become the best interpreter of Willard's personal and public life. Gifford writes, "It is my contention that Willard's two most recent biographers [Earhart and Bordin][e] have not taken seriously enough Willard's religious faith nor her immersion in a particular religious culture. . . [with few exceptions] American women's historians in general do not adequately recognize, understand, or deal with the category of religion. When biographers and historians attempt to discuss Willard's life and assess its significance, this lack of understanding results in a serious misrepresentation of that life."[10]

Willard was a devout and loyal Methodist. She described her process of accepting Christian salvation in her journal. Listening to a sermon preached on the text of Proverbs 23:7, "As a man thinks in his heart, so is he," caused Willard to reflect deeply on her spiritual condition in her journal After pondering her life, she came to this humiliating conclusion,

> "Mine is an unregenerate, a totally depraved nature when I have, in my blindness, dared to think that I had some noble qualities, some generous impulses, some attributes worthy of respect & love, I deceived myself—ah how woefully…underlying all my ideas & wishes, has been the idea that Christ would love & pardon me, if I rightly asked him…As yet, I have no light, but, I will not, if God will help me, be wearied in striving."[10]

---

[e] Mary Earhart [Dillon] Frances Willard: From Prayers to Politics [Chicago: University of Chicago, 1944] and Ruth Bordin, Frances Willard; A Biography [Chapel Hill, North Carolina: University of North Carolina, 1986

This is the Methodist understanding of the conviction of sin. Wishing to gain control of her life and direct it toward a faithful and moral aim, she knew the first step would be make a public declaration of her intent to lead a Christian life. But she vacillated for weeks. She read the Bible, prayed, and poured out her uncertainties in her journal.

During her first year in Evanston, Willard listened to Bishop Simpson (chapter ten) preach. He was a family neighbor and she was impressed by his personal holiness. Her decision for salvation came to a head as Willard attended a week-long revival preached at the Evanston Methodist church in December 1859. "No argument that he could bring in favor of Christianity would weigh with me more than his [i.e., Simpson's] presence—his earnestness—his life."

The example of Rev Simpson's life helped to enable her to take the step of becoming a Christian. I have commenced! O Lord!" she announced in her journal, the day after making her decision."[10]

Simpson also influenced Frances Willard as a young adult. His daughter, Ella Simpson, is described in Frances Willard's journal as being her "friend" and one "tried and true."[11]

One can surmise that Bishop Simpson strongly influenced Frances Willard's life directly and indirectly through his daughter Ella. While the author could not find direct evidence of Simpson speaking about women's suffrage in Evanston or to Ella and Frances about the matter, he was known to possess those views at the time.[f]

---

[f] More work needs to be done here. Newspaper accounts of Evanston events in the time when Simpson lived there have not been searched by the author for talks about women suffrage. He was speaking in other geographic areas on the topic, so it seems likely Frances Willard heard him speak on the topic. It is clear in her journal that Willard felt strongly in favor of women's suffrage as early as 1869. The author speculates that Simpson was one source of her pro-suffrage thinking.

He undoubtedly influenced Frances Willard in the formation of her ideas; or, at the least, represented an authoritarian example that such views were well within Wesleyan thinking.

THE 1888 GENERAL CONFERENCE

Willard would need all her experience in Christian grace to remain strong in an unusual contest later in life. In 1880, the General Conference of the AMEC allowed women to join the governing body of local churches that voted for the "Electoral Conference"; the Electoral Conference was responsible for choosing delegates for the Quadrennial General Conference. The next logical step was the election of women delegates to the General Conference. This came in 1888.

In October 1887, Frances Willard was elected by her home district, the Rock River Conference, as a delegate to the Methodist General Conference scheduled to meet in New York City in April 1888. Although by far the most eminent, she was one of only five women delegates that year. Mary Ninde of Minnesota, president of the Methodist Women's Foreign Missionary Society and WCTU leader; Angie Newman, of Nebraska, National Superintendent of Prison Work (for an eventual 27 years) in the WCTU; Amanda C. Rippey, head of the Kansas Conference delegation; and Lizzie Van Kirk of Pittsburgh were the other four. The five states represented a decidedly western United States tilt.

Frances was pleased. Anna Gordon, her secretary, wrote to Willard's mother,

> "I wish you could have heard her praise of those noble men who were the means of her election, and seen her delight when the news came. We were at the breakfast table. When she tried to tell her hostess, she could hardly speak for tears."[12]

Willard later wrote that it did not occur to her that women, who "constitute at least two-thirds of the church membership, bear more than one-half its burdens, and have patiently conceded to the brethren, during all generations, its emoluments and honors," would prove unacceptable as delegates.[13]

Nonetheless, Willard must have received warnings about the opposition forming to the seating of the women delegates. She corresponded with John M. Hamilton, founder of the People's Church in Boston, whom she knew since her work with Moody in 1877. Hamilton was to lead the pro-woman forces on the Conference floor. Hamilton assured her that, if objections were raised, he would challenge the objections on a point of order; his motion being that only a delegate's constituency could object, not the Conference.

As the meeting approached, the Methodist establishment became divided on the question of woman delegates. *Zion's Herald*, a Chicago publication representing the progressive West, believed women could certainly be delegates, pointing to the long tradition of their participation in the electoral conferences where they helped choose General Conference delegates. The *Christian Advocate* and the *Methodist Review* both opposed the admission of women, but the *Western Christian Advocate* lined up with *Zion's Herald* on the pro-women's side.[12]

On 1 May 1888, the national legislative body of the Methodist church was called to order in the Metropolitan Opera House. Since the Conference assembled for only a month every four years, there was a lengthy list for the agenda. The 25th General Conference was faced with numerous problems: could the mandatory time of shifting ministers between locations every three years be lengthened? Could presiding elders of the Conference be elected rather than having them appointed by the bishops? Could laymen be added as delegates to the 103 regional annual conferences that were now entirely ministerial? And then, of course, the question of the eligibility of women to be seated as delegates to the current conference. The woman question was first on the agenda, and the *New York Times* saw this issue as the major decision the Conference would make in 1888.[14]

Two women delegates, Mary Ninde and Angie Newman, were in their seats on the floor when the presiding bishop's gavel opened the first session. Frances Willard, however, was not. The day before the meeting, Willard had received a telegram that her mother was worsening with pneumonia; she immediately returned to Evanston. Willard kept her personal secretary, Anna Gordon, in New York City and attempted to use her as surrogate. Gordon was told to keep careful account of the votes, and to urge "the women to sit it out and never withdraw until forced to it."[12] General Fisk gave Gordon a seat in his Opera House box. From here, Gordon sent Willard "constant bulletins" during the debate.[15]

Willard's absence from the convention was a severe setback to the cause of the women delegates. The *Times* wondered, "They can't think of putting Miss Willard out, can they?"[14] The *Times* described the fight as a "battle royal," which "brought such an audience to the Metropolitan Opera House as is seldom drawn to it by the profane attractions which are usually there presented," and emphasized that ladies were in the majority.[16]

Opponents of seating the women argued narrow technical points such as the pronoun "laymen" meaning "male" only, and procedural issues. Didn't the church *Discipline* only authorize a rule change by taking a national member referendum?

On the other hand, pro-suffrage speakers emphasized solid logic: if you can vote for a position then you are also eligible to be in that position.

Arguing from the viewpoint of Christian love, General Fisk (chapter ten) ended his speech with "Let us rather strengthen our guarantee of loving protection of every right and privilege of every member of our Church without distinction of race, color or sex. Amen and Amen [Applause]."[17]

The issue dragged for seven days and the delaying tactics of the opposition began to wear the assembly down. Interest had begun to lag when the vote was finally taken. Both sides had reiterated the same old arguments the delegates had heard many times before. In the end, the resolution to seat women was defeated by small margins in both lay and ministerial votes.[g]

On the long-term, the two sides reflected about the meaning of the 1888 vote.

Willard addressed the question in her annual message to the WCTU at its fall meeting in the same New York hall where her cause had failed in May. She urged her followers to work in the church for a "voice in all its circles of power." She saw the recent "unprecedented discussion relative to woman's church relations" as a positive gain. Women had won considerable support. In closing, Willard reiterated her devotion to Methodism,

> "I love my mother church so well and
> recognize so thoroughly that the base and
> body of the great pyramid she forms is
> broader than its apex, that I would fain give
> her a little time in which to deal justly by the
> great household of her loving, loyal, and
> devoted daughters."[12]

On the other side, the AMEC Conference determined that the issue of women delegates seated at the General Conference had been so contentious that the delegates referred the choice to the membership of the entire church for voting on a constitutional amendment of the *Discipline*.

---

[g] It seems clear that had Matthew Simpson or Gilbert Haven still been alive, the vote would have been in favor of the women. Another "what if" of history.

The call for the vote read,
> "*Resolved*, that in the month of October 1890, there shall be in every place of public worship of the Methodist Episcopal Church an election, at which every member in full connection [i.e., not probationary], who is not less than 21 years of age, shall be permitted to vote upon the following proposition: *Shall women be eligible as lay delegates to the Electoral and General Conferences of the Methodist Episcopal Church?*"[18]

Women members were part of this vote. A separate vote was taken by the ministers, who, by definition, were all male. The tally of votes reported at the next quadrennial conference in 1892 indicated that 235,668 members of individual churches voted for the eligibility of women, and 163,843 against (a 60% majority in favor!), while 5,609 ministers were in favor of women delegates, and 5144 against (54% in favor!). Though a large plurality of the membership and ministers affirmed the change, the necessary three-fourths majority for amendment of the *Discipline* had not been attained.

Nonetheless, the strongly positive nature of the national church vote influenced the AMEC. The leadership saw the handwriting on the wall and over time changed the procedural rules, so women could be seated at the General Conference in 1904.

The result, though, raises the metaphorical question: "Is the glass half empty or half full?" The latter vote of 409,862 Methodists represents the first positive plebiscite on the "woman question" in the history of American society and culture. It was not merely the seating of Methodist Episcopal women delegates, but that these women would vote in the most important legislative body of the largest denomination in America.

The preceding 23 years had seen many state referendums on women suffrage that lost by large margins. Moreover, the large sample size of Methodists tallied more voters than all the state voter referendum totals combined until 1892.[h] Nationally, it seems clear that Methodist men were out in front on women's suffrage compared to secular men.

What was Frances Willard's legacy? She singlehandedly moved the WCTU into placing women's suffrage as the number one issue. However, it was male voters that had to be convinced to give suffrage to women. It was in this area that Frances Willard, with her home protection motto, made Methodist men comfortable with the idea that women could vote in the church; then with the next logical step of general suffrage. She often encouraged men by expecting the best,

> "So, I find it everywhere. The men best educated—most gifted— liberated most from prejudice & the unillumined past, think of woman as a human soul placed by a kind Creator on the earth to do & be all that she can—unfettered by any law or custom so long as her freedom touches on the just rights of no other human soul. May I live to see the day when this choice leaven shall "raise" the lump of public opinion nearer hope & Heaven! And may I be brave enough to speak in a womanly voice my honest word in this behalf!"[19]

---

[h] See table 17.1 in chapter 17.

References
Chapter 11

1. Smith RM. Civic Ideals: Conflicting Visions of Citizenship in US History: Yale University Press; 1997, p. 386.
2. Bordin R. Woman and Temperance: The Quest for Power and Liberty, 1873-1900: Temple University Press; 1981, p. xv.
3. Ibid, p. 169.
4. Gifford CDS. For God and Native Land. In: Thomasa H, ed. Women in New Worlds: Historical Perspectives on the Wesleyan Tradition. Nashville: Abingdon; 1981: p. 310-2.
5. Gifford CDS. Writing Out My Heart. Chicago: University of Illinois Press, pp. 273, 295.
6. Bordin, pp. 50-58.
7. Bordin, pp. 87-90.
8. Bordin, pp. 99-100.
9. Bordin, pp. 102-103.
10. Gifford CDS, American Society of Church History Meeting. "My Own Methodist Hive" : the Nurturing Community of Frances Willard's Young Womanhood 1997.
11. Frances Willard Digital Journal: October 12, 1862. In: http://willard.historyit.com/
12. Bordin R. Frances Willard: A Biography: UNC Press Books; 2014, p. 163-168.
13. Willard F. Glimpses of Fifty Years: The Autobiography of an American Woman: Chicago: Women's Temperance Publication Association; 1889, p. 617-622.
14. A Great Church Council - The National Conference of the Methodists - Questions which will be brought up at the Coming Meeting. New York Times April 28, 1888, p. 11.
15. Willard, p. 620.

16 Sex in Church Councils: A Great Discussion Begun in the Conference. New York Times May 4, 1888, p. 9.

17. Speech of Clinton Fisk. The Christian Advocate June 14, 1888, pp. 10-11.

18. Election of Women as Lay Delegates. Christian Advocate supplement August 9, 1888.

19. Gifford, Writing out My Heart, p. 298.

Chapter 12 Women's Suffrage and Race

A great contrast existed between NAWSA and the WCTU over racial inclusion. Despite NAWSA's statement of universal suffrage, NAWSA shied away from allowing black women (or black men) to join. NAWSA even refused to allow bids for membership by blacks in white NAWSA clubs, they denied separate black women's chapters or to even acknowledge affiliation of auxiliary black women's groups.[1] The reason given was that many southern white women would object.

Examples include Susan Anthony's asking her friend, Frederick Douglass to stay away from the 1895 NAWSA convention in Atlanta for fear his presence would cause dissension. Elizabeth Cady Stanton's suffrage requirement to include literacy in reading and writing English had racial implications; Susan B Anthony disagreed with Stanton on requiring literacy for voting.[2]

In retrospect, beyond racial objections, the reasons for NAWSA not including black women sounded cliquish. The presence of blacks would hinder the recruitment of "prominent women" and the effort to gain "respectability" throughout the nation.[1] To some degree, the latter fears likely sprang from the ever-present money woes of NAWSA. "Prominent women" would of course be more likely to contribute money than lower class whites and blacks.

Fears of schism over the issue dogged NAWSA leadership for decades. The executive committee of NAWSA in 1903 issued a statement about black membership to the press that read in part,

> "The association as such has no view on this subject…The doctrine of state's rights is recognized in the national body and each auxiliary State association arranges its own affairs in accordance with its own ideas and in

harmony with the customs of its own section."[3] [a]

In vivid contrast to the NAWSA, the WCTU welcomed black women into membership. But, even more dramatically, the WCTU actively recruited black women into their ranks.

The position of the WCTU will become clear from an extended quote from Frances Ellen Watkins Harper, the first national Superintendent of [WCTU] Work among black people. In her position, she led the effort to recruit black women into the WCTU and promote temperance work among African Americans. Harper was a well-known speaker, writer and reformer.

THE WOMAN'S CHRISTIAN TEMPERANCE UNION AND THE COLORED WOMAN.[b]
By Mrs. F.E.W. Harper

"A woman sat beneath the shadow of her home, while the dark waves of intemperance dashed against human hearts and hearth-stones, but there came an hour when she found that she could do something else besides wring her hands and weep over the ravages of the liquor traffic, which had darkened so many lives and desolated so many homes.

---

[a] The interested scholar should read the entire executive statement. The only subject of the entire statement is a justification of NAWSA's (functional) policy of not accepting blacks. Also, the two sentences quoted in the text do not form a logical sequence. That is, NAWSA nationally did have a view and that was "the doctrine of state's rights," code words for racial exclusion. And, while the national leadership of the WCTU took a strong stance on racial inclusion and equality for blacks and native Americans ([see farther down in text], their statement that they could not control what local Unions did in regard to race (i.e. inclusion or exclusion) is not equivalent, since there was no recognition of the "doctrine of state's rights" by the national leadership of the WCTU. Frances Willard fostered inclusion by speech and example and state Unions were well aware of her leadership on the issue.

[b] This quote is extensive and is intentionally not indented.

Where the enemy spreads his snares for the feet of the unwary, inexperienced and tempted, she, too, could go and strive to stay the tide of ruin which was sending its floods of sorrow, shame and death to the habitations of men, and 1873 witnessed the strange and wondrous sight of the Woman's Crusade [i.e., WCTU], when the mother heart was roused up in defense of the home and all that the home held dearest. A Divine impulse seemed to fan into sudden flame and touch with living fire earnest hearts, which rose to meet the great occasion. Lips that had been silent in the prayer meeting were loosened to take part in the wonderful uprising. Saloons were visited, hardships encountered, insults, violence and even imprisonment endured by women, brave to suffer and strong to endure. Thousands of saloon visits were made, many were closed. Grand enthusiasms were aroused, moral earnestness awakened, and a fire kindled whose beacon lights still stream o'er the gloomy track of our monster evil. Victor Hugo has spoken of the nineteenth century as being woman's era, and among the most noticeable epochs in this era is the uprising of women against the twin evils of slavery and intemperance, which had foisted themselves like leeches upon the civilization of the present age. In the great anti-slavery conflict women had borne a part, but after the storm cloud of battle had rolled away, it was found that an enemy, old and strong and deceptive, was warring against the best interests of society; not simply an enemy to one race, but an enemy to all races--an enemy that had entrenched itself in the strongholds of appetite and avarice, and was upheld by fashion, custom and legislation. To dislodge this enemy, to put prohibition not simply on the statute book, but in the heart and conscience of a nation, embracing within itself such heterogeneous masses, is no child's play, nor the work of a few short moons. Men who were subjects in their own country and legislated for by others, become citizens here, with the power to help legislate for native born Americans. Hundreds of thousands of new citizens have been translated from the old oligarchy of slavery into the new commonwealth of freedom and are numerically strong enough to hold the balance of power in many States and sway its legislators for good or evil. With all these conditions, something more is needed than grand enthusiasms lighting up a few consecrated lives with hallowed brightness. We need patient, persevering, Christly endeavor, a consecration of the moral earnestness, spiritual power and numerical strength of the nation to grapple with this evil and accomplish its overthrow.

After the knowledge and experience gained by the crusade, women, instead of letting all their pure enthusiasms become dissipated by expending in feeling what they should utilize in action, came together and formed the Woman's Christian Temperance Union…. For years I knew very little of its proceedings and was not sure that colored comradeship was very desirable, but having attended a local Union in Philadelphia, I was asked to join and acceded to the request and was made city and afterwards State Superintendent of work among colored people. Since then, for several years I have held the position of National Superintendent of work among the colored people of the North. When I became National Superintendent, there were no colored women on the Executive Committee or Board of Superintendents. Now there are two colored women on the Executive Committee and two on the Board of Superintendents…The race question has arisen, and some members of different Unions have met the question in a liberal and Christian manner; others have not seemed to have so fully outgrown the old shards and shells of the past as to make the distinction between Christian affiliation and social equality, but still the leaven of more liberal sentiments has been at work in the Union and produced some hopeful results.

One of the pleasantest remembrances of my connection with the Woman's Christian Temperance Union was the kind and hospitable reception I met in the Missouri State Convention, and the memorable words of their President, Mrs. Hoffman, who declared that the color-line was eliminated. A Superintendent was chosen at that meeting for colored work in the State, at whose home in St. Louis the National Superintendent I was for some time a Guest. The State Superintendent said in one of the meetings to the colored sisters, 'You can come with us, or you can go by yourselves.' There was self-reliance and ability enough among them to form a Union of their own, which was named after the National Superintendent. Our work is divided into about forty departments, and among them they chose several lines of work, and had departments for parlor meetings, juvenile and evangelistic work, all of which have been in working order. The Union held meetings in Methodist and Baptist churches and opened in the African Methodist Episcopal Church an industrial school for children…. This Union has gathered into its association seventeen schoolteachers, and I think comprises some of the best brain and heart of the race in the city. From West Virginia a lady informs the national Superintendent that her Union has invited the colored sisters to join with them, and adds, 'Praise God, from whom all blessings flow.' There are local Unions in the North where the doors have been opened to colored women, but in the farther South separate State Unions have been formed. Southern white women, it may be, fail to make in their minds the discrimination between social equality and Christian affiliation. Social equality is the outgrowth of social affinities and social conditions, and may be based on talent, ability, or wealth. Christian affiliation is the union of Christians to do help build up the kingdom of Christ amid the sin and misery of the world, under the spiritual leadership of the Lord Jesus Christ. At our last national Convention two States were

represented by colored representatives. The colored
President of an Alabama Union represented a Union
composed of white and colored people, and is called No.
2, instead of Colored Union, as it was not composed
entirely of colored people, and in making its advent into
the National Union brought more than twice the amount
of State dues which was paid by the white Alabama
Union, No. 1. The question of admission into the White
Ribbon Army [i.e., WCTU] was brought before the
national President, through a card sent from Atlanta.
Twenty-three women [in Georgia] had formed a Union
and had written to the National Superintendent of colored
work in the North asking about their admission, and if
black sheep must climb up some other way to tell them
how. I showed the card to Miss Willard, who gave it as
her opinion 'That the National could not make laws for a
State. If the colored women of Georgia will meet and
form a Woman's Christian Temperance Union for the
State, it is my opinion that their officers and delegates
will have the same representation in the National.' The
President of the Second Alabama was received and
recognized in the National as a member of the Executive
Committee, and had a place, as I was informed, on the
Committee of Resolutions. Believing in human solidarity,
the Woman's Christian Temperance Union has in its
hands one of the grandest opportunities that God ever
pressed into the hands of the womanhood of any country.
Its conflict is not the contest of a social club, but a moral
warfare for an imperiled civilization. Whether or not the
members of the farther South will subordinate the spirit of
caste to the spirit of Christ, time will show. Once between
them and the Negro were vast disparities, which have
been melting and disappearing. The war obliterated the
disparity between freedom and slavery. The civil law
blotted out the difference between disfranchisement and
manhood suffrage. Schools have sprung up like wells in
the desert dust, bringing the races nearer together on the

intellectual plane, while as a participant in the wealth of society the colored man has, I believe, in some instances, left his former master behind [in] the race for wealth. With these old landmarks going and gone, one relic remains from the dead past: 'Our social customs.' In clinging to them let them remember that the most ignorant, vicious and degraded voter outranks, politically, the purest, best and most cultured woman in the South, and learn to look at the question of Christian affiliation on this subject, not in the shadows of the fashion of this world that fades away, but in the light of the face of Jesus Christ. And can anyone despise the least of Christ's brethren without despising Him? Is there any path that the slave once trod that Jesus did not tread before him, and leave luminous with the light of His Steps? Was the Negro bought and sold? Christ was sold for thirty pieces of silver. Has he been poor? 'The birds had nests, the foxes had holes, but the Son of man had nowhere to lay His head.' Were they beaten in the house of bondage? They took Jesus and scourged Him. Have they occupied a low social position? 'He made himself of no reputation and was numbered with the transgressors.' Despised and trodden under foot? He was despised and rejected of men; spit upon by the rabble, crucified between thieves, and died as died Rome's meanest criminal slave. Oh, my brothers and sisters, if God chastens everyone whom He receives, let your past be a stimulus for the future. Join with the great army who are on the side of our God and His Christ."[4]

Lucy Simpson Thurman, a feminist, was national Superintendent of Black Work for the WCTU in the 1890s, reported that she had "always favored the organization of unions among the black women for it will be to them just what it has been to our white sisters, the greatest training school for the development of women."[5] The Michigan State Federation of Black Women commended the WCTU at their 1900 state convention because "they have shown the absence of prejudice against us by appointing such women of the race as Lucy Thurman . . . and others to positions of trust."[6]

Nonetheless, despite the avant-garde racial position of the WCTU, Frances Willard was criticized by non-Union sources from both directions on their efforts to include black women. Some black adversaries criticized the existence of segregated unions. On the other hand, some racist women resented even the presence of black women, let alone their equal positions at national WCTU conventions.

In response to these critics, Frances Willard penned the following letter to an editor. (It is reproduced here in its entirety).

RE: BLACK INCLUSION IN WCTU AND LYNCHING

"TO THE EDITOR, --It would be impossible for an association like the W.C.T.U., the central object of which is the recognition and development of the brotherhood of man, to be other than in warm sympathy with those who declare the substantial unity of humans, and endeavor to influence public opinion in the promotion of justice and sympathy between all races, classes, creeds, and communities. It is our purpose, not only by words, but deeds, to invest our lives in the effort to help on every member of the human family toward freedom, opportunity, and every brotherly consideration.

Two principles underlie all our efforts in the nearly fifty countries in which the society has obtained a foothold. The first has just been stated; and the second recognizes the autonomy of each nation and state in respect to the way its work shall be conducted. In some of the Northern States it is thought best to organize in societies by themselves groups of women who speak the Scandinavian tongue, and in the Southern States black women are organized in separate groups in the same way, by their own wish and will. They realize that by working in this manner they will develop more rapidly than they would if associated with white women, even as the W.C.T.U. itself does not admit men, because we wish to become drilled and disciplined by having the entire management of the society, so that when we are enfranchised, we shall be prepared to co-operate with men in the wider circle of Government.

So far as the World's and National W.C.T.U. officers are concerned they would gladly see white and black women in the same societies, and no distinction is made between white and black delegates at the Conventions. From the first, black women have been among the Superintendents and Organizers of the National W.C.T.U. We are aware that in the Southern States, it would not be practicable to group our local members in this way, and we have reason to believe that black women, as a class, much prefer to affiliate with those of their own race. We have been told this repeatedly by them, and while there are exceptions to this statement, we believe it represents the current opinion of the black people up to the present time, but we think the development that will come to the women who form these helpful groups of workers will at some time in the future lead to the closer affiliation of the two groups of women in their work. We were obliged to choose either not to organize in the South at all, or else to organize on this basis. We have done the best we could under the circumstances, and we think those who have criticized us so severely (i.e., in Great Britain) would take an altogether different view if they were better informed concerning the local situation at the South.

The General Officers of the W.C.T.U. make no distinction on account of race, and the attitude of the society toward the barbarity of lynching has been more pronounced than that of any other association in the United States, for not only has a resolution against lynching been repeatedly enacted in the general society, but in many of its State branches, while the utterances of its leaders have been made clear and unmistakable. With such a record as this, White Ribboners [i.e., WCTU members] need not fear to abide the verdict of fair-minded men and women."
--Believe me, Yours sincerely,
FRANCES WILLARD

AMERICAN INDIANS

The WCTU also worked with American Indians. In 1888, Frances Willard traveled to the Indian Territory (now Oklahoma). Willard was impressed with the leadership ability of Jane Stapler (1844-1899) a Cherokee woman who had married John Stapler, a Quaker. While growing up, Stapler had been educated at missionary schools.

Briefly, the relevant history of the Cherokees begins for us in 1836 when they were forced to move by the

"Indian Removal Act" pushed through Congress by Andrew Jackson. The Cherokees were to exchange their land in Georgia for land in the Indian Territory. Gold had been discovered on their reservations in Georgia and the miner's greed, along with corrupt Georgia state officials, worked to dislodge the Cherokees and other tribes.

On the side of the Cherokees trying to help them keep their land were Protestant missionaries, Congressional supporters, and the US Supreme Court. The Methodist Episcopal Church was the first church to pass a resolution supporting the rights of the Indians.

The State of Georgia threatened 14 missionaries with four years hard labor in the penitentiary if they persisted in helping the Indians, or they could leave the state. Two missionaries accepted the four-year sentence of the Supreme Court of Georgia rather than depart. Even citizens wishing Indian removal "were filled with revulsion at the treatment meted out to the missionaries" by the state. The injustice suffered by the missionaries did much to swing a certain measure of public feeling in favor of the Cherokees.[7]

There were two key treaties signed by the US government prior to 1836 giving the Cherokees rights to their ancestral homeland. The US Supreme Court, led by Chief Justice John Marshall, ruled the treaties were still in force. Andrew Jackson infamously replied, "John Marshall has made his decision; now let him enforce it."[c]

In the end, Jackson and the Georgian officials instigated the ejection of 20,000 Cherokees. Elijah Hicks was the leader of the second 1,000 Indian contingent to leave in the wagons and horses provided by the US government. The move has been aptly called the "Trail of Tears." There were many hardships. The Hicks' contingent left Athens, Georgia September 9, 1838, and

---

[c] While white people referred to Jackson as "Old Hickory," the Cherokees nicknamed him "Chicken Snake." (Duvall DL. The Cherokee Nation and Tahlequah: Arcadia Publishing; 1999, p. 8)

did not arrive in the Indian Territory until January 4, 1839, during a snowstorm. Fifty-four members of the original 1,000 party died in route to the Indian Territory.[8]

The eleven-year-old daughter of Chief Elijah Hicks, the future Jane Stapler, was one of those who landed safely in the new Territory.

Frances Willard made Stapler leader of the first Union in Indian Territory which was organized in Muskogee in 1888. The first territorial meeting for the WCTU took place in Jane Stapler's home in Tahlequah on June 4, 1889. Willard stayed in her Oklahoma home in 1888 and 1889 when visiting the Indian Territory. The Indian Territory sent Jane Stapler to the 1890 WCTU national convention as a delegate. She was received warmly.[9] Stapler remained as WCTU president of the Indian Territory until 1899.

Willard visited reservations whenever she traveled the American West and was received enthusiastically.[10]

It is important to record what contemporary suffragettes thought of the WCTU's record of racial inclusion. Carrie Chapman Catt, Chairman (sic), Campaign Organization Committee, National American Woman's Suffrage Association, brought greetings to the 1899 WCTU convention and stated, "that the WCTU more than any other agency had broken down the intolerance of the past."[11]

Upon Frances Willard's death, Rev. Ransom described Willard in his eulogy as a friend of the "colored race." "This queen among women has fought their battles, championed their cause, and numbered many of them among her personal friends."[12]

References
Chapter 12

1. Graham SH. Woman Suffrage and the New Democracy. New Haven: Yale Univeresity Press; 1996, p. 9-25.
2. Stanton EC, Anthony SB, Gage MJ, Harper IH. History of Woman Suffrage, Volume 5: Susan B. Anthony; 1886, p. 5.
3. Ibid, p. 60.
4. Harper FEW. "The Woman's Christian Temperance Union and the Colored Woman (1888)" In: Boyd MJ, ed. (Reprinted in) Discarded Legacy: Politics and Poetics of Frances EW Harper. Detroit: Wayne State University Press; 1994: p. 203-7.
5. Bordin RBA. Woman and temperance: The Quest for Power and Liberty, 1873-1900: Temple University Press; 1981, p. 84.
6. Ibid, p. 53.
7. Wilkins T. Cherokee Tragedy: The Ridge Family and the Decimation of a People: University of Oklahoma Press; 1989, p. 227
8. Biography of E.D. Hicks. https://www.accessgenealogy.com/native/biographical-sketch-of-e-d-hicks.htm2012.
9. Woman's Christian Temperance Union. Minutes of the National Woman's Christian Temperance Union. 1890, p. 34-35.
10. Bordin, p. 85.
11. Woman's Christian Temperance Union. Report of the National Woman's Christian Temperance Union. 1899, p. 34.
12. Ransom, RR. They Mourn for Miss Willard. February 1898. Frances Willard death scrapbook. Frances Willard Library, Evanston, IL. Included in: Why Did African-American Women Join the WCTU, 1880-1900? By Thomas Dublin and Angela Scheuerer.

Chapter 13 WCTU: A Single-issue Group?

In some quarters, it has been alleged that the WCTU became a single-issue organization after the death of Francis Willard in 1898. The purported shrinkage was to one solely of temperance.

> "For whatever reason, the WCTU's program emphasis changed after Willard's death. The Union shifted to a single-issue approach, and emphasis on temperance…. The change in tone from Willard's last presidential address in 1897 to the subsequent president, Lillian Stevens, first presidential address is even more dramatic…[to] where Stevens first address [1898] was confined almost entirely to endorsing legislation to cure the liquor problem."[1] [a]

Catherine Clinton also stated, "When the WCTU lost Willard, it reverted to a single-issue organization. By 1900 the WCTU rescinded its commitment to suffrage. The new leaders concentrated on their original aim of temperance."[2]

These authors are mistaken about the WCTU becoming a single-issue organization after Willard's death. Data to the contrary can be presented in four ways. One, performing a larger sample of the annual addresses of the succeeding leader, Lillian Stevens. Two, citing Lillian Stevens own description of how she limited topics when composing her own speeches. Three, the continuing interest in suffrage can be quantitated by the frequency of the terms "suffrage" and "franchise" in WCTU national

---

[a] While normally a good scholar on Frances Willard, Borden is mistaken here. This shows the deficiency of a limited sample and not attempting a quantitative assessment. Sampling only the first two or three of Lillian Stevens' national addresses is woefully inadequate for a woman who gave 15 annual national addresses.

annual convention reports for the years from 1891 to 1914. (Table 13.1). Finally, the 37 departments involved in the "do everything" continued their reporting for many years during and beyond the ensuing 15-year tenure of Lillian Stevens.

Lillian Stevens (1844-1914) was Frances Willard's successor as President of the national WCTU from 1898 until her own death in 1914. A 23-page biography written in 1921 gives a snapshot of her life centered in her birth state of Maine. Known for her commitment to charitable causes, Stevens met Willard on the latter's first trip to Portland, Maine in 1874. The two became instant friends. Willard organized a state chapter of the WCTU with Stevens elected as treasurer. In 1878, Stevens became the President of the Maine WCTU, a position she held until her death.[3]

Maine was unusual in the temperance movement by being the first state to enact a temperance law in 1855. Because of constant challenges to the law by the liquor cartel, Stevens was among several anti-alcohol workers who helped Maine adopt a constitutional amendment banning the recreational use of alcohol. Because of this success, the WCTU in Maine was much less focused on temperance than other state chapters of the WCTU. The fact that the Maine WCTU did not dissolve after achieving the constitutional amendment success, shows the "do everything" approach continued to help women with multiple endeavors beyond temperance.

Favorite causes of Stevens were prison reform for women and the humane treatment of animals. At the time, there were no separate prison facilities apart from men. The first state reformatory institution for women in Maine named its first building for Lillian Stevens in recognition of her efforts for women. The American Humane Education Society and the Massachusetts Society for the Prevention of Cruelty to Animals awarded Stevens a silver medal for her efforts in advancing the humane treatment of animals.[3]

The greatest interest Lillian Stevens had as national WCTU President was temperance. However, the issue that was likely of greatest concern to Stevens in Maine was her indefatigable efforts towards suffrage for women. Her biographers noted, "Mrs. Stevens was an advocate of the enfranchisement of women and worked long and earnestly for this cause, arranging and conducting many hearings at the Maine legislature in behalf of this just measure."[3]

It should be noted that the term "just measure" was used here; that Maine women needed this right by itself, as a matter of fairness was advocated by Stevens. The right was not needed to vote for alcohol control.

The conclusion to this section on the many interests of Stevens for reform and charity in Maine and elsewhere helps to deny the idea in some quarters that she was a "single-issue" woman interested in only prohibition.

What about her silence on suffrage in the Presidential speeches for the WCTU in 1898 and 1899 cited by Bordin? In contrast to Willard's addresses, Stevens did not attempt to talk about everything the WCTU was doing in her annual report. Each of the 37 departments that would benefit women presented a speech by the national chairwoman of that department. Stevens saw no reason to repeat the substance of these reports. Her annual Presidential Address in 1902 provides a clue to her approach. "I almost wished the first order of this Convention might be to hear the year's work story related by the State Presidents—all combined a record too long to review here, but parts of which I shall weave into to what is said later."[4] Instead of repeating information, she gave an overview of events that would highlight national efforts and weave a coherent address. Even so, in her 1902 presidential address, Stevens used 570 words to discuss the advancement of women's suffrage.[5]

The annual national WCTU reports consistently contained about 400 pages. As one can see from Table 13.1, the frequency of the terms "suffrage" and "franchise" remain about the same. Moreover, there appears to even be a notable increase of the frequency of these terms a few years after Willard's death in 1901 and 1902!

One need only peruse the yearly WCTU National

Year	Place	Total pages report	Franchise Report #pages	Suffrage Word count	Franchise Word count
1891	Louisville	185	4.5	10	9
1895	Baltimore	402	5	26	19
1896	St Louis	440	5	26	18
1898	St Paul	382	4.6	27	11
1899	Seattle	332	6.5	19	19
1900	Wash D.C.	347	5	30	59
1902	Portland, ME	340	4	25	61
1906	Hartford	379	6.0	20	13
1907	Nashville	365	6.9	13	12
1908	Denver	389	2*	13	15
1909	Omaha	391	2*	21	14
1911	Milwaukee	383	4	154	47
1913	New Jersey	401	3	45	14
1914	Atlanta	338	3	31	11
*The franchise president chose to summarize her report. (Some yearly reports not available to author).					
Table 13.1 Suffrage Word Count in Reports for Annual Meetings of the National WCTU					

convention reports from 1898 to 1914 available online to verify the numerous departments of the "do everything" continuing vigorous efforts to help women in many ways.

On a qualitative level, there are numerous descriptions that illustrate the ongoing and even increasing interest in suffrage; this attention was not merely for the sake of prohibition, but also for justice. What one can also ascertain is the close cooperation of the WCTU and NAWSA for suffrage, an alliance usually ignored by later suffrage writers.

In another of many efforts, the March 29, 1906 issue of the national WCTU publication, *The Union Signal*, was given over entirely to suffrage. Copies of this issue were handed out in different states by WCTU Union members where suffrage was an issue in 1906.

The front of the issue is a full-page encomium and obituary on the recent death (two weeks earlier, March 13, 1906) of Susan B Anthony and her devotion to suffrage and temperance. The issue then devotes a large amount of space to explaining how Colorado women have been using the franchise responsibly since Colorado became the first state to approve suffrage with a popular vote of adult males and not merely by fiat of the state legislature. Included are the testimonies of many prominent Colorado men who tabulate the many good things that the vote of women have achieved; these men also debunk the rumors circulating in other states about the dangers of women voting. Nearly a full page was written by Ellis Meredith, a *Rocky Mountain News* reporter (chapters 16-18) entitled "Opportunities for Enfranchised Women." The franchise issue also updated the status of woman's suffrage in every state.

HUMOR AND THE WCTU

Twenty-first century readers may tend to think of suffragettes or white ribbon women (i.e., WCTU women) as being humorless, but this was not the case. In 1911, Sophie L.W. Clark produced a comedy play entitled "*An Entertainment to Make Votes for Women*" for the WCTU Franchise department for which she was national president.[b] It is a 14-page script set in the future year of 2099 where women are now in complete control of

---

[b] (Library of Congress http://hdl.loc.gov/loc.gdc/ scd0001.20060809006en.2) Sophie Clark produced at least a second comedy play and perhaps more but these cannot be found by the Library of Congress or the WCTU library.

politics and males no longer have the franchise. The scene is a legislative chamber where men and sympathetic women argue for male suffrage and the dour female opposition to suffrage for men argue against the male franchise. It contains much humor in the line of Jane Austen.[c] The brightest humor comes when the male franchise bill keeps getting referred out to dead end committees such as the "fishery committee" where the bill will surely die. The analogy is clear to anyone who followed the shenanigans of corrupt legislators (chapter 22) who conspired to have female suffrage bills die.

Stevens uttered perhaps some of her best oratory in her Presidential Address at the National WCTU convention in 1913. Extended excerpts follow,

> "The latest, and in some respects the greatest woman suffrage victory, was achieved in June, by the action of the Illinois Legislature in granting to the women of the state all voting privileges the Legislature can bestow. Illinois women can now vote for presidential electors, mayor, aldermen, city clerk, supervisor, town clerk, assessors, collectors, highway commissioners, trustees of the sanitary district, members of the Board of Review and State Board of Equalization; in fact, for all city and town officers except police magistrates. No wonder there was gnashing of teeth among the liquor sellers, gamblers, the keepers of dance halls, and the white slave traffickers when on June 11 the

---

[c] The author and his wife, Marilyn, have studied Jane Austen extensively, and have written two sequels to Austen's Pride and Prejudice, Desire and Duty and Virtue and Vanity (available Amazon). The current author contributed a study for the *CS Lewis Society of New York Bulletin* on Jane Austen's Influence of CS Lewis entitled, "Desire and Duty: Metaphors Borrowed by Lewis from Jane Austen's Pride and Prejudice." April 1997 issue. Available: http://www.nycslsociety.com/back-issues.html

suffrage victory came. The *Chicago Evening Post* announced that 'state-wide woman suffrage had crossed the Mississippi. The women as well as the men of Illinois will vote for the next president of the United States'…The figure of Miss Frances Willard stands in the background. Around her are grouped the memories of even an earlier generation of high minded women who fought for suffrage when the fight meant ridicule and abuse… [then there are] the trooping ranks of women, young and old, who went to twenty-six legislatures at Springfield to make the plea that was granted yesterday at last. The story of how the women worked and won in Illinois has appeared in newspaper and magazine, and reads like a thrilling romance, eliciting admiration, as well as gratification, from all who believe in the enfranchisement of women. In Illinois, as in other states, the liquor interests fought the suffrage bill. The following from the *Chicago Daily News* is in accord with the public expressions on this point: 'It is interesting to observe that the fight against woman-suffrage at Springfield was mainly a fight by friends of the liquor interests. The feeling that women should be permitted to express themselves at the polls on the liquor question and on many other questions directly affecting the financial, physical, and moral welfare of the communities in which they live has had much to do with the outcome of their hard-fought campaign.'

Many women who had felt no special interest in the temperance cause have through their suffrage work been led to a knowledge of the

strength and evil of the liquor element. After
the passage of the Illinois law a test soon
came to the Illinois Equal Suffrage
Association. It was in reference to publishing
liquor advertisements in the woman suffrage
edition of the Daily Chicago Examiner of
August 4. The Suffrage Association, with
characteristic courage and wisdom, declined
to have any such alliance with the liquor
traffic, refusing to publish not only their
proffered advertisements but also a flattering
greeting from the brewers…unmistakably it
has been a great year for the cause of woman
suffrage as well as for the temperance cause.
In fact, these causes are closely intertwined,
and we expect similar triumphs are to rapidly
follow. Old time prejudices are fading away
and if the woman suffragists of our country
continue to conduct their campaigns with the
dignity, consistent, courtesy and intelligence
thus far displayed, and they will, we are sure
to keep on the winning side."[6] [d]

With a longer period sampled, and by using key word
frequency and speech content, it is clear that the WCTU
did not revert to a single-issue organization after the time
of Frances Willard. In many ways, under the 15 -year
reign of Lillian Stevens, the WCTU expanded its efforts
in advocating women's suffrage. This backing was not for
utility alone (i.e., to vote for liquor control), but because
women deserved equal justice.

---

[d] the opposition of the liquor interests to women's suffrage was a
subject of growing awareness by NAWSA and the public at large.

References
Chapter 13

1. Bordin RBA. Woman and Temperance: The Quest for Power and Liberty, 1873-1900: Temple University Press; 1981, p. 151-152.
2. Clinton C. The other civil war: American Women in the Nineteenth Century: Macmillan; 1999, p. 170.
3. Stevens G. Lillian M. N. Stevens a life sketch. http://nrs.harvard.edu/urn-3:FHCL:520167: Repository: Collection Development Department. Widener Library. HCL Institution: Harvard University. 1921. Accessed August 10, 2017.
4. Woman's Christian Temperance Union. Report of the National Woman's Christian Temperance Union ... annual meeting. Chicago: Woman's Temperance Pub. Ass'n; 1902, p. 118
5. Ibid, pp. 132-133.
6. Woman's Christian Temperance Union. Report of the National Woman's Christian Temperance Union ... annual meeting. Chicago: Woman's Temperance Pub. Ass'n; 1913, p. 110-111.

Chapter 14 Science and Suffrage

Elizabeth Cady Stanton, and other so-called "freethinkers" of the late 19th century, attacked the validity of Christianity by quoting "scientific" sources. This same group, despite lacking classical scholarship or knowledge of the ancient languages, wrote their own interpretation of the Christian Bible called *The Woman's Bible*. In doing so, they supposed that they would advance women's rights and suffrage. The purpose of this chapter is to examine these ideas and respond to them.[a]

THE MYTH BEGINS

On December 18, 1869, Andrew Dickson White (1832-1918 AD) strode to the podium at the Cooper Union Hall in New York City to give a melodramatic lecture entitled, *The Battlefields of Science*. His thesis was, "Interference with Science in the supposed interest of religion… has [invariably] resulted in the direst evils both to Religion and Science." White spoke of the "great war" between science and Christianity. He regaled the audience about the Italian scientist, Giordino Bruno, being "burned alive as a monster of impiety;" and, of Galileo being "tortured" and imprisoned as the "worst of unbelievers." Over the next 27 years, White expanded his ideas into a huge two-volume work, *A History of the Warfare of Science with Theology in Christendom* (1896).[1,2]

A similar tone was advanced by John William Draper (1811-1882 AD) in 1874 in his book, *History of the Conflict between Religion and Science*:

---

[a] The relevance for women's history is that these allegations have been oft repeated in an uncritical manner by subsequent authors who have no background in the history of science or biblical criticism.

"The antagonism we thus witness between Religion and Science is the continuation of a struggle that commenced when Christianity began to attain political power ... The history of Science is not a mere record of isolated discoveries; it is a narrative of the conflict of two contending powers, the expansive force of the human intellect on one side, and the compression arising from traditionary (sic) faith and human interests on the other."[3]

Elizabeth Cady Stanton admiringly wrote,

"[The] Hon. Andrew D. White, formerly President of Cornell University shows us in his great work, 'A History of the Warfare of Science with Theology that the Bible with its fables, allegories and endless contradictions, has been the great block in the way of civilization. All through the centuries scholars and scientists have been imprisoned, tortured and burned alive for some discovery which seemed to conflict with a petty text of Scripture."[4]

Really? The reader should peruse *Galileo Goes to Jail and Other Myths about Science and Religion*, written by Ronald Numbers and 24 other scholars in 2009 [Harvard University Press]. In his introduction, Numbers writes:

"Historians of science have known for years that White's and Draper's accounts are more propaganda than history…Unlike the master mythmakers White and Draper, the contributors to this volume have no obvious scientific or theological axes to grind. Nearly half, twelve of twenty-five, self-identify as agnostic or atheist (that is, unbelievers in religion). Among the remaining thirteen there are five mainstream Protestants, two evangelical Protestants, one Roman Catholic,

one Jew, one Muslim, one Buddhist—and two
whose beliefs fit no conventional category
(including one pious Spinozist)"[5]

The term "myth" is used by Numbers, et al to
"designate a claim that is false."[5]

"The greatest myth in the history of science and
religion holds that they have been in a state of constant
conflict. No one bears more responsibility for promoting
this notion than two nineteenth-century American
polemicists: Andrew Dickson White and John William
Draper."[6]

"Perhaps the most influential and most
frequently published book ever written about
science and religion, John William Draper's
*History of the Conflict between Religion and
Science* (1874), is…so slanted and hysterical
that it is difficult for an educated person today
to read it without smirking; Draper's work
plays fast and loose with the facts and
contains barely a shred of reliable historical
information. Nonetheless, it continues to be
read and cited by some, and a generation ago
even some historians of science referenced it
uncritically. More significantly, its claims
have become "common knowledge" for a
great number of people"[8]

Three topics are presented to illustrate the
disinformation from the latter sources: the persecution of
Bruno and Galileo; the assertion that the medieval church
believed in a flat earth; and that the church opposed
anesthesia for childbirth.

BRUNO EXECUTED, AND GALILEO IMPRISONED?

An entire legend has grown around the myth that
Giordano Bruno (1548-1600 AD) was put to death for his

assertion that the earth circled the sun; an idea first promoted by the mathematician Copernicus [1473-1543 AD].[b] This allegation is simply not true. Moreover, as far as the team of Ronald Numbers, et al can determine, no scientist at any time in history has been put to death by the church for his scientific beliefs.

The fable of Galileo's torture and imprisonment in the 17th century by the ecclesiastical authorities has persisted for a long time. Many opponents of the church have maintained something on the order of Voltaire's statement, "[T]he great Galileo, at age of fourscore, groaned away his days in the dungeons of the Inquisition, because he had demonstrated by irrefragable proofs the motion of the earth." —Voltaire, "Descartes and Newton" (1728 AD).[7][c]

Maurice Finocchiaro reviews the allegations about Galileo in detail.[7] Interestingly, before 1609, Galileo himself felt the evidence of anti-Copernican arguments outweighed the pro-Copernican ones. He changed positions by thinking through a process of using the direct evidence of the senses, astronomical observation, traditional physics and scriptural passages.

In 1609, Galileo perfected the newly invented telescope and proceeded to make startling discoveries such as mountains on the moon, and the four satellites of Jupiter. As he did so, he shifted his paradigm to the heliocentric movement of the Earth.

Volunteering to go to Rome in 1615 to answer complaints against him for his thinking, a long series of investigations and judicial proceedings then took place over 18 years about his ideas. Except for possibly three days, Galileo was never held in prison, either during the

---

[b] versus a universe that revolved around the earth.

[c] Voltaire (1694-1778) was a famous French skeptic who vehemently attacked the Catholic Church. Paradoxically, though, he told his mistress, Marguerite, "Whatever you do, don't tell the servants there is no God or they'll steal the silver."

trial (as was custom) or afterwards as the sentence decreed. Even for the three days under question, he was likely lodged in the prosecutor's apartment. Finally, considering the available evidence, Galileo was never tortured.

Thus, "the myths of Galileo's torture and imprisonment are genuine myths: ideas that are in fact false but once seemed true—and continue to be accepted as true by poorly educated persons and careless scholars."[7]

FLAT EARTH VERSUS ROUND GLOBE?

Draper also asserted,
> "In Christendom, the greater part of this long period [2nd to 16th centuries A.D.] was consumed in disputes respecting the nature of God, and in struggles for ecclesiastical power. The authority of the Fathers, and the prevailing belief that the Scriptures contain the sum of all knowledge, discouraged any investigation of Nature... This indifference continued until the close of the fifteenth century. Even then there was no scientific inducement. The inciting motives were altogether of a different kind. They originated in commercial rivalries, and the question of the shape of the earth was finally settled by three sailors, Columbus, Da Gama, and above all, by Ferdinand Magellan."[9]

Or more blatantly, Boise Penrose (*Travel and Discovery in the Renaissance*, 1955) stated,
> "Strict Biblical interpretations plus unbending patristic bigotry resulted in the theory of a flat earth with Jerusalem in its center, and the Garden of Eden somewhere up country, from which flowed the four Rivers of Paradise."[9]

Did people living in the Middle Ages and early exploration period really think the world was flat? The author and his wife were taught in widely disparate public-school locations that Columbus and his men "were afraid of sailing off the edge of the world." When they did not fall off, his voyages proved "the earth was round." Nonsense.

In his world travels, the author has encountered striking visual proof that flat-earth thinking has never been the case over the past two millennia. Figure 14.1 shows the sculpted foot of the Roman emperor, Trajan (reign 97-117 AD) with his foot resting on a three-dimensional globe expressing his rule of the world; Figure 14.2 shows a Byzantium painting dated from 1300 to 1350 of the Archangel Michael holding a spherical globe representing the earth in his hand.[d]

Cormak states,

> "From the seventh century to the fourteenth, every important medieval thinker concerned about the natural world stated more or less explicitly that the world was a round globe, many of them incorporating Ptolemy's astronomy and Aristotle's physics into their work."[10]

Pierre d'Ailly (1350-1410), archbishop of Cambrai, wrote about the sphericity of the earth in his book, Imago Mundi in 1410. The latter tome was read by early explorers like Columbus. Even vernacular writers like Chaucer (1340-1400) in *The Franklin's Tale*, spoke of "This wyde world, which men seye is round."[10]

---

[d] After the fall of Rome in 548 A.D., the central administration of Christianity resided in Constantinople as the Byzantium Church until the city's fall to Islam in the year 1453.

Figure 14.1 **Roman Emperor Trajan's foot demonstrating his rule over the global world (Reign 97-117 AD). The rest of the statue is in the Ephesus Museum, Vienna Austria. Photo taken by author at Ephesus in Turkey. Museum in Vienna also visited by author.**

Apart from isolated individuals, there is no historical evidence to support the myth of an ancient or medieval flat earth being held by any group. Christian clerics neither suppressed the truth nor stifled debate on this subject. Cormak concludes, "A good son of the church who believed his work was revealing God's plan, Columbus didn't prove the earth was round—he stumbled on a continent that happened to be in his way."[10]

Figure 14.2 Icon of the Archangel Michael holding the earth as a globe. Circa 14th century. Permission granted Byzantine and Christian Museum, Athens.

ANESTHESIA FOR CHILDBIRTH?

The reader may be surprised at the late development of obstetrical anesthesia or painless childbirth. Prior to 1846, attempts to ameliorate the horror of surgery were ineffectual and dangerous. Different forms of narcotics had been known for over three millennia. The use of opium (extracted from the poppy plant) is described by most ancient civilizations, who readily appreciated the fact that opium induced sleep, relieved cough, alleviated pain and caused constipation. Unfortunately, the oblivion which can be achieved with high dose narcotics is often permanent.

Alcohol is even worse for anesthesia than narcotics. While a large amount of alcohol can render one stuporous, it does little to mask pain. Alcohol in high doses depresses heart and lung function and the fatal dose of alcohol, as for opiates, is not much higher than the coma inducing dose. When alcohol and narcotics were combined, they become even more erratic.

The first advance in anesthesia was promoted by William Morton, a dental surgeon in Boston, who took a well-known compound, ether, and researched its ability to induce dental anesthesia both on animals and himself. Morton finally convinced Dr Warren at the Massachusetts General Hospital to use it, with Morton as the anesthesiologist, for a young man with thyroid tumors needing surgery. On the day of surgery, October 16, 1846, Morton put his patient to sleep. Warren began operating on what would have been a nearly impossible task previously of cutting extensively in the neck.

When the patient was fully restored to consciousness and able to answer questions, he gave the gratifying intelligence, "I have experienced no pain, but only a sensation like that of scraping the part with a blunt instrument."[11]

A year later, a gynecologist in Edinburgh, James Young Simpson was to try another agent for anesthesia, chloroform. He used it on November 4, 1847 on a mother who had been in labor for three days. The child was delivered painlessly 25 minutes later.

Andrew Dickson White thundered 50 years later,
> "From pulpit after pulpit Simpson's use of
> chloroform was denounced as impious and
> contrary to Holy Writ; texts were cited
> abundantly, the ordinary declaration being
> that to use chloroform was "to avoid one part
> of the primeval curse on woman."[12]

This anti-Christian myth persists into the 21st century: "When 19th-century doctors began using chloroform to alleviate the pain of childbirth, the Scottish Calvinist church declared it a "Satanic invention" intended to frustrate the Lord's design."[13]

The truth is the great majority of theologians welcomed general anesthesia for themselves and their spouses. And why not? Favorable reasoning came from a story in *Genesis* chapter two: God put Adam asleep to remove a rib from him to fashion woman to stand at his side (not his feet).

Nonetheless, within weeks of his use of chloroform, James Simpson published a pamphlet entitled, *Answer to the Religious Objections Advanced against the Employment of Anesthetic Agents in Midwifery and Surgery*. The missive was directed primarily to medical professionals. Simpson argued on exegetical, logical, historical, and moral grounds against those who "believe that the practice in question ought in any degree to be opposed and rejected on religious grounds." Typical of many scientific contemporaries, Simpson denied any inherent conflict between religion and science. Theologians from Presbyterian, Anglican and other Protestant churches sent overwhelmingly positive responses to Simpson for his 1847 pamphlet.[14]

Six years later, Queen Victoria set the style. The Queen had made James Simpson her Physician-in-Ordinary in Scotland. She accepted chloroform anesthesia with the birth of her seventh child in April 1853. In the time, it certainly would have been disloyal for any subject to accuse the Queen, the head of the English Church, of engaging in a harmful or sinful act.

A.D. Farr, a historian and physician, conducted an exhaustive study of the matter. He found only fleeting published evidence,

> "either for theological opposition to
> anesthesia from the institutional churches or
> of any widely held (or express) opposition on
> the part of individuals.' Farr concluded that 'it
> is almost certain that Simpson's pamphlet . . .
> was written to forestall objections which, in
> the event, did not arise, and that its
> publication has subsequently been
> misinterpreted by other commentators as
> evidence for a non-existent opposition."[15]

RECEPTION OF THE WOMAN'S BIBLE

Elizabeth Cady Stanton started a project to rewrite the Bible in her own fashion. She called it *The Woman's Bible*. Stanton's idea was to have "two or three Greek and Hebrew scholars devote themselves to translation" and numerous committees review the written material of both the translators and commentators.

Stanton, as managing editor and principal contributor, was clear as to her bias,

> "Women meet in convention and denounce
> *The Woman's Bible*, while clinging to the
> Church and their Scriptures. The only
> difference between us is, we say these
> degrading ideas of woman emanated from the
> brain of man, while the Church says they

came from God. Now to my mind, the
Revising Committee of *The Woman's Bible,*
in denying divine inspiration for such
demoralizing ideas shows a more worshipful
reverence for the great Spirit of All Good than
does the Church. We have made a fetich (sic)
of the Bible long enough. The time has come
to read it as we do all other books, accepting
the good and rejecting the evil it teaches."[16] [e]

Early on, Stanton played fast and loose with her
suffrage friends by appointing many to the editorial board
for *The Woman's Bible* without asking their permission!
Among many, was Frances Willard, who withdrew her
name with a strenuous objection.

Susan Anthony also refused Stanton's call for the
project. In addition, Anthony cautioned Stanton to recruit
at least a few editors "who have read the Bible once
through, consecutively, in their lives."[17] That even one
panel member had ever done so was never clear. Not a
high bar for an editor, one would think.

Stanton repeatedly voiced her *a priori* disbelief of
events of the Bible without any reference to factual
support for the episodes. These statements were not going
to endear her to the religious culture of the 1890s.

Despite the claims in the introduction to her book
about Greek and Hebrew translators and review
committees, these groups never materialized.
Nonetheless, she left these claims in her preface. Not a
good ethical start.

Elizabeth Cady Stanton's Bible was not well received
by the public.

Even though Stanton was a former president, the
National American Woman's Suffrage Association
became enmeshed in severe controversy over *The*

---

[e] The reader should examine the peculiar book written almost entirely
by Stanton. Kathi Kern is right—the project should be called Mrs.
Stanton's Bible.[17]

Woman's Bible. Leaders, such as Carrie Chapman Catt, claimed that the book had driven potential suffragists from the movement. Criticism of the project had been "seriously injurious to the work of organizing." In southern Illinois, for example, the publication of *The Woman's Bible* had ended the suffrage campaign. "We had to withdraw," Catt said simply.[18]

The controversy came to a final head in the 1896 NAWSA convention in Washington, D.C., where a vote of 53 to 41 censored the project by pointing out NAWSA had "no official connection with the so-called 'Woman's Bible.'"[19]

The national WCTU followed NAWSA later in 1896. Temperance women took issue with Stanton's title, stating,

> "While we recognize the right of women to make commentaries on the Bible, as men have done from the beginning until now, we regret the name 'Woman's Bible' to any volume, and we farther deplore the misapprehension of the Bible only relating to woman as a new version of the Scriptures."[20]

Undaunted, Stanton continued the project. Her perfidy continued. Stanton had promised to share the copyright, and presumably the royalties, for the project with Matilda Joselyn Gage. Gage had been a strong supporter, also a "freethinker," and a key writer on the project. Gage eventually found out from the associate responsible for filing the copyright with the Library of Congress that her name was not on the paperwork. Gage fired off a letter to Stanton about the "mistake" and included instructions how to file an amended copyright application. Details from Stanton's viewpoint are not completely known. Perhaps, the abundant number of copies of the self-published book left sitting in her [Stanton's] storage meant there were no royalties to share. In any case,

Stanton never shared the copyright or royalties. The dispute resolved itself with Gage's death in 1898.[21]

DARWIN AND THE INFERIORITY OF WOMEN

There is a curious episode in the history of science in the 19th century that women rights advocates had to tussle with: namely, the allegation by Darwin in his book, *The Descent of Man,* (1871) that women were both physically and mentally inferior to men.[f]

Lest there be any misunderstanding, Darwin repeats his dogma of the inferiority of human females to human males numerous times. For example,

> "The chief distinction is the intellectual powers of the two sexes is shewn by man's attaining to a higher eminence, in whatever he takes up, than can woman—whether requiring deep thought, reason, or imagination, or merely the use of the senses and hands. If two lists were made of the most eminent men and women in poetry, painting, sculpture, music (inclusive both of composition and performance), history, science and philosophy, with a half-a-dozen names under each subject, the two lists would not bear comparison."[21]

Some men used Darwin's ideas as a "scientific" basis for rejecting suffrage for women.

Four years later in 1875, Antoinette Brown Blackwell (chapter eight), published a response to Darwin. Her book was titled *The Sexes Throughout Nature*. In it, she replies that,

> "These approximate equations are largely collated from Mr. Darwin's extended

---

[f] Even for the author who has a college degree in biology and chemistry, and who is steeped in 19th century vocabulary, Darwin's book is a dense and sleep-inducing book.

comparisons of secondary sexual characters. Fixing attention, as he does, upon masculine characters only, there seems to be no equilibrium of sex; but, holding the feminine characters up beside the others in a balanced view, the equilibrium is restored."[23]

Blackwell took up Darwin's challenge and created a chart (Table 14.3).[23] Again, the comedic wit of Jane Austen seems to jump out at the current author when reviewing Blackwell's chart.

Regardless of one's level of engagement with biologic evolution, Darwin's hypothesis on the inferior status of women compared to men was scientific nonsense.[g] The author hopes that future researchers will carefully evaluate claims concerning science or the Christian Bible from the late 19th century or early 20th century. We have shown many of the claims made during the latter time period have no basis in fact.

---

[g] Interested readers may be interested in referring to an essay by the author in Appendix B entitled: *Soviet Science and Suffrage*. Stanton and the freethinkers wished for communism to become a reality. If they had only waited a few years, they could have seen the absurdity of the way Soviet communism defined science and how the ideology led to the violent death of more women (and men) than any other movement in history (in just 72 years).

Characteristic		
	Male Advantage	Female Advantage
		Structure
	Size	
	Strength	
	Amount of Activity	
		Rate of Activity
	Amount of Circulation	
		Rate of Circulation
		Endurance
		Products
		Direct Nurture
	Indirect Nurture	
	Sexual Love	
	Parental Love	Parental Love
	Reasoning Powers	
		Direct Insight of Facts
		Direct Insight of Relations
	Thought	Thought
	Feeling	Feeling
	Moral Powers	Moral Powers
Overall Result in every species--Females equal males		
Organic Equilibrium in Physiological and Psychological Equivalence of the Sexes		

Table 14.3 Characteristics of the sexes as determined by Antoinette Brown Blackwell. Shaded characteristics were thought to be equivalent by Blackwell. From Rossi and Blackwell.[23]

References
Chapter 14

1. Professor White on the Battlefields of Science. New York Daily Tribune 1869; p. 4.
2. White AD. A History of the Warfare of Science with Theology in Christendom: Appleton; 1896.
3. Draper JW. History of the Conflict between Religion and Science: New York, Appleton; 1875. Preface. p. vi.
4. Gordon AD. The Selected Papers of Elizabeth Cady Stanton and Susan B. Anthony: An Awful Hush, 1895 to 1906: Rutgers University Press; 2013, p. 114.
5. Numbers RL. Galileo Goes to Jail and other Myths about Science and Religion. Harvard University Press; 2009, location 3%.
6. Ibid, location 3%.
7. Finocchiaro M. Myth 8: That Galileo was Imprisoned and Tortured for Advocating Copernicanism. In: Numbers R, ed. Galileo Goes to Jail and Other Myths about Science and Religion: Harvard University Press; 2009, location 23-26%.
8. Numbers, location 33%.
9. Numbers, location 10%
10. Cormack LB. Myth 3: That Medieval Christians Taught that the Earth was Flat. In: Numbers R, ed. Galileo Goes to Jail and Other Myths about Science and Religion: Harvard University Press; 2009, location 11-2%.
11. Senate USC. Reports of Committees: 30th Congress, 1st Session - 48th Congress, 2nd Session 1863, p. 23-24.
12. Numbers, location 18%.
13. Schoepflin R. Myth 16, That the Church Denounced Anesthesia in Childbirth on Biblical Grounds. In: Numbers R, ed. Galileo Goes to Jail and other Myths about Science and Religion. ebook ed. Cambridge. MA: Harvard University Press; 2009, location 41%.
14. Ibid.
15. Schoepflin, location 41-42%.

16. Stanton EC. The Woman's Bible. Self-published. 1898. P. 187.
17. Kern K. Mrs. Stanton's Bible: Cornell University Press; 2002, p. 137.
18. Ibid, p. 184.
19. Kern, p. 189.
20. Kern, p. 207.
21. Kern, p. 170.
22. Darwin C. The Descent of Man and Selection in Relation to Sex: Murray; 1888, p. 560.
23. Blackwell AB. Antoinette Brown Blackwell: Sex and Evolution (1875). In: Rossi A, ed. The Feminist Papers: from Adams to de Beauvoir. 1973 ed. New York: Columbia University Press; 1875: p. 356-77.

Chapter 15 John Wesley and Science

Few Methodists are aware of John Wesley's great interest in science. The scientific revolution of the 18th century created shockwaves. Its repercussions engaged Wesley.

> "The newly discovered facts, and the theories generated to explain them, aroused Wesley's curiosity. As a theologian, he had to meet the challenges…which the new science posed, and in his role as 'cultural middleman,' he felt obliged to keep the Methodist preachers and societies informed."[1]

Wesley taught logic and Greek at Oxford for six years. During his Oxford years, he set aside one day a week for the study of metaphysics and natural philosophy; the latter phrase includes what we call "science" today." Wesley has a strong sense of logic in his writings. He often relied on formal syllogisms in his writings and insisted on the importance of logic. "What is there, then," he asked, "in the whole compass of science, to be desired in comparison of it?"[1]

Wesley's major effort in practical science was to supply a book of medical remedies called *Primitive Physic*, first released in 1747. The need for this stemmed from the woeful lack of university trained physicians in England. Donat notes,

> "[the] three principal medical schools of United Kingdom in the 18th century, Oxford, Cambridge, and Edinburgh, all together, were graduating slightly more than two dozen physicians a year, plus a few more [were] arriving from Leiden and other Continental medical schools, to service a growing population of five to nine million people."[2]

The bulk of this expanding population in England was poor. The poor could not afford the care of a physician let alone find one. Noting the need among his Methodists, Wesley moved to fill this gap and considered medical advice to be part of his pastoral responsibility. He read widely among the medical works available to him from the 17th and 18th centuries and followed trends in the field. He did not perform surgery and passed on complicated cases to physicians. His goal was to recommend easily available and inexpensive treatments.

Wesley's emphasis was on preventative methods that encouraged fresh air, exercise, diet, and early rising. Further, his philosophy with respect to remedies is based on the principle that simple "receipts" heal as well as "compound medicines;" that local botanical substances are cheaper and as effective as exotic imports.[a] And, when possible, he identifies substances by their English vernacular names instead of the traditional medical Latin.

Wesley continually revised this latter work, with the 23rd edition appearing in 1791. These editions contain what Wesley thought to be the best available remedies. They were gathered from a variety of sources, many of which he himself tried. *Primitive Physic* was the most popular book of its kind in England and North America well into the 19th century.[3] It continues to be reprinted again and again in the 21st century.[b]

Like a majority of current medical therapies, most of the Wesleyan medical manual is neither proven nor disproven. The current author is a therapeutic skeptic. Proposed therapies need to be tested in randomized controlled trials to prove their worth. Wesley used the standard of the day to evaluate his regimens; namely, anecdotal case trial and error. In any case, the fact that Wesley lived to be 87 years-old, despite constant travel

---

[a] A simple receipt was a single item versus the multiple ingredients of a compound prescription.

[b] For example, see Amazon.com accessed 4-25-2016.

and pastoral activity, would seem to lend support to his ideas on health.

Wesley studiously avoided recommending bloodletting and use of quicksilver (i.e., mercury); these were common practices of contemporary physicians that often led to immediate mortality.

The nature and uses of electricity discussed in the 18th century caught Wesley's attention. In 1753, he read Benjamin Franklin's letters on electricity and printed excerpts in his journal: the notion that electricity is normally diffused in "nearly equal proportions through all substances," "that lightning is no other than electrical fire," and "that anything pointed, as a spire or tree, attracts the lightning just as a needle does the electrical fire." (the prior statements remain substantially true). Wesley came to feel that the subject was important enough to impress on his followers, and, in 1760, published his book on electricity: *The Desideratum: or Electricity made Plain and Useful.* This work went through at least five editions by 1781.[4] [c]

Wesley's major concern with electricity was over the practical applications to medicine. He was so convinced of its medicinal powers that he purchased an "electrical machine" for each of his four free medical clinics in London. (Figure 15.1).

---

[c]It is interesting that Benjamin Franklin published John Wesley's sermon, "On Free Grace," in 1741. It was never recorded that the two men met, but they were often in close proximity during many of Franklin's prolonged stays in London. They were obviously aware of each other.

How did this machine work? The rotating glass cylinder rubbed the leather pad and created static

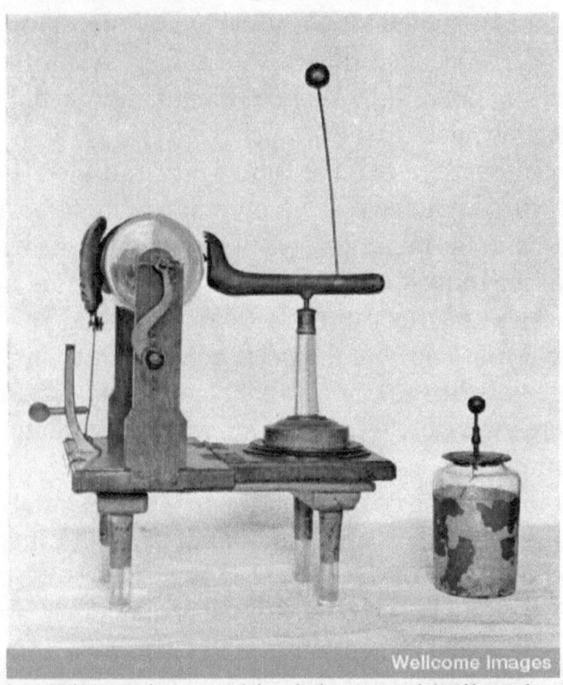

electricity. The patient grabbed the metal ball and received a small shock. Or, electricity could be stored in the Leyden jar to deliver a larger shock. These were momentary shocks; as electrical current, as we know it today, would not begin until Alessandro Volt created the first battery in 1800.

Figure 15.1 Electrical machine designed by John Wesley. A Leyden jar is at the right. Wesley had four machines, one of which is on display at his house in London. Used by permission. Wellcome.

Wesley listed 44 conditions in which he thought electrical stimulation might help. He also produced 45 case reports of patients helped with this treatment.[5] More than 3,000 patients were treated for free when many other clinics were charging substantial fees for the electrical treatment.

What can we conclude from Wesley's involvement with the science of his day? Wesley saw science in two ways. One, it helped to reveal the nature of God and was therefore a subject worthy of study. Two, scientific advances improved the service of humanity (and thus love) with better care of the sick.

Wesley insisted that the Bible was not a literal source of scientific knowledge: "No other ideas are to be affixt to the words of Scripture than such as occur to one who looks at the thing spoken of;"[4] that is, one should not create scientific theories from what are ethical or historical passages. On the other hand, Wesley insisted that true knowledge came by revelation, and that the Scriptures were the words of God revealed through divine inspiration.

Did these ideas of the founder of Methodism become integrated into later Wesleyan thought? Yes. A hundred years after John Wesley, Rev. Matthew Simpson (chapter ten), Bishop in the Methodist Episcopal Church, asserted that, "Science is nothing more than catching a glimpse of some of the thoughts of God."[6] As a younger man, Simpson had been a professor of Mathematics and Science at DePauw University, and was in a unique position to consider the overlap of topics.

Simpson was not troubled when geologists asserted that the world had existed for myriads of ages: "I am willing to admit all of| that." The "true spirit of Christianity welcomes all investigation." It is better for humanity "that inquiry should not be repressed." The result, he believed, would be that "Revelation and Nature would be found to be in harmony in the end."[7] Finally, the thinking processes of John Wesley helped free himself regarding his ideas about the status of women in society.

In his sermon, "The Imperfections of Human Knowledge" (1784), Wesley showed that science and reason are both needed to show God's sovereignty over the human world. The text, taken from 1 Corinthians 13:9, is "We know in part," is a reminder that humankind's knowledge is limited. Reason affirms God's sovereignty. Reason alone, however, cannot offer enough answers to satisfy the thinking man. In the discourse "The Case of Reason Impartially Considered" (1781) Wesley explained that reason has a significant purpose since it helps mankind understand the natural world created by God. But reason cannot give faith, love, virtue, happiness, or salvation; these things can only be given through the love of God and scriptural hope. Thus, reason falls short of replacing religion. Wesley steered a course between those who undervalued and those who overvalued reason; he thought reason and religion must exist in tandem. In both sermons, Wesley promoted scientific inquiry and rational thinking while simultaneously providing a place for scriptural revelation in history.[8]

The result of Wesley's thinking was to place reason at one of the four cornerstones of thinking about life and religion. Wesley was aware of the fallibility of his opinions and he found in dialogue a means to test his views, seeking those most adequate. When confronted with an apparent conflict between reason, experience, tradition and scripture, he did not simply debate which format was more authoritative; but engaged in the difficult, and often lengthy, reconsideration of his interpretations. He was frequently prodded by alternatives defended by others. This process continued until an equitable interpretation emerged.[9] Simply put, Wesley endeavored to advocate the best of science and the best of religion.

The current author believes that all the foregoing reasons form the best explanation for the progressive change in Wesley's thinking about women serving as ministers. Early in his career he was against lay ministers, whether men or women. He then moved to using laymen as ministers; finally, in the last three decades of his life, he approved using women as lay ministers. Thus, Wesley moved to achieve an understanding of women and the Bible that did justice to all.

References
Chapter 15

1. English J. John Wesley's Scientific Education. Methodist History 1991; 30; p. 42-51.
2. Donat J. Empirical Medicine in the 18th Century: The Rev. John Wesley's Search for Remedies that Work. Methodist History 2006; 44; p. 216-26.
3. Malony Jr HN. The Amazing John Wesley: An Unusual Look at an Uncommon Life: InterVarsity Press; 2012, p. location 3%.
4. Schofield R. John Wesley and Science in 18th Century England. Isis 1953; 44; p. 331-40.
5. Schwab L. "This Curious and Important Subject": John Wesley and *The Desideratum*. In: Madden D, ed. "Inward and Outward Health": John Wesley's Holistic Concept of Medical Science, the Environment, and Holy Living. London: Epworth; 2008, p. 169-212.
6. Clark R. The Life of Matthew Simpson. New York: Macmillan; 1956, p. 268.
7. Ibid. p. 300.
8. MacMillan K. John Wesley and the Enlighted Historians. Methodist History 2000;38; p. 121-32.
9. Maddox RL. John Wesley's Precedent for Theological Engagement with the Natural Sciences. Wesleyan Theological Journal 2009.

Chapter 16 Prelude to Colorado: B.F. Crary

The *History of Woman's Suffrage* gives the honor of a "true apostolic helper" to Rev Benjamin Franklin Crary. However, little more information is given about this Methodist minister.[1]

B.F. Crary (1821-1895) attended Belmont College during which he became fluent in Latin, Greek, French and German. After graduation, he passed the bar. A few years into a thriving law practice, he felt called to become a Methodist (AMEC) minister.

> "To his friends, it doubtless appeared like folly to leave the bar for the pulpit. A lawyer was then the popular idol, the dazzling center of the social circle; a Methodist preacher was little more than a homeless wanderer, laboring without compensation, [and] derided by men."[2]

Crary pastored from 1845 to 1857 in the Indiana Conference. He had a practical view of personal sanctification and holiness. If a man had this blessing from God, "What would he be like?" Crary asked.

> "He would begin at home and set his house in order. If he was a good, kind, liberal, loving, devoted husband and father, he would be better now in all these respects. His charity would have amazing expansion, and his neighbors would all see the mighty change. He would have an increase of all amiable and admirable qualities, and would be every way more lovable, agreeable, companionable, and liberal. He would be absolutely devoted to his wife and family and Church, next to God. He would give freely to every good and worthy cause and be more earnest for the success of every church enterprise. His quickened zeal

would be seen in the social meetings of the
church, and in the entire work of God's
people. He would make paradise of home, and
sunshine in every assembly… [he would
show] his abounding love, his deeper interest,
his increasing gifts and sacrifices, that he had
been with Christ. He would extend to his
pastor the warmest greetings and most earnest
support; would pray for him, and invite him to
his house, and welcome him, and gladly
attend his ministry."

Crary then goes on to cite Methodists such as Mary
Bosanquet (chapter three) who had exhibited the
characteristics of such a loving life.[3]

HAMLINE UNIVERSITY AND METHODIST HIGHER EDUCATION

Crary, who also had a doctorate in Divinity, was
elected in 1857 to become the second president of the first
co-educational college in Minnesota, Hamline University.
Upon Crary's arrival in 1857, Hamline organized as a
university.

While Oberlin has the honor of being the first co-
educational college in the United States, the regents of
Oberlin and supporters did not seek to build other
colleges. For the first few decades, women at Oberlin
could take some but not all the courses and degrees open
to men. In 1857, by contrast, there were more than a
dozen coeducational Methodist colleges and universities
in the United States. These Universities granted classical
and scientific degrees to both men and women in a unified
academic program.[4] Moreover, Methodism was
sponsoring the great majority of women in the United
States graduating from coeducational colleges and
universities.

"Nineteenth-century American Methodists underscored rationality and social functionality in learning, and this underpinned the raison d'etre for women's education, distinguishing it from women's fashionable ornamental education. [The latter studies were] designed to prepare late-eighteenth and early-nineteenth-century women for marriage. This type of education was, in the Methodist view, simply a waste of women's intellectual and spiritual powers, condemning her to a sinful life of disuse and rendering her incapable of understanding the dynamic complexities of God's world and the place of humans in it."[4] [a]

P. S. Donelson, also a Methodist writer, in 1857 noted in the *Ladies Repository*, "it is well to free beings with brains from the drudgery which belongs to brainless wheels."[4]

Women students at Methodist universities in the 19th century were expected to take the same courses as their male counterparts. That is, Philosophy, Languages, Chemistry, and Mathematics, for example. There was no separate curriculum for women.

Even so, Crary's leadership produced unique results among Methodist institutions of higher education. Hamline University had an extraordinary proportion of women faculty members and women students. During the early years of Hamline, 12 of 27 faculty were women. Women college teachers were uncommon at the time, and were usually hired as Preceptress (i.e., Dean of Women). Just as importantly, women professors taught both male and female students at Hamline.

---

[a] "Decorative" female education involved playing a musical instrument, drawing on paper, dancing, how to walk gracefully, wear corsets and false curls. These ideas are explored in the novels of Jane Austen written earlier in the 19th century.

It is impressive that in its first decades Hamline University granted about seven out of ten degrees (70%) to women students. While comparative numbers are hard to come by, the first set of statistics published by the United States Commissioner of Education in 1870 estimated that about one in five (20%) students in post-secondary education in the United States was a woman.[4]

The president of a small university would be closely involved in recruitment of faculty and students. Thus, Crary was both an ardent supporter of higher education for women, but also supported their role as University professors.

The strongest lifelong effect of Hamline University on B.F. Crary was undoubtedly his marriage in 1861 to Mary Sorin, a graduate of Hamline in 1860. They would remain together until his death 35 years later.[4]

During the Civil War, Hamline University greatly slowed down its activities as many students enlisted. On May 4, 1862, Crary was commissioned as an army chaplain of the Third Minnesota Volunteers. In July 1862, his Minnesota Regiment was captured by the Confederates. The order was given that the officers should be sent to Libby Prison in Richmond, Virginia. Wearing a surgeon's scarf and assisting in the care of the wounded of both sides, Chaplain Crary avoided being sent to the death camp in the south. The following year he lost a significant amount of hearing from the concussion of a cannon and for his disability was honorably discharged in July 1863.[5]

CRARY AS COLORADO DISTRICT SUPERINTENDENT

Crary was called to become the Presiding Elder of the Colorado Methodist Episcopal Conference in 1872 and ministered until 1880. His wife, Mary, would serve as the first lady of Methodism in Colorado. Crary also supervised the Methodist churches in the Territory of Wyoming from 1872-1876.

The life of a frontier presiding elder was not easy. Biographer F.D. Bovard wrote,

> "Crary came to Colorado in 1872 and reentered the pastoral work as a presiding elder. He was a stranger, but he walked right into the esteem and affections of his brethren. During the eight years of his service no more heroic pioneer work has been done in the history of the Church. He would drive forty or fifty miles to be at the reception of his preachers in hard and discouraging fields of labor. There seemed to be no limit to his endurance. Through storms and over swollen streams he went; across the sandy desert under a broiling sun he journeyed, facing withering winds hot as if from the mouth of a furnace; over parched and rainless plateaus he rode toward the distant mountains, up whose serpentine grades he toiled into the clouds. Dusty, hungry, and thirsty, he often found himself with his supper to prepare, his team to care for, and his bed to make alone under the stars."[2][b]

Crary would be what was called in the Old West a "man's man." No dilettante was he. He did not come to his position of unequivocal support for women's suffrage from weakness.[c]

---

[b]It should be noted that by 1872, most of the principal cities of the front range of Colorado (i.e., Ft Collins, Denver, Colorado Springs, and Crary's three charges in southern Wyoming) had regular train service. However, this description of travel for Crary with a horse team to distant smaller towns in Colorado would be relevant.
[c]Crary's numerous activities supporting the 1877 referendum for women's suffrage in Colorado are included in chapter 17 where all the issues for the referendum are grouped together.

He was elected by the Methodist General Conference to the prestigious position of editor of the California Christian Advocate in 1880. He was to remain editor for 14 years until his disabling stroke. In 1894, his wife, Mary Sorin Crary, took over the duties of the California Advocate, after the "earnest solicitation" of the Conference ministers.[6]

The most striking women's rights proposal of Crary comes from 1888. He proposed a gender-neutral rewriting of the Methodist *Discipline,* the rule book for the AMEC. His proposal to the 1888 General Conference of the AMEC is as follows,

> "Whereas, Women are already in numerous instances filling the offices of stewards, trustees, leaders of classes, etc.; and, Whereas, Presiding Elders have been compelled to decide that the words 'man' and 'men' in the Discipline were generic, and included woman as simply female man; and, Whereas, the work of God would be greatly hindered if they did not so decide and put women in these offices, some of our Churches in the West being composed chiefly of women; therefore,
>
> Resolved, 1. That the Committee on Revisals be and hereby are instructed to change all names and pronouns in the Discipline that seem to conflict with this understanding of its import in this behalf.
>
> Resolved, 2. That the administration of pastors and Presiding Elders who have been under the necessity of employing women's help in organizing and building up Churches is hereby approved."[7]

THE LEGACY OF B.F. CRARY

Two sisters were among the first graduates from Hamline University. Already mentioned was Mary Sorin Crary. Her sister, Emily Sorin Meredith obtained an undergraduate and graduate degree (A.B. 1859, A.M. 1863) and was married in 1860 to Frederick Meredith. Frederick was an early proprietor of the local *Red Wing Republican* newspaper. Both Emily and Frederick Meredith believed in the power of an educated citizenry. They would eventually settle in Denver in the 1870s where Frederick would become managing editor of the *Rocky Mountain News*; Emily was both the Literary Editor and a contributor on women's suffrage topics.[8,9] [d]

Emily would become a leader in the Colorado state WCTU; and with her daughter, Ellis, rose to prominence in the woman suffrage movement in Colorado. Ellis also worked for the *Rocky Mountain News*. Later, mother and daughter Meredith would co-author a chapter detailing events of the Colorado Suffrage movement for the *History of Woman Suffrage*. The first page of the latter chapter gives credit as: "The *History* is indebted for this chapter to Mrs. Emily R Meredith and her daughter, Ellis Meredith of Denver, both strong factors in securing suffrage for the women of their State."[10]

When Frederick Meredith died in 1911, the Colorado Equal Suffrage Association took out a three inches of newspaper column space in the Denver Republican noting his contributions.

"The Colorado Equal Suffrage Association has adopted resolutions on the death of Frederick A. Meredith. . .whereas the pen and voice of Mr. Meredith were always employed in the cause of freedom, justice and equality,

---

[d] the A.B. degree was like the modern Bachelor of Arts degree; the A.M. degree was similar to the modern Master of Arts degree.

the enfranchisement of the women of
Colorado having possessed in him a
champion of high ability and much devotion.
Therefore, be it resolved, that the Colorado
Equal Suffrage Association hereby expresses
its gratitude for the fine example afforded by
the career of Frederick A. Meredith. And its
sense of personal loss in the withdrawal of
that brave spirit from the activities of this
life…Resolved, that a copy of these
resolutions be sent to the family and
forwarded to the press of Denver and the
Woman's Journal, the organ of the National
American Women's Suffrage Association."
Signed Mary C Bradford, Helen Grenfell, Harriet
Wright[11]

The influence of B.F. Crary seems unmistakable in
helping to nurture the Meredith's position on suffrage.
His wife, Mrs. Mary Crary, sister of Emily, undoubtedly
represented a familial attraction for Frederick and Emily
Meredith's to re-locate in Denver. Together, over nearly
20 years, the five family members worked for the
enfranchisement of women in Colorado until it succeeded.

References
Chapter 16

1. Stanton EC, Anthony SB, Gage MJ, Harper IH. History of Woman Suffrage, Volume 3: 1886, p. 720.
2. Bovard FD. Benjamin Franklin Crary, D.D. The Methodist Review 1896, p. 171-90.
3. Crary B. Entire Sanctification. Asbury Theological Seminary eplace;1889, 2011.
4. Bloomberg KM. Nineteenth-century Methodists and Coeducation: the Case of Hamline University. 2008, pp. 50-6.
5. Ward WH. Records of Members of the Grand Army of the Republic: With a Complete Account of the Twentieth National Encampment ... A History of the Growth, Usefulness, and Important Events of The Grand Army of the Republic, from Its Origin to the Present Time: H. S. Crocker & Company; 1886, pp. 422-423.
6. Bloomberg, p. 61.
7. Methodist Episcopal Church General Conference. Journal of the General Conference of the Methodist Episcopal Church: G. Lane & C. B. Tippett; 1880, p. 182.
8. Bloomberg, p. 60.
9. Association Alumni. History of the Hamline University when located at Red Wing, MInnesota from 1854 to 1869. Saint Paul, MN: Alumni Association; 1907, pp. 71-72.
10. Stanton EC, Anthony SB, Gage MJ, Harper IH. History of Woman Suffrage, Volume 4: 1902, p. 509.
11. Colorado Equal Suffrage Association and Frederick A. Meredith. Denver Republican, March 9, 1911, p. 5.

Chapter 17 Suffrage in the American West

Efforts for suffrage took place exclusively in the American West prior to 1890. Seven Western legislatures tried to introduce suffrage for women by fiat or allowing men to vote. Only Wyoming Territory still stood for women's suffrage at the end of the 1880s; "still" since two successful efforts were reversed (Table 17.1). But at least Westerners were exercising democracy. By contrast, in the Eastern United States, women's suffrage rarely rose to a vote in the state assembly.[a] That is, legislative chairmen in the East would not allow a bill for women's suffrage out of committee. There were two exceptions. A Michigan referendum in 1874 lost by a 3:1 margin. In 1887, intense citizen pressure on a legislative committee in Rhode Island led to an assembly floor vote where it was beaten by a 3 to 1 margin (Table 17.1).[b]

KANSAS 1867

The first state referendum on enfranchisement of women and/or black males took place in Kansas in 1867.[c] The General Conference of the Wesleyan Methodist Church in the same year adopted a "Report on the State of the Country" which supported Kansas in its attempt to give the franchise to women.[1] Lucy Stone, Susan B.

---

[a] The definition of eastern and western United States is a later one of using the Mississippi River as the dividing line. In 1874, Michigan would have been considered a western state. Eastern historians and feminists have long been chagrined at the suppressed suffrage efforts in the East.
[b] The reader should note this remarkable fact. This helps to support the idea of widespread corruption by the "unseen enemy" written about by Carrie Chapman Catt in Chapter 22 and Appendix C.
[c] The 15th Federal Amendment giving the right to vote for black males was not enacted until 1870.

Anthony, and Elizabeth Cady Stanton traversed the Jayhawk state and spoke in favor of women's suffrage.

The Wesleyans and women's rights leadership were swimming upstream, however. Kansas was a Republican state and it was thought that the women's suffrage measure might pass. However, it was overwhelmed by a 21,000 to 9,000 margin. A further sting to suffragettes was that black male suffrage lost, but by a much closer margin of 2,000 votes.

WYOMING TERRITORY

Women's suffrage in the United States was first granted by the Wyoming Territorial Legislature on December 10, 1869. No records were kept of the legislative deliberations, so many unofficial stories abound. The motivation, by some accounts, seemed to be one more of a lonely-hearts club by the 20 men in the legislature: there was a 6:1 ratio of men to women in the territory. However, in 1871, the legislature had second thoughts about the radical idea and voted to repeal the law they had just passed. The governor vetoed the repeal effort, and the subsequent attempt at override with two-thirds vote needed by each chamber, fell one vote short.[2]

Nonetheless, the ploy to attract women worked. Women flocked to Wyoming as the total population more than doubled from 9,100 in 1869 to 20,789 in 1880; in the same period, the population of women rose from 1,899 to 6,637, improving the ratio of men to women at 2:1.[3]

When Wyoming achieved statehood in 1890, the provision for women's rights stuck, but this was only by legislative fiat. Popular referendums by men to give women the right to vote in other states had produced lopsided margins against the proposition.

Year	State	Type of Vote	Outcome
1867	Kansas	Popular Vote	No: 21,000 Yes: 9,000
1869	Wyoming Territory	Legislative Vote	Legislature reversed itself but did not override governor's veto.
1870	Utah Territory	Legislature	Reversed itself 1887
1874	Michigan	Popular Vote	No: 130,500 Yes: 40,000
1883	Washington Territory	Legislative	Supreme Court reversed statute 1887
1884	Oregon Territory	Popular Vote	No: 28,176, Yes: 11,223
1889	Washington Territory	Popular Vote	No: 35,917, Yes: 16,527
1886	US Senate	Congressional	Lost 2:1
1887	Rhode Island	Legislative	Lost 3:1
1890	South Dakota	Popular Vote	No: 45,972 Yes: 22,972

Figure 17.1 Outcomes of Women's Suffrage Bills or Referendums 1867-1892, United States.

COLORADO 1870

Wyoming forms two-thirds of Colorado's northern border. The territorial governor of Colorado, Edward McCook, requested that the territorial legislature follow Wyoming's lead in granting women's suffrage. The measure lost. George Hinsdale, president of the territorial council, maintained that giving women the right to vote would "destroy the symmetry of her character."[4]

Colorado men did not have the scarcity of women that Wyoming had. The census for Colorado in 1870 showed the number of men and women in the Territory was 24,820 and 15,044, respectively; a 5 to 3 ratio of men to women compared to Wyoming's 6 to 1.

Eastern suffragettes did not give up. Elizabeth Cady Stanton and Susan B Anthony toured Colorado in 1871 hoping to win converts. "Dane," an anonymous newspaper correspondent from Wisconsin, warned that "Colorado appears to be the vineyard wherein the female suffragists are laboring assiduously, probably expecting to reap the harvest of another territory victimized into committing itself to their cause." In Greeley, Dane heard Stanton engage "in the customary pathos when speaking of the galling serfdom of women and how they are tyrannized over by the monster, man"[4]

REFERENDUM OF 1877

"Not all men were monsters."[4] The Colorado state constitutional convention in January 1876 gave supporters of women's suffrage another opportunity. On January 10, supporters hastily formed the Colorado Equal Suffrage Association (CESA) for purposes of addressing the constitutional committee on January 12, 1877.

CESA placed two people on their executive committee of whom we wish to take note: B.F. Crary, the Presiding

Elder for Colorado Methodists (AMEC); and Mary F. Shields, age 48, from Colorado Springs.

Mary F. Shields was the "only [woman] resident speaker of the state known as a public speaker."[5] Mary was one of five mobilized by CESA to speak on behalf of women's suffrage on January 12, 1876. The actual wording for suffrage proposed by the CESA speakers was that "no distinction be made on account of sex."

A Denver newspaper summarized her speech: "Mrs. Shields said she represented a large class of women who were taxed and had no voice in the amount assessed, or the use made of their money. The women of Colorado Springs pay one-third of the taxes in that town. The Constitution will be much more popular in the southern part of the Territory if women are not shut out of its provisions."[6]

Shields ended her presentation with encouragement, "no assembly of men ever had so fine an opportunity to distinguish themselves."[7]

After the presentations were made, the committee asked no questions and remained quiet. Later, discussion within the committee led to the majority (three of five) report denying suffrage to women. There were concerns that the U.S. Congress might reject such a provision and thus the entire effort. Judge Bromwell, a well-known constitutional expert on the committee, disagreed but was unable to carry his point.

Two of the five committee men, Judge Bromwell and Agapeta Vigil presented the minority report. Vigil represented the counties of southern Colorado. Bromwell and Vigil argued in part that "in no class of business is such discrimination allowed… [Only in the] government of the commonwealth [do] we go on refusing the exercise of the plainest and most fundamental right to half the people."

Mr. Vigil was the first to urge the full convention to give the franchise to women. He spoke only Spanish and his talk was interpreted as he spoke. Mr. Vigil gave credit to Mary Shields for his conversion to women's suffrage. When asked by adversaries about his support, he replied he had been talking through his interpreter to the "nice old lady, who smiled so much" [meaning Mrs. Shields], and he knew what they asked was all right, and he should vote for it."[8]

Despite the loss, Bromwell and Vigil won two concessions. The 1876 Colorado State Constitution approved by the U.S. Congress contained two provisions relevant to women's suffrage. It empowered women immediately to vote in local school elections. Also, complete suffrage for women could be placed on a referendum ballot once the legislature passed the enabling measure by simple majority. Or, both houses of the legislature could pass women's suffrage by a two-thirds majority as a constitutional amendment.

The Colorado people and U.S. Congress approved the new constitution and Colorado became the 38th state on August 1, 1876. The legislature quickly passed the enabling statute. The first popular vote by Colorado men for women's suffrage was scheduled for mid-October 1877.

Mary Shields stormed the state. "The *Colorado Springs Gazette* notices that Mrs. M. F. Shields has been charged by the Colorado Woman Suffrage Association with the duty of visiting the various cities and towns in State, to awaken interest in the subject of woman suffrage and forming clubs in different localities. She will probably be ready to start on her mission in two weeks"[9]

She was a one woman show in the beginning. The *Woman's Journal* distinguished Shields as "prosecuting her work with marked success."

She was noted to be,

> "an ardent, unceasing, unselfish laborer in the
> church, in suffrage and temperance, for more
> than ten years. She did not lecture, but

'talked;' talked to five hundred men at a time
as if they were her own sons, and only needed
to be shown they were conniving at injustice,
in order to turn about and do the right thing.
This same element of 'motherliness' it was,
which gained her the respectful attention of an
audience of the roughest and most ignorant
Cornish miners up in Caribou, who would
listen to no other woman speaking upon the
subject."[8]

Shields' efforts did not go unnoticed. The minutes of
CESA note that when she stood to address the suffrage
rally at the Lawrence Street Methodist Church, "Mary
Shields received loud applause. She delivered her address
in a free and easy manner. Her remarks were good and
occasionally brought forth applause."[10] [d]

Catholic Influence on the 1877 referendum

In Colorado, the two largest religious groups in the late
19th century were the Catholics and Methodists (AMEC).
Their numbers were about the same.[11] [e]

The history of Catholicism in Colorado realistically
began when Joseph Machebeuf became Bishop of
Colorado in 1868. Born in France in 1812, he came to the
United States in 1839 to assume pastoral work in

---

[d] In the third volume of the History of Women's suffrage, there is
footnote describing Mary Shields, "Mrs. Shields is one of the most
lovable women to be seen in the suffrage panorama; a tower of
strength in her own family, where she is at once the comrade and
commander of her children—the help-meet of her husband. She
inspires immediate confidence whenever she confronts an audience."
(p. 717)

[e] Catholics usually report members of all ages, whereas Protestants
report only their adult members. In 1890, the numbers reported for
Catholics and Methodists (AMEC) in Colorado were 55,425 and
8,560. Depending upon what the size of the average large Catholic
family was, the adult members of the Methodists and Catholics in
Colorado can be estimated to be about equal. (Baker).

Cincinnati followed by work in Santa Fe, New Mexico. In Colorado, he accomplished much with meager finances and built many churches. He also helped to build a sense of belonging and culture to a wild frontier society in Denver. On the other hand, Machebeuf had little interest in reforming a society he was trying to stabilize.

Machebeuf vigorously opposed the 1877 referendum. Machebeuf toured his Colorado diocese and gave a series of sermons and lectures in which he cited his reasons for resisting the measure. On February 6, 1877, in a Catholic Church in Denver, he stated, in part,

> "The class of women wanting suffrage are battalions of old maids disappointed in love. [These are] women separated from their husbands or divorced by men from their sacred obligations-women who, though married, wish to hold the reins of the family government, for there never was a woman happy in her home who wished for female suffrage."[8]

Machebeuf also wrote several pamphlets against the issue.[f]

Catholics in Colorado in the 19th century were not a monolithic block.

> "Machebeuf tried to humor all the nationalities among his Colorado flock but did not hide his special fondness for the oldest and poorest group, the Mexican-Americans. He liked their custom of donating one day a week labor—or equivalent money—to the Church. He also admired their farming skill and the irrigation systems that they introduced to Colorado. 'The American, the German and the Irish Catholic are really good,' Machebeuf

---

[f] lest the current author is accused of being anti-Catholic, it should be noted that these statements by Machebeuf are also cited in a Catholic supported publication (see Noel).

once told another priest, 'but give me the childlike and incomparable faith of the good Mexican... the ardent faith that moves mountains."[12]

On the other hand, "My Irish Catholics," Machebeuf wrote to Archbishop John B. Purcell of Cincinnati on March 26, 1868 "have frequently manifested a strong dislike to my administration, caused first by my quick and passionate temper [and] by a scandalous Irish priest who I had to dismiss."[12]

Moreover, since they spoke English, Irish Catholics considered themselves "American." This contrasted with the many Mexican Catholics who still spoke Spanish, or the German Catholics who spoke German. It is of interest that European 19th century immigrants, such as the Germans, often self-classified themselves as "German" or "American" (not German-American) depending on whether they still used the old country's tongue or had learned to speak English, respectively.

Demographic facts are relevant. The Irish-Americans were almost exclusively located in the mountainous counties, where they worked the gold and silver lodes.[13] On the other hand, the Mexican-American Catholics were predominantly in southern Colorado. They formed a very large majority in the five south central counties of Costilla, Huerfano, Las Animas, Conejos and Pueblo. The German-American Catholics settled largely in the Denver area.

Finally, Irish-Catholics had a distinct cultural heritage towards suffrage for women. Daniel O'Connell, their Irish folk hero, was well known for his push for universal suffrage. This attitude was unique for Ireland during the 1830s and 1840s compared to other Catholic countries at the time.

These differences among Catholics help to explain variability in their support for women's suffrage in

Colorado. County tabulations of the suffrage vote in 1877 reveal these differences.

Wesleyan Influence on the 1877 Referendum

In contrast, the Methodists (AMEC) gave unwavering support of women's suffrage during the 1877 referendum.

The first major rally for pro-suffrage forces in Colorado for the referendum of Women's Suffrage, scheduled took place in the Lawrence Street Methodist Church on January 15, 1877. It would also be the first annual meeting of the Colorado Suffrage Association. This church, no longer standing, was a large facility which seated 475 people and included a balcony.[14] It seems certain that the pastor of the church, Rev. Eads, would have asked his Presiding Elder, Rev. Crary, for use of the building for the rally. The Presiding Elder of the Conference could have denied the venue. Instead, Crary encouraged the use of the largest Methodist building in Denver for the women's suffrage rally. However, not only did Eads, and Crary permit such use, they also spoke in favor of the issue at the rally.

January 15, 1877 arrived as a bitterly cold day in Denver. Organizers were worried about the turnout that evening. Nonetheless, the Lawrence Street Methodist Church was "packed to its utmost capacity." The pastor of the church, Rev. Eads, opened the meeting with a prayer. There were several speakers. The next morning there was a business meeting. That afternoon, Rev. B.F. Crary gave a speech,

> "I have not come hastily to the conviction that woman (sic) ought to be allowed to vote. My attention once called to the subject, two facts impressed my mind: one, the arguments in favor of woman suffrage were generally answered by sneers. Two, some of these

arguments I found it impossible to answer
satisfactorily.
Generally, whatever is sneered at has some
good in it. One cannot fail to remember that
the noblest men and best revelations ever
made to man were met by scoffs and made the
subject of ridicule. The arguments that
seemed to have some force, and that I had
never heard answered were many, among
which these seemed to me to be fair:
One, the ballot may properly represent all the
wealth of a State.
Taxation without representation has always
seemed to Americans unjust. Women own
and represent a large amount of property, yet
have no representation in our legislatures and
courts, no voice in the selection of public
officers who have control of questions of
property; A hundred tramps, paupers, and
vagabonds are gathered up from streets, lanes,
jails and police courts, and are led to the polls
and vote, while women, however worthy,
honorable or wealthy, are excluded from the
ballot because they are not males. The justice
of this we have never been able to see.
Nobody refuses to tax women. With what
possible excuse can we refuse them the
ballot?
Two, it has occurred to us that the ballot
should also represent the patriotism of the
State. If that be so, then the women are
entitled to vote, for our nation's history
proves the patriotism of the women of
America. They have born their full share of
all the burdens of the State, in peace and in
war, from the first great revolution to the last
great war...

We have heard some objections to this movement. It is said that it would break up domestic peace. We answer: There are only two classes of men that it could possibly affect. One is composed of tyrants who are not willing anybody should do anything contrary to their wishes. There are bullies who now lord it over their families and make slaves of their wives. If their wives could vote they would probably vote against their husbands, but this would not change things at home. Another class is made up of men addicted to vices which their wives hate and would vote against if they could. There is but little love or hope in such households now. Women voting would not increase the trouble but might help it.

Recently we have examined the subject of woman suffrage in Wyoming Territory, where, as all know, women vote.[g] We cannot see any evil effects predicted by the enemies of this movement. On the other hand, there seems to be in Wyoming as much domestic happiness as anywhere else, and we know many charming households where every refinement and blessing of Christian civilization is fully illustrated. The women of Wyoming vote as intelligently as men and generally vote right. For these and other reasons, we have concluded to vote for

---

[g] The AMEC churches of Wyoming Territory were part of the annual Colorado AMEC Conference for the first four years (i.e., 1872-1876) of B.F. Crary's leadership. As Presiding Elder visiting Methodist churches in Evanston, Green River and Rock Springs, Crary would have been one of the few people in the nation with extensive first-hand knowledge of the sparsely populated state. Thus, his comments deserve respect.

woman suffrage whenever the opportunity offers."[15] [h]

Crary was indefatigable in working for women's suffrage in Colorado. The *New Northwest* in Oregon, reported on July 20, 1877,

> "The suffragists of Colorado are vigilant, quick to perceive an opportunity, and ready to seize upon it. The Catholic Bishop Machebeuf of Colorado has recently delivered two lectures in Denver against Woman Suffrage, and these have called out a vigorous reply from Rev. Dr. Crary. The Colorado Woman Suffrage Association immediately had five thousand of this reply struck off on convenient size for gratuitous distribution. Among many people the Bible argument against Woman Suffrage is the most potent of all, as they deem it sacrilegious to attempt to disturb the status of woman as expounded to them by priests and ministers who interpret certain Scriptural texts to suit their own narrow ideas. When, however, these are fairly met by more enlightened ministers, and the absurdity of arguments shown up and refuted, hundreds whose conscientious scruples have caused them to array themselves with the opposition see that there are no Biblical reasons for assigning to woman a menial or subordinate position, and truly converted,

---

[h] It is interesting that after the introduction of the speech, where Crary used the pronoun "I," the speech shifts to the "we" pronoun throughout the remainder of the speech. The current author deduces that Crary was articulating "official" Methodist posture in his conference. As the highest-ranking Methodist clergy for more than 500 miles, and the fact that the rally was in the largest Methodist church in Denver, the frequent use of the pronoun "we" is full of intended and rich meaning. Having started his adult life as a lawyer, Crary used words very carefully.

make public profession of their belief in woman's political freedom.

The reply of Dr. Crary is an able review of and answer to the so-called Bible argument against equal rights. It's distribution throughout Colorado at this juncture will be most opportune. Thus, the labored effort of the Catholic Bishop will add strength to the cause of women's enfranchisement, instead of being an instrument of warfare against it. It is therefore quite apparent that His Grace the [Catholic] Bishop builded (sic) better than he knew when attempting to strengthen the old citadel of error."[15]

Unfortunately, a copy of the pamphlet by Dr. Rev. B.F. Crary printed by the Colorado Woman Suffrage Association has not yet been found. Crary is known to have replied in one setting to Bishop Machebeuf as follows, "Women should not usurp authority; therefore, men should usurp all authority.' This is the sort of [bad] logic we have always heard from men who are trotting along in the wake of progress and howling because the centuries do not stop rolling onward."[8]

In Golden, Colorado on Sept. 19, 1877, it was reported,

"At a woman's suffrage rally in this city last night the Baptist church was crowded to its utmost capacity, a large number being unable to find admittance. Rev. Dr. Crary presided and made the opening speech. Dr. Henry B. Blackwell [husband of Lucy Stone] followed with a strong and convincing speech, reviewing the political history of the country. and appealing to both parties for support. Woman suffrage tracts were distributed, and after joining in singing the doxology adjourned."[16]

On October 1, 1877, a "monster" meeting was held once again (earlier ones being Jan 15, 1877 and Sept 13, 1877) in the Lawrence Street Methodist Church. Among others, the audience was addressed by Lucy Stone and two Colorado women, Mrs. Campbell and Dr Avery. "The most intense interest was manifested, and the excellent speeches heartily applauded."[17] [i]

Religious opposition to the 1877 Referendum was not limited to Catholics. A Denver Presbyterian minister of the "old school" (chapter eight), Rev. Dr. T.E. Bliss, preached on Sunday, October 7, 1877, a sermon entitled, "Woman Suffrage and the Model Wife and Mother," in which he alluded to "certain brawling, ranting women, bristling for their rights," and said that,

> "God had intended woman to be a wife and
> mother, and the eternal fitness of things
> forbade her to be anything else. If women
> could vote, those who were wives now would
> live in endless bickering with their husbands
> over politics, and those who were not wives
> would not marry."[17]

On another occasion, Bliss declared in his pulpit that "the only two women in the Bible mentioned as having meddled in politics were Jezebel and Herodias." Bliss

---

[i] Not much is reported for this meeting other than the few facts listed. The meeting was notable for calling out the rebuke of the Rev Bliss on October 7, 1877 against the suffrage ideas presented at the Methodist Church (see later in main text). The word "monster" is a curious word choice here and refers to the political meetings held by the Irishman Daniel O'Connell held in the 1840s to induce the British Government to consider the independence of Ireland. These meetings had more than a 100,000 Irish in attendance. Obviously, since there were only about 30,000 people in Denver at the time, this usage cannot indicate such a crowd size. Thus, the use of the word 'monster" probably relates to the idea that it was an effort to convince a government to change policy. It seems to imply that the 475 seat Methodist church was filled to capacity.

made it point to persuade men heading towards the polling booth on election day not to vote for woman suffrage.[18] [j]

In summarizing the attitude towards women's suffrage by religious groups in Colorado in 1877, we see variable support among Catholic ethnic groups for suffrage. The Methodists were strong supporters as the Wesleyans enunciated unequivocal support. The third largest group, the Presbyterians did not seem excited to support the issue and at least one leader was against it.

Southern Colorado in 1877

The five south Central counties of Colorado: Costilla, Huerfano, Las Animas, Conejos and Pueblo, were chiefly populated by Mexican-Americans. No disrespect is intended in the term "Mexican" and 19th century inhabitants in southern Colorado would have proudly labeled themselves as Mexicans. Anglo-centric American histories often fail to note continuous Spanish settlements in the Santa Fe area from 1598 AD onwards. These settlements existed before the failed Jamestown settlement and long before continuous settlements in Massachusetts. Mexico gained its independence from Spain in 1821. After all, the Treaty of Guadalupe had only been signed in 1848. This treaty ended the Mexican-American war and provided for resolution of property issues.

Land Grants made by the Spanish, and subsequently by the Mexican government, were not easily resolved by American land courts. The Spanish-Mexican land grants

---

[j] this statement is simply not true as anyone with reasonable knowledge of the Bible would know. Deborah, as sole leader and judge of the nation of Israel, would be the best example to cite in disagreement. She was far more political than either of his cited women (Judges 4: 4-5). The mention of Herodias was an irrelevant and incoherent citation by Bliss since she was neither a Jew or Christian.

often had no written documentation and were based on widespread community oral tradition. Moreover, the boundaries were often notable topographic points such as hills, rivers, etc. The Americans, on the other hand, made maps divided into artificial grids without regard to landmarks. They desired fee simple transactions with notarized paperwork. It isn't difficult to understand why the two systems would clash and land ownership disputes would plague the region for more than a hundred years. The obvious effect was resentment on the part of Mexican-Americans, particularly in the 19th century.

In the year 1877, only 29 years had passed since the resolution of the Mexican-American war. Most adults in southern Colorado had originally been Mexicans. Americans had come and conquered them. At least to the first generation, the inhabitants of the five southern Colorado counties must have felt like they were living in a territory occupied by a foreign invader.

In addition, Everett notes in the summer of 1877 that southern Colorado was dissatisfied with the leadership in northern Colorado and Denver.[19] The Anglo miners in the surrounding San Juan Mountains were talking of joining with the five southern counties and forming a new territory. The leadership of the largest southern city, Pueblo, was envious of Denver and longed to be a capital of the state. Numerous meetings and newspaper articles expressed the desire of southern Colorado to secede and form a new territory called the San Juan Territory.

> "In the secession talk, Puebloans saw an opportunity to dominate a vast, wealthy new territory liberated from Denver… The *Chieftain*, Pueblo's most prominent newspaper, adopted the mantle of secession and became its most dedicated supporter. Fanning the flames for several months, the *Chieftain* touted political divorce and the

obviousness of Pueblo to serve as the seat of
San Juan's government."[19]

The secessionist rhetoric burned during the summer of
1877. The bombast began to fade in the fall. The two
reasons it would not become entrenched were the vivid
memory of what succession had plunged the nation into
during the recent civil war. People were still exhausted
from the trauma. Second, the Denver and Rio Grande
railroad brought rail service to the area in 1876 thereby
lessening the sense of isolation.[19]

Susan B Anthony toured southern Colorado in 1877
stumping for the women's suffrage referendum. She felt
the resentment and recorded the disinterest interest locals
had in the issue. It is difficult to know, in retrospect, how
much of this antipathy was due to women's suffrage or
the fact that she was a representative of the Anglo-
American conquerors.

On the other hand, the experience Mary Shields had
upon lecturing in the southern counties was much more
positive.

> "A correspondent of the *Denver Tribune*,
> writing from Trinidad under the date of
> [March 1877] the 10th, says Mrs. Mary F.
> Shields, of Colorado Springs, lectured on
> woman suffrage last evening in the Methodist
> church, which was crowded to suffocation.[k]
> Everyone appeared well pleased and went
> away with a flea in the ear. She has the
> sympathy of a majority of the women of this
> place, and I think when the time comes for
> voting on the question, Las Animas County

---

[k] This was a thriving and growing church in Southern Colorado. The
seating capacity was enlarged to 600 in 1891. The seating capacity is
unknown in 1877, but it was of some notable size to be "enlarged" 14
years later. (Methodist Episcopal Church. The Christian Advocate
1893; p. 90).

will be found all right. She speaks again this evening this evening in the courtroom."[20]

Another source notes that Shields lectured twice in Trinidad where "several influential Spanish-speaking citizens" persuaded Shields to delay departure to have her appeal interpreted for the Spanish-speaking audiences.[21]

1877 Referendum Results

In a letter written the evening of Election day, but before the results of the 1877 Referendum were known, Mrs. H.S. Mendenhall of Georgetown gave a lengthy description of what she encountered outside the election booth area. She had urged an affirmative ballot to men entering the polling area. The entire letter is worthy to review.

> "The Methodist men were for us; the Presbyterians and Episcopalians very fairly so, and the Roman Catholics were not all against us, some of the prominent members of that church working and voting for woman suffrage."[22] [1]

Statewide, the referendum measure failed; 6,612 in favor and 14,053 against.

The only county to vote favorably on the measure was Boulder County and it decisively did so by 1,011 to 804 margin. As detailed more in the next chapter, the cities of Boulder and especially Longmont in Boulder County, were bastions of support for temperance; an issue that went hand in hand with support for women's suffrage.

Denver, as a part of the largest county, Arapahoe, at the time voted 1,173 yes and 2,048 no. The five southern

---

[1] The hometown writer in Georgetown would have known which church the men belonged to. The secret ballot had not yet been instituted in America. Yes and no votes were color coded on paper. The poll observer could easily have noted the color of the ticket going into the large glass container.

counties in Colorado voted overwhelmingly against suffrage by an astounding 12:1 margin (3,707 to 314). The mining counties of Colorado: Boulder, Clear Creek, Park and Lake, were closer (1691 yes, 2310 no) than the state suggesting that Irish-American Catholic miners were voting yes.

Inevitably there were charges of voting fraud. Henry Blackwell noted,

> "Now when the political managers of both parties take pains to place in the hands of every voter, a ticket printed with the words "Woman Suffrage not approved," as was done to my knowledge in a number of counties in Colorado, nine voters out of ten do not stop even to read it."[23]

Mrs. Archibald, in testimony at the Congressional Hearings on Woman suffrage in 1884, charged,

> "In the county of Las Animas, where there is a large population of Mexicans…tickets must be printed for those people in Spanish. The gentleman in Trinidad, who had the charge of the printing of those tickets, being averse to us, had every ticket printed against woman suffrage. The samples sent to us from Denver were "for" or 'against,' but the tickets that were printed [for Trinidad] only had the word 'against' on them. Our friends had to scratch their tickets, and all those Mexican people who could not understand this trick and did not know the facts of the case voted against woman suffrage. [As a result], we lost a great many votes."[24] [m]

One editorial after the election carried the headline: "Good-bye to the Female Tramps of Boston." The author angrily told the Massachusetts "carpetbaggers" and

---

[m] Las Animas county voted 127 for, 995 against.

"political hacks" to depart… He also attacked the changes that the campaign brought in women's roles such as campaigning at the polls, speaking in public, and encouraging new thought on women's roles. Finally, he charged the women with having "prostituted the churches" with their lectures on Sunday evenings.[25]

The purpose of this chapter is to provide a basis of comparison with the referendum for women's suffrage of 1893 in Colorado. In retrospect, the 1877 campaign for suffrage was too little and too late. Apart from the Methodists, the small group forming the Colorado Equal Suffrage Association, and Boulder County, there were few bright spots to remark upon.

References

Chapter 17

1. Caldwell W. ed. Reformers and Revivalists: History of the Wesleyan Church. Indianapolis, Indiana: Wesley Press; 1992, p. 57
2. Right Choice, Wrong Reasons: Wyoming Women Win the Right to Vote 2015.
http://www.wyohistory.org/essays/right-choice-wrong-reasons-wyoming-women-win-right-vote)
(Accessed November 1, 2016).
3. Hoyt JW. Report of the Governor of Wyoming Territory, Made to the Secretary of the Interior, for the Year 1878: U.S. Government Printing Office; 1880.
4. Leonard, S. Bristling for Their Rights: Colorado's Women and the Mandate of 1893. Colorado Heritage 1993; Spring 1993; pp. 7-15.
5. Vaile AW, Meredith E. Woman's Contribution. In: Baker JH, Hafen LR, eds. History of Colorado, 3 vols. Denver: Linderman1927, p. 1105.
6. Minutes (handwritten). In: Colorado Equal Suffrage Association. 1876-1877. Availble from History Colorado Center, Denver.
7. Marilley SM. Woman Suffrage and the Origins of Liberal Feminism in the United States, 1820-1920: Harvard University Press; 1996, p. 90.
8. Stanton EC, Anthony SB, Gage MJ, Harper IH. History of Woman Suffrage, Volume 3, 1886, pp. 720-721.
9. Minutes, CESA, p. 50.
10. Minutes, CESA, p.44.
11. Baker JH, Hafen LR. History of Colorado. 5 vols. Denver: Linderman Co. Inc; 1927; vol 3, p. 1204.
12. Noel TJ. Colorado Catholicism and the Archdiocese of Denver, 1857-1989: University Press of Colorado; 1989, p. 37.
13. Wright JE. The Politics of Populism: Dissent in Colorado: Yale University Press; 1974, p. 157.

14. History of Methodism in Denver. In:
https://history.denverlibrary.org/sites/history/files/History
of_MethodisminDenver.pdf, ed. February 19, 2018; p 21.
15. Woman Suffrage: Address of Rev. Dr. B.F. Crary at
the Suffrage Convention. The Denver Daily Times;
January 29, 1877, p. 2.
16. Suffrage at Golden. Denver Daily Times September
19, 1877, p.1
17. Stanton, p. 723.
18. Stanton, p. 725.
19. Everett DR. Creating the American West: Boundaries
and Borderlands: University of Oklahoma Press; 2014,
pp. 183-185.
20. Mary Shields. Colorado Springs Gazette 1877
Colorado Springs Gazette, March 17, 1877 p. 1.
21. Marilley, p. 94.
22. Stanton, p. 724.
23. Blackwell H. The Lesson of Colorado. Woman's
Journal. womhist.alexanderstreet.com/
colosuff/doc7.htm1877:332.
24.   Woman Suffrage, Senate Hearings. Select
Committe on Woman Suffrage, US Senate, March 7,
1884. Washington, DC: Government Printing Office,
Document 1035, 1913; 1884, p. 40.
25.   Marilley, p. 98.

Chapter 18 Colorado- Winning in 1893

Colorado no longer had frontier status in 1893. Since 1877, its population had doubled to 413,000. Out-of-staters poured mostly into the northern counties of the state.

In sixteen years, leisure time expanded for the middle class. Interest in rifling and rowing had changed to bicycling and baseball. Women demonstrated their independence by riding bicycles. Fifty-three-year-old Frances Willard took up bicycling in 1893. She subsequently wrote a book, *A Wheel within a Wheel: How I Learned to Ride a Bicycle*, which became a bestseller. Pantaloons helped women ride bicycles more gracefully.

Charles Dana Gibson influenced women with drawings of an idealized American woman known as the "Gibson girl." The Gibson girl wore a high-necked, fitted blouse with full puff sleeves. A long skirt with a flared bottom and a tightly fitted waistline finished the figure. Gibson girls were "new women" pushing against the limits placed on them.

In 1877, the nation was in economic depression. Colorado bounced back in the 1880s. There was good rainfall for dry farming methods (i.e., non-irrigation) on the eastern plains. The area under cultivation in Colorado during the decade quadrupled from 200,000 acres to 800,000 acres. The Colorado mountains gave up huge amounts of silver.

In the 1880s, the silver market was thriving in the American West. The British overseas were minting silver coins. For reasons, usually unprovable in any slowdown, a national credit crunch started in 1890. Eastern bankers lobbied the U.S. government to stop the regular purchases of silver. Congress passed the Sherman Act in 1890 that halted required silver buying. President Grover Cleveland signed the anti-silver Sherman act over the strenuous objections of Western U.S. congressional delegations. The national political parties wanted to adhere to the gold standard alone. The Westerners derisively called these Eastern U.S. bankers and politicians "goldbugs." Silver mining slowed. Crop prices fell in Colorado.

Single issue suffrage groups disappeared from Colorado after the devastating defeat of the 1877 referendum in Colorado. The state chapter of the Women's Christian Temperance Union organized in 1880 in Longmont, Colorado. Members from six local chapters attended. Residual members from the disintegration of the single-issue suffrage groups in Colorado joined the WCTU. The WCTU was so strong for the franchise that contemporaries felt it precluded a need for other suffrage organizations.[a] Frances Willard remarked by letter on the strong beginning of the Colorado WCTU, "yours is the only state chapter that has not needed help from the national organization to get started."[1]

Mary Shields was elected the first state president. From 1880 until her death in 1887, Shields toured Colorado to speak on suffrage and other WCTU issues. As a tough pioneer woman Shields traveled 800 miles over desert plains and up mountain trails, by lumber wagon and horseback, to organize unions.[2] Shields also became an active member of the executive committee of the national WCTU.

WCTU women did not wish to wait for the vote in some uncertain future decade; they rolled up their sleeves to help women in the here and now. In Colorado, to mention only a few of many social projects, the WCTU agitated for a jail matron in 1888 in Denver. The matron examined and provided care for newly arrested women. The WCTU then paid the salary of the jail matron for several years. The Colorado Union supported daycare for working women; promoted literacy; trained women how

---

[a] WCTU was the only suffrage group in Colorado from 1877 until 1891.

to get a better job; ran a home for unwed pregnant women; and operated a homeless shelter and soup lines for unemployed women (and some men).[3]

This was the genius of Frances Willard and the national WCTU leadership. Local unions were not required to follow a set of directions determined by the national leadership. If the local WCTU women saw problems they wished to address, then their chapter's resources could be directed at those needs. Local Unions were not required to spend time on temperance issues; though most did.

A NAWSA member, Louise Tyler moved to Denver from Boston in 1890. In 1891, she revived the Colorado Equal Suffrage Association (CESA) and became its president; in 1892, she was elected to the state WCTU Superintendent of the Franchise Department. Tyler then added to her dual leadership the role of chair of the executive committee of CESA for the 1893 campaign. Louis Tyler's efforts represented remarkable cooperation of the two suffrage organizations.[1]

Further demonstrating the crossover, Lenora Lake, under the auspices of the WCTU in 1891, gave a lecture that appealed to women to also join the suffrage association. The WCTU members, Mrs. Emily Meredith and her daughter, Ellis, decided to also join CESA, the small band affiliated with NAWSA.[4]

SETTING THE STAGE-1892-THE WCTU NATIONAL CONVENTION

On October 28, 1892, the WCTU held their annual five-day national convention in Denver at the Trinity Methodist Episcopal Church. Trinity Church building had succeeded the 475 seat Lawrence Street Methodist Church. The auditorium and balconies of the newer Methodist Church seated 2,000 adults. The WCTU convention overflowed the church capacity.[b]

After the first day of the WCTU convention, Ellis Meredith noted in the Rocky Mountain News, "It is the grandest gathering of women ever assembled in the West and the grandest welcome, as the visitors themselves are fond of saying, ever accorded a [national] WCTU convention."[5]

The Republican Governor, John Routt offered a generous welcome to the Convention, indorsing with all heartiness the enfranchisement of women, of which he said he had been an advocate for twenty years.

Routt said: "You will never be able to accomplish this grand work you have undertaken until you are allowed the ballot; and if I had it in my power, I would give every one of you the ballot before I left my present position."

Miss Willard replied: "I don't think we ever had any speech we liked any better than that."

Governor Routt: "That is right. I am going to vote for you." (Laughter).

Miss Willard: "We have had a welcome from a Governor with a good big head on his shoulders, and who has the manliness to say he used to shove the jack plane. We are now going to be addressed by the pastor of this church, who-I am going to get ahead of him and tell you-used to handle the trowel."

Robert McIntyre: "These women have come from various parts of the Earth, come from many church circles and firesides; they have made their way by many paths to our door, and I stand here to bid them welcome…You do not know how we honor and respect you. Sometimes in the act of welcome, we say more than we mean, but this time we mean ten times more than we can say. And tonight, we offer you a mountain welcome, as generous as the hills, as pure as the snow on yonder mountain, as true as the love we have for you. We pray that no accident may come to you…and go home and remember this as a

---

[b] Compare the national NAWSA convention of 1896 in Washington, D.C. where there were perhaps 100 attendees (chapter ten).

place where goodwill followed you and where they heartily bade you "God-speed."

Miss Willard: "I think the mountain welcome beats all the others."[6]

Willard's Presidential speech at the convention stated in part,

> "Now in our cause the movement against the saloon was the Genesis, and the first formation of that W. C. T. U. was the Exodus. But we did not cross Jordan until we proclaimed the right of women to vote, and we shall not enter into the Promised Land to possess it until the full right of women to full citizenship is fully recognized in every State in our land and in the federal government…the right to vote in a democratic age is an acknowledgment by the States of the value of the individual…The voteless adult is nowhere, whose rights, whose individuality, whose common nature, even, are all held by sufferance, permitted rather than recognized, and as a consequence, minimized beyond endurance. But we all know that anything that minimizes the self-respect of any class is an offense and injury to that class. Women are never treated as if they were citizens except in bearing liabilities, paying taxes, and suffering the mischief which mismanagement brings upon the community. If we are ever to save the State, we must enfranchise the sex which at this moment has to bear the most painful burdens imposed by nature upon humanity, and which is much more acclimatized to self-sacrifice for others than the sex which at present monopolizes the franchise. What lies at the root of everything? Give us the vote, that we may be recognized as if we were

capable citizens. Give us the vote, in order
that we may help in purifying politics, which
at present can hardly be said to be so ideally
pure that you can afford to refuse a helping
hand. Give us the vote, in order that we may
use it, and in using it exercise ourselves in the
discharge of responsible duties, in the
administration of affairs which form so large
a part of the realms of most men."[7] [c]

Ellis Meredith as reporter, wrote –

"The Women's Christian association has
roused in them the instinct of self-
preservation, which sometimes seems last in a
woman. It has always been taken for granted
that women were all right, without any effort
to encourage or sustain them. The Women's
Christian association recognizes the
undoubted fact that women need the home
feeling even more than men in the desolation
of a great city. The Women's Christian
Temperance Union, the strongest association
of women in the world, is bound together by a
thousand kindred hopes and prayers. It has
outposts all over the world, its sentinels are
never off guard. Vice and crime slink by on
the other side muttering vain imprecations, as
little by little they are driven slowly back into
the confines that grow narrower every
day…Sooner or later, it is only a question of
time, womanly fingers will pick up the
'weapon that comes down as still as
snowflakes fall upon the sod' in defense of
themselves, their homes and children."[8]

---

[c] The metaphor from Exodus, the "voteless adult," and thrice
repetition "give us the vote," makes for great rhetoric. The crowd was
unlikely to stay quiet.

The closing ceremony for the WCTU convention took place only five days before the national and state election day of November 8, 1892.

THE POPULIST PARTY

The economic slowdown, status of silver, and depressed markets for farm goods led to the rise of a third political party in Colorado, the Populists. It was to be the Populist's year. The national and state Populists voiced a strong pro-silver sentiment that reflected the attitude of most Coloradoans. However, for political survival, the Democratic and Republican Colorado state parties also adopted statements in 1892 that were pro-silver; the latter positions of the old parties in Colorado differed sharply from their respective national anti-silver platforms.

Willard, a platform leader at the 1892 national Populist party convention in Omaha, introduced a woman suffrage plank that she had been promised would pass. Despite assurances from several key leaders of support, other delegates mobilized to defeat the measure. Delegates were in part afraid of southern voter displeasure.[d]

During the Colorado gubernatorial campaign of 1892, Aspen lawyer and Populist candidate Davis Waite alternately called the suffrage issue "excellent" or

---

[d] Frances Willard made a grand movement to lead a fusion of the Prohibition Party and the People's Party. The Prohibition party's main issue was of course alcohol. However, it was the only political party in U.S. history to unequivocally support women's suffrage during its entire 50-year existence. The Prohibition party had garnered 250,000 votes in the 1888 presidential election. Willard was interested in fusion of the two reform parties. In the spring of 1892, she called a summit of key leaders from both parties to St. Louis, She was even willing to compromise on temperance. The group agreed to suffrage, and a watered-down plank that would advocate the suppression of saloons, but not alcohol itself. The compromise broke down at both party conventions in the summer of 1892. (Earhart M. Party Politics. Frances Willard From Prayers to Politics. University of Chicago Press; 1944, p. 227-44).

"unnecessary". He wrote that the Populist party stood for "equal rights for all and special privileges to none."[9] Some suffragists were hopeful and others skeptical about his candidacy.

The well-liked and strong supporter of women's suffrage, John Routt stepped down as Republican governor. His nominee replacement lost badly by 6,000 votes to the Populist Waite. Colorado also returned a plurality of votes for the Populist presidential candidate, James Weaver. Weaver garnered the electoral votes of Kansas, Idaho and Nevada.

After his election, Governor Waite confirmed his less-than-wholehearted support and confusion about suffrage for women: "About eight years ago [i.e., 1885] a law was passed giving the women of Colorado the right to vote at school district elections.[e] On that basis, Waite was willing to recommend "a law extending to the women of Colorado the right of suffrage at all municipal elections."[9] He seemed to think the next step of voting in city elections reasonable.

Colorado suffragists took strong exception to this incremental approach. The following spring of 1893 saw five bills introduced into the legislature for women's suffrage. Louise Tyler carefully monitored the progress of every bill. House Bill 118 went forward as "that every female person be entitled to vote at all elections, in the same manner in all respects as male persons." The bill specified that a referendum be held during the November election day of November 7, 1893. When the bill underwent discussion in the House, a "large delegation of ladies" from the WCTU, plus a few members of the recently revived CESA, were present to signify their support.[9]

---

[e] the right to vote in school district elections had been enshrined in the 1876 Colorado Constitution, not in an 1885 law.

The Colorado Senate passed the bill on April 3, 1893. Governor Waite signed the bill for a suffrage referendum four days later.

HELP FROM CHICAGO?

The scene shifted temporarily to Chicago. The Colorado Equal Suffrage Association, desperate for assistance, sent their vice-president, Ellis Meredith, to the Chicago World's Fair looking for help from national NAWSA leaders.[f] The Chicago World's Fair opened May 1, 1893, and represented the largest world's fair in history. Among 200 new buildings, the fair contained a major building representing the achievements of women. Chicago would be the site for the World Congress of Representative Women convention which started May 15, 1893.

The World's Fair could not have started with any gloomier news than with the crash of the New York Stock Exchange on May 3, 1893. The news worsened daily as more stocks collapsed.

The national suffrage leadership at the Fair had many duties during the Women's Congress. For example, Susan B Anthony, Lucy Stone were on a Conference committee entitled "Civil Law and Government" chaired by Carrie Lane Catt. Presumably, they were known for their understanding of civic affairs. The three women and others appointed an ad hoc committee to listen to appeals

---

[f] At the spring meeting of the Colorado Equal Suffrage Association (CESA), Ellis Meredith moved that the name be changed to the Non-Partisan Equal Suffrage Association of Colorado; the name change was accepted. Some historians have stayed with the CESA acronym. To prevent confusion, we will use only the designation "CESA." CESA was a small organization in the spring of 1893. Exact membership numbers could not be found, but the author estimates fewer than 100 members; this would include men. Even in September, the Denver branch only numbered 100. (4th vol Woman Suffrage p 515).

for help in different state suffrage campaigns. Seventy-five-year-old Lucy Stone was ill and would die from cancer five months later. Susan Anthony was 73 years old and appeared like an old warrior.

Catt was 34 years-old and raised in Iowa, graduated from what is now Iowa State University; moved to San Francisco where her first husband died suddenly; and then back to Iowa before coming to the Chicago World's Fair. Self-described as having a "foghorn" voice, her pictures, young and old, all seem to show eyes deep in thought with eye strain and/or fatigue present. If one deduced that Catt was tired, however, as a first impression, they would soon find out otherwise; she exhibited boundless energy. While she and her husband, Leo Chapman, would be married by a Methodist minister, she was never a member of any church.[10]

Women from New York were there to ask for aid for a petition drive and possible constitutional convention in New York. Likewise, women from Kansas were there to ask assistance in the more distant, but real event, the 1894 Kansas Constitutional Amendment Campaign. Eastern women disdained the Colorado effort. Similarly, the ad hoc committee thought the embryonic New York effort and the Kansas movement were much more likely to yield an advancement in suffrage compared to the hopeless effort in Colorado.

Lucy Stone asked Ellis Meredith, "Why was your campaign precipitated when our hands are so full?"

Susan Anthony, referring to the heavy vote against suffrage in 1877 southern Colorado, followed with, "Are all those Mexicans dead?"[11]

"No," said Mrs. Meredith, "the Mexicans are all there yet;" but she explained that women now voted in the labor unions; the ruling political party was favorable; and that the WCTU was organized throughout the state and was a firm friend and advocate of the franchise for women.

The most difficult issue by Ellis Meredith to get across to the committee was their mistaken idea was that the upcoming vote in Colorado was a referendum and not a constitutional amendment. The difference being that a referendum requires only a simple majority to pass; a constitutional amendment needs a two-thirds majority for passage. The vote in Kansas was to be for a constitutional amendment. New York had yet to budge in any manner out of legislative committee. When the ad hoc committee finally appreciated this difference, their opinion became more open minded in discussing the possibilities for Colorado.

In any case, the ad hoc national leadership either could not or would not send any resources to help the suffrage cause in Colorado. Later, the group decided to send Carrie Chapman Catt on the condition that the national group would make up for any expenses that Catt could not raise with her speeches in Colorado; an unlikely need as Catt had a track record of bringing in more than her expenses.[g]

The ad hoc committee misread the favorable situation that was developing in Colorado. The committee continued to have illusions about possibilities for suffrage in New York State. New York State would not adopt women's suffrage until 21 years later in 1914. In the committee's defense, the national economic news was terrible. To NAWSA, an organization never flush with money, the idea of new fundraising for Colorado must have seemed quixotic.

The lack of lecturing help from the East, in a period when Westerners blamed Easterners for their regional economic problems, may have been a blessing in disguise. As in the 1877 loss, suffrage might have been linked with

---

[g] This was the extent of what can only be considered a feeble response by the NAWSA leadership. "Feeble" is the correct adjective here since four national members went to Colorado in 1877 to crisscross the state to speak to a state with half the population it would have 16 years later.

Eastern "carpetbaggers." Catt, with her foghorn voice, may have passed for a local resident.[h]

THE COLORADO DEPRESSION

The bottom fell out for the Colorado economy when Great Britain stopped minting silver coins in June 1893. Within four days the price of silver bullion dropped from 80 cents to 62 cents an ounce. Prior to this action in India, marginal silver mines had shut down in Colorado, but now even the most productive mines ceased operations. In the Leadville district, every mine was closed. The huge smelters for processing the silver at Aspen, Pueblo and Leadville banked their fires.[12]

To add insult to injury, the rainfall in 1893 in Colorado was significantly lower than in previous years. Farmers struggled. Without silver or grain, railroad receipts plummeted; most Colorado railroads were in receivership by the end of the year.

Economic hard times worsened during July 1893. For three days, beginning on July 17, there were runs on all banks in Denver by panicked depositors. Twelve banks, or half of the Mile High's city banks were forced to close. One observer reported a "continuous mass of humanity stretched down all of the streets near Denver's banks."[13] The depression of 1893 was becoming far worse than the previous record 1873 Depression. Bank closures nationwide quintupled the number in 1873; the national total of 503 banks that closed would not be matched again until the U.S. depression of the 1930s.

The closure of banks further exacerbated the credit crunch. Money drying up popped the real estate "bubble" in Denver, an overpriced market from speculation on properties.

---

[h] Also, with Catt growing up in Iowa and living in California, she could not be construed an Easterner.

Reliable unemployment statistics are not available from the Federal government in the 19th century, but state officials in Colorado attempted to assess the damage. Leadville had 4,300 adult males in 1890. A report indicated 2,500 were unemployed in July 1893; of whom, 1,500 had left town. In Aspen, 2,000 males out of 2,200 lost their jobs in July.

Even in Denver, with a more diversified economy, 14,000 men lost their jobs out of an estimated 43,000 adult men.[12] Many took advantage of the offer by idle railroads to leave Denver for six dollars. The population of Denver dropped from 116,000 in 1890 to 90,000 in 1895.

THE WCTU IN 1893

The Colorado WCTU sponsored their president, Eva Higgins of La Veta, Colorado, to embark on a five-month speaking tour prior to the November election to support suffrage.[14][i]

By early autumn 1893, women were quick to draw the connection between silver and suffrage in the public eye. The state WCTU, for example, passed a resolution at its September convention stating,

> "The Silver and the Suffrage questions are
> vitally connected. A vote for equal suffrage is
> a vote for free silver. The man who goes to
> the polls on the seventh day of next

---

[i] The only other information the author could find on Eva Higgins is that she wrote to express her regrets to the National WCTU meeting in Denver in 1892 that she was recovering from an illness and could not attend. It is striking to note that La Veta is in Huerfano County, Colorado, one of the five stronghold counties against suffrage in 1877. The state WCTU likely had several choices for this duty; the selection of a local woman might help the county become "converted" for suffrage; in doing so, the selection may have represented significant strategical thinking about the upcoming campaign by the WCTU.

November and votes to exclude the ballots of
half the citizens of Colorado from the ballot
box, on account of sex, is a traitor to the white
metal and to the best interests of the state."[9]

As a symbol of solidarity advocating the vote for
women, Colorado WCTU members traded their white
ribbons that symbolized purity for yellow ribbons that
symbolized support for suffrage in Colorado.[9] Yellow
ribbons were first worn by Kansas women in their failed
1867 suffrage campaign. The color was taken from the
Kansas state flower, the wild sunflower. The Yellow
ribbons generally had artwork or printing on them, in
contrast to the plain white ribbons usually worn by
WCTU women.

Showing crossover between the Colorado WCTU and
CESA, the three-page franchise report of the September
Colorado State WCTU Convention in September 1893
reflects the activities of many of the local Unions. A
sampling is summarized below.

Denver Highlands Union (west Denver) sponsored a
yellow ribbon contest [artwork]. Suffrage articles were
published in the local paper and one public meeting was
held for the vote.

Colorado Springs branch formed an "Equal Suffrage
League."

Boulder members distributed 80 copies of the
Woman's Column and 26 copies of the *Woman's Journal*.[j]

Canon City formed an Equal Suffrage Association.

Sterling's "Madame Willard" Union was sponsoring
franchise articles in the weekly paper.

---

[j] These were publications of NAWSA. The former being a four-page
weekly summary on current suffrage news designed to be sent to 100-
200 national newspapers that agreed to receive it. It was also
designed as a self-contained handout. The Woman's Journal was a
larger 12-14-page weekly newspaper containing many topics of
interest to women

Denver Central Union secured space for franchise articles in the *South Denver Eye.*

Fort Collins Union first secured subscribers for the *Woman's Column.* This union was the most active. The last third of their report stated, "Public meetings are held in the churches in the interest of the amendment, addressed by our own citizens, with papers by our women. These are requested for publication in our weeklies. A school-house campaign [i.e., for adults] was arranged to last until the 7th of November. Nearly a score of our public speakers, including ministers, judges, attorneys, businessmen, and college students have cheerfully accepted our invitations to address these schoolhouse audiences. We have secured a franchise committee of two persons, usually a man and a woman, in nearly all the different organizations, including five church societies; the young people's societies, the Y.M.C.A and Y.W.C.A. of the College, of the faculty and students, the literary societies, and the two women's clubs, besides the W.C.T.U, the W.R.C., the G.A.R.[k] and sons of Veterans. The work is to distribute suffrage literature among the members, to interest and invite them to join the franchise association.

An important resolution at the September state convention was, "From now until election day, [all] our forces be turned towards equal suffrage."[15]

RELIGIOUS INFLUENCES ON THE 1893 ELECTION

Catholic Bishop Joseph Machebeuf died in 1889. The number two man during much of Machebeuf's leadership, Rev. Nicholas Matz (1850-1917), was also born in France. Matz became the second Bishop Sof Colorado, which changed its name to the Archdiocese of Denver.

---

[k] The Woman's Relief Corps was an auxiliary to the Grand Army of the Republic (the name of the northern civil war army)

Matz was an "authoritative" Catholic bishop. He "sternly promulgated the Council of Baltimore's decree that parents, under pain of mortal sin, must send their children to Catholic schools if they were available. Furthermore, parents could be deprived of the sacraments for such a sin"[16]

Matz had a low view of Protestant clergy. He was reported in a Denver newspaper to have said, "not one Protestant minister in one hundred believes in the Divinity of our Lord and Savior Jesus Christ." At the time, Matz's most loyal Catholic layman and huge financial giver was J.K. Mullen. In a letter to Matz, Mullen expressed his dismay over Matz's statement and wrote that many of his best friends were among the Protestant clergy; Mullen concluded by asking Matz to retract his statement. Matz wrote back to Mullen and politely refused.[17]

Matz continued to struggle with his Irish-American priests like his predecessor.

Finally, Matz was known to be anti-trade union, especially the Western Federation of Miners; this was distinctly an anti-populist stance in Colorado at the time.

The wonder about the outspoken Bishop Matz is that the current author could not find his stance on the woman suffrage referendum of 1893. Because of his attitude on other issues, we can infer his private viewpoint; but what is important is that he withheld his opinion, whatever it was, from the public concerning his attitude towards suffrage.

Years in the making, the monumental Catholic Encyclopedia was published in 1907. The article states "the Catholic Church has made no doctrinal pronouncement on the question of women's rights in the present meaning of the term." Nonetheless, most, but not all, American prelates were thought to hold a negative view of women's suffrage. The article candidly points out that American Bishops were choosing to keep their views private on woman suffrage rather than making public statements. This may have been what Matz choose to do.[18] One can also speculate that the Catholic flock had changed their views since 1877 on women's suffrage. Thus, the Bishops had decided the issue was not germane to be a good Catholic and left it up to individual conscience.

On the other hand, at least one Catholic priest in Denver argued publicly for passage of the woman suffrage referendum. Reverend O'Ryan, of St Leo's Church, an Irish parish, argued that women during apostolic times occupied the "highest positions in the ministrations of the church." In an extensive review of history, Pastor O'Ryan continued,

> "The church has always given a woman a place in its management…In all ages our church has acknowledged the right of our women to hold and dispose of property at will. The jurisdiction given woman by the church went away beyond domestic limits; it extended to the widest expanses of temporal affairs, and their advice was always coveted in spiritual matters."[19]

Also, in contrast to the earlier 1877 referendum, one cannot find any outspoken opposition from the Presbyterian community. Moreover, a Presbyterian minister from Loveland published a favorable opinion for suffrage.[1]

Thus, the religious influence on the 1893 ballot issue was much more favorable. While the Methodist's support remained strongly positive, the two other largest religious bodies in Colorado moved from a negative position to at least a neutral stance. Thus, the Catholics and old school Presbyterians became more susceptible of being "converted" by pro-suffragist logic.

RESULT OF THE ELECTION

On election day, November 7, 1893, the final vote was 35,698 for and 29,461 against. Frances Willard heard the news while convalescing from pernicious anemia at her friend's estate in England. She wrote and underlined in her journal, "<u>News to stir the blood</u> – Colorado enfranchised its women – four thousand majority!" (Diary, November 10, 1893).[1]

After defeat in nine other state contests, the suffragists and the good men who supported them rejoiced. The *Denver Republican* newspaper may have summed up the victory best,

> "We thank the men of Colorado who showed
> the world yesterday that they were neither
> afraid nor ashamed to give their women equal
> rights with themselves…This was the first
> time in history [in which] the class in power
> enfranchised a class not in power without
> being forced to do it."[20]

References
Chapter 18

---

[1] This majority difference was perhaps an early return. She would eventually succumb in 1898, at age 58, to pernicious anemia; a disease first cured with eating liver in 1926, and now with vitamin B12.

1. Marilley SM. An Exceptional Victory: The Colorado Campaign of 1893. Woman Suffrage and the Origins of Liberal Feminism in the United States, 1820-1920: Harvard University Press; 1996, pp. 124-58.
2. WCTU. History of the Colorado WCTU letters. Box 1. WCTU Archives, Norlin Library, Boulder, Colorado1880-1893: Box 1.
3. Stefanco C. Pathways to Power: Women and Voluntary Associations in Denver, Colorado, 1876-1893. Doctoral Thesis. Duke University: 1987, pp. 118-126.
4. Stanton EC, Anthony SB, Gage MJ, Harper IH. History of Woman Suffrage, Volume 3, 1886, p. 517.
5. Meredith E. To Protect Homes: Women of the White Ribbon Army Meet at Trinity [Methodist] Church Rocky Mountain News; 1892, p. 2.
6. Union WCTU. Minutes of the National Woman's Christian Temperance Union at the... Annual Meeting in ... with Addresses, Reports, and Constitutions. Chicago: WCTU; 1892, pp. 25-26.
7. Ibid, pp. 113-114.
8. Meredith E. Women's World: What Does it Mean? : Rocky Mountain News; 1892, p. 18.
9. Stefanco C. Harvest of Discontent. Colorado Heritage 1993, pp. 16-21.
10. Van Voris J. Carrie Chapman Catt: a Public Life: Feminist Press at CUNY; 1996, p. 10.
11. Stanton EC, Anthony SB, Gage MJ, Harper IH, Association NAWS. History of Woman Suffrage, Volume 4, 1902, pp. 513-513.
12. Wright JE. The Politics of Populism: Dissent in Colorado: Yale University Press; 1974, pp. 166-167.
13. Wicker E. Banking Panics of the Gilded Age: Cambridge University Press; 2006, pp. 53, 70.
14. Beeton B. Women Vote in the West: The Woman Suffrage Movement, 1869-1896. New York: Garland Publishing; 1986, p. 113.

15. WCTU. Fourteenth Annnual Convention of the
Woman's Christian Temperance Union of Colorado.
1893; WCTU Archives, Norlin Library, Boulder,
Colorado, p. 48.
16. Noel TJ. Colorado Catholicism and the Archdiocese
of Denver, 1857-1989: University Press of Colorado;
1989, p. 64.
17. Ibid, p. 68.
18. Herbermann CG. The Catholic Encyclopedia; an
International Work of Reference on the Constitution,
Doctrine, Discipline, and History of the Catholic Church;
Edited by Charles G. Herbermann.: New York, Robert
Appleton Company; 1907, volume 4, p. 696.
19. Denver Republican, Nov. 6, 1893.
20. Leonard S. Bristling for Their Rights: Colorado's
Women and the Mandate of 1893. Colorado Heritage
1993; Spring 1993, p. 15.

Chapter 19 Why Victory in 1893 Colorado?

Wesleyans were a positive factor in the success. No prior study has analyzed this influence.

Arapahoe County, which included Denver, returned the largest difference in the absolute number of affirmative votes (n=913); however, as a percentage, it was a close call at 53%. The Wesleyans and WCTU had the greatest number of members in Denver, but then Denver contained ¼ of the state population.

The next four counties with the greatest difference in vote totals contained a large Wesleyan membership (Table 19.1).[1,2] Moreover, 89% of Colorado WCTU membership was in these five northern counties.[3] As it had in 1877, Boulder County, a bastion of temperance and suffrage support, once again nodded yes. Weld County was even more favorable. Considering the numerous and intense pre-election support activities by the local Weld County WCTU mentioned in chapter 18, this outcome is no surprise.

One can speculate as to the vote margin that Wesleyans contributed. We can take the 1892 vote of the national AMEC churches concerning the franchise status of women at the Church General Assembly as a surrogate index. The latter vote represents an incredible cross section of a cultural group unparalleled in 19th century US history. The vote was 235,668 in favor and 163,843 against (chapter 11); this can be used to estimate one factor.

If we take half of the Colorado Wesleyan membership to be men and postulate them to vote at the same percentage as the national AMEC group (60% versus 40%), then the result would have been 4,159 to 2773; providing a yes vote margin of 1,386 among Wesleyan men.

The correlation factor of the number of Methodists and the number of county votes for women's suffrage is 0.16

(Table 19.2). This is a mild to moderate correlation, suggesting an association. Analytical statistics often fail to reveal the whole story. With visual inspection thru tabulation (Table 19.1), one appreciates a stronger association in the five counties that delivered the largest positive vote difference for suffrage.

In any case, these data mean that the Wesleyans did not win the suffrage ballot alone. Nonetheless, the data provide numerical support for this subgroup in Colorado known to be extremely supportive of suffrage for women.

Counties	Yes Vote	No Vote	Margin Yes Votes	Per Cent Yes*	Wesleyan Members[+]	WCTU Members
Arapahoe	8816	7901	915	53% (13)	5404 (1)	651
Weld	1385	612	773	69% (2)	503 (5)	49
Boulder	1629	918	711	64% (5)	811 (4)	381
El Paso	2000	1313	687	60% (9)	1065 (2)	25
Larimer	1136	556	580	67% (3)	425 (6)	98
Total 5 counties	14966	11300	3666**		8208[++]	1204
Total State	35788	29451	6337		13863	1350

*Rank order of 21 counties with more than 1,000 vote totals in parentheses (Total of 53 Colorado Counties, 1893)

** % of total state yes votes were 58% in these 5 counties alone.

89% of total state WCTU members in these 5 counties

+ Wesleyan-type membership adds the totals of the Methodist Episcopal Church (1893), Methodist Episcopal South (1890) African Methodist Episcopal (1890), 1890 Free Methodists (1890), and United Brethren Church (1890).[2]

Rank order is the number of Wesleyan-type members of all 53 Colorado counties.

++ % of total state Wesleyans 59% in these 5 counties

Interpretation: correlation values can range from -1.0 to +1.0 (-1.0 means factors are completely independent; that is, when one factor increases the other factor decreases) A value of zero shows the factors have no relatedness. (+1.0 means the two factors increase exactly in the same amount at all times). Correlation values do not "prove" causation. They can help to interpret the possible quantitative association.

Table 19.1 Top Five Counties in Colorado by Absolute Vote Totals, WCTU members, and Wesleyan Congregants.

Factor	Correlation 1893 County Suffrage vote and factor	
Populist	0.6	Strong correlation
Republican	0.46	Strong correlation
Democrat	0.04	No correlation
Methodist membership	0.16	Mild-moderate correlation
Catholic membership	-0.24	Mild-moderate negative correlation
Methodology: for political parties, the vote totals in each county were averaged between the 1892 and 1894 elections for governor (two-year terms at the time); then the mean was correlated with the 1893 suffrage vote. For religious bodies, the membership in each county (1890 Catholic and 1893 Methodist) were used Thanks to Chris Aston, Ph.D., statistician.		

Table 19.2 Correlation Values in 1893 Colorado Suffrage Referendum.

IMPROVEMENT IN NEGATIVE VOTE AREAS

Using the 1877 suffrage vote for comparison, we can see significant shifts in the opposition. Improvement in the support of the five southern counties for suffrage proved helpful. The five counties had voted 12 to 1 against the measure in 1877. In 1893, it was only 3 to 1. What does this mean? If we postulate that the five southern counties had again voted in a 12 to 1 ratio, the 1893 suffrage referendum would have barely passed by 899 votes, instead of a margin of 6,237. The latter margin was important to establish legitimacy.

What changed in southern Colorado? These counties were predominantly Mexican-American Catholics, and this group was no longer being urged by their hierarchy to vote no. As the two largest religious denominations in Colorado at the time, the Catholics kept an eye on the Methodists; they were likely influenced by the predominant Methodist culture, but this cannot be measured. Or, perhaps the Irish Catholic miners influenced their southern cousins.

The demographic shift from first generation Mexicans to the second or third generation Mexican-Americans healed memories of the Mexican War. The vanquished no longer felt so.

Resolution of some land grant issues helped. For example, the City of Trinidad, the most populous city in the five-county south, had been engaged in a long-term struggle with the American land courts since the inception of statehood. At issue was whether the land the city stood on belonged to the municipality or to an individual American claimant. The court decided the issue in 1892 in favor of the City of Trinidad; this ruling likely improved attitudes towards the capitol in Denver.[4]

CARRIE CHAPMAN CATT'S ANALYSIS

Carrie Chapman Catt gave a lecture in Boston on December 23, 1893 listing her reasons why Colorado was the first state to vote in women's suffrage by male plebiscite.[5] As she was intimately involved with the campaign, her stated reasons deserve review. Her major points summarized were,

1. Colorado bordered Wyoming which had legislatively passed women's suffrage.
2. Labor unions supported women's rights.
3. The Farmer's Alliances and the Grange supported equal rights
4. Populist Party endorsed suffrage as did many of the Republicans and Democratic county committees did.
5. The newly instituted secret ballot
6. Men were allowed on every organizing committee. Eastern women usually did not allow men on local committees.

7. The liquor industry, "As the influences against us, we had, first, the brewers and saloon-keepers. Although there was no effort made on the part of the workers for woman suffrage to attack them, and although there never has been any very extensive temperance movement in Colorado, yet the liquor interest seemed to feel instinctively that the women were their enemies, and they organized against us, sending their people out over the State, raising money, printing circulars, and putting up placards in their saloons, urging their customers to vote against equal suffrage."

8. Christian "orthodoxy" was against suffrage, but this caused "unorthodox" Christianity to speak for suffrage. The only example cited was the Young Men's Christian Association (YMCA); the YMCA was "our third enemy, and one that did a great deal of work against us."

9. Newspapers were on our side.

10. German-Americans were against us.

11. The depression of the economy was implied in many of the issues, though she did not cite this influence directly.

Catt's points are listed in the order of her speech and do not seem to be in order of importance. Our focus here is on religious factors and the influence of the WCTU. Catt's reference to "orthodox" and "unorthodox" Christianity being opposed and in favor of suffrage, respectively, is incomprehensible. Methodists, the cultural pacesetter of American society in the 1890s, were strongly in favor of women's suffrage. Catholic leaders either abstained or came out in favor as did the Presbyterians. These three branches of Christianity were by far the most numerous in Colorado at the time. If they do not represent "orthodox" Christianity, the current author cannot determine who would otherwise win this nod. Likewise, the label "unorthodox" Christianity refers to a not yet understood grouping of Catt's.

Given that the YMCA was a charitable non-denominational organization dependent on donations, it is unimaginable that the YMCA would take an official position against suffrage. Individual Methodists likely represented a large segment of donors.

> G.M. Varnum replied to the *Woman's Journal*, "The Young Men's Association of Denver was not and is not an "enemy" of woman suffrage… [the YMCA] is absolutely non-partisan on this and all other political questions…The Association did not do 'a great deal of work against' woman suffrage, nor any work for woman suffrage. I am President of the Debating Club organized under the auspices of the YMCA of this city. Pursuant to a custom of five or six year's standing, we gave a public debate on the woman suffrage question, to which we invited the suffrage leagues of the city, together with the public, giving the ladies the privilege of the floor to advocate their principles. A debate must have two sides – hence speakers were assigned to oppose woman suffrage…It was simply a debate…After the speeches, eight ladies gave expression to their views. Upon a vote of the merits of the debate, suffrage won by a large majority – most of the men present voting for the reform."

Varnum felt that the debate, which had attracted wide attention, had "indirectly assisted the cause [of suffrage]."[6]

A gaffe that Catt would likely regret was "there has never been any extensive temperance movement in Colorado."

Ella Beecher Gittings, corresponding secretary of the Colorado WCTU, published a reply in the *Woman's Journal*. Gittings reminded readers that CESA had existed for only two years, whereas the state WCTU had been organized more than 13 years. Local unions began in 1875. Since its inception, the WCTU's franchise department stoutly advocated suffrage.

"Not a convention has been held, not a speaker appeared before the public, without urging the claims of women upon the ballot. Petitions have been circulated, literature has been distributed, mass meetings have been held – in short, for nearly two decades the "white ribbon" women of Colorado have been earnestly and untiringly hammering at the adamantine wall of prejudice which barred women from her rightful place in political affairs. 'White-ribbon' women did the pioneer work in 1875, which resulted in the constitutional clause which made it possible for equal suffrage to carry in 1893 by a simple majority vote. The recent campaign the whole energy of the seventy local unions of Colorado was focused upon the equal suffrage movement… and a weight of personal influence brought to bear which no one can estimate…we have no desire to be hypercritical, but we think it scarcely fair that the equal suffrage leagues who, with fresh steeds and burnished trappings, rode gallantly 'in at the death,' should seek to wrest all the honors from the toiling 'beaters of the bush.' But, beyond and above all this, we are unwilling that the blot of 'never any extensive temperance movement' should rest upon Colorado's fair name."[7]

Julia A. Sabine, a former superintendent of the franchise department in Colorado's WCTU, also wrote to the *Woman's Journal*. She had organized a woman suffrage league in Colorado Springs in 1885 and its members were "composed almost wholly of WCTU women." The group eventually decided that "work could be better done in connection" with the temperance organization "and the separate organization was dropped."

Moreover, voting mattered to Colorado temperance women, "The work of electing women to the place of School Directors, and of arousing the women of Colorado to vote at school elections, was begun by the WCTU, and was one of their most treasured projects."

She also observed that Mary Jewett Telford, editor of the *Challenge*, a Colorado temperance journal made it, from the first issue, a "suffrage paper." Sabine continued,

> "I never attended a convention of the WCTU [in Colorado] where woman suffrage was not endorsed, and plans made for its success. At one convention, two thousand copies of the *Woman's Journal* were given away. Money was appropriated by the State, by the county, and by the local unions to purchase literature, mostly *Woman's Journal* leaflets, for distribution. How much of the final triumph is due to this quiet educational work, carried on so long in face of discouragements, matters not, but it is rather hard to be accused of 'coming forward now with the assurance that we have worked a long time for the cause' so satirically, in a paper which we recommended to all the unions and tried our best to circulate, for years before the fight was on."[8]

Catt replied in a letter to the *Woman's Journal* that "no slight was intended by her to the WCTU." Current readers can judge for themselves.[9]

Catt, while she worked hard for the accomplishment, may have perhaps overstated her labors in Colorado as the reason for victory. She was fond of saying after the Colorado victory, that she felt like a frog that fell into a milk pail, then struggled until it had churned "a fine pot of butter" and climbed out.[10]

Given her criteria for victory in Colorado, we can speculate that Catt looked forward to adding another state to the suffrage column with the vote in Kansas coming 11 months later. Most of the conditions thought favorable by Catt in Colorado would be nearly identical in Kansas. Kansas is a state contiguous to Colorado and very close to Wyoming. The People's Party was more popular in Kansas than it was in Colorado. The depression was worse in 1894 than it was in 1893.

In contrast, the WCTU was not likely to campaign as hard in Kansas for suffrage as there had been a statewide prohibition amendment in place since 1881; but, since Catt seemed to have not understood the degree of long-term and peri-election effort the Colorado WCTU had given in the Centennial State, this discordant factor in Kansas might not have concerned her.

Yet come November 6, 1894, women's suffrage was crushed with 130,000 no votes to 95,000 yes ballots. Catt deserves credit for her effort in campaigning in 1894 in Kansas. However, she must have been greatly disappointed in the decisive loss. Her hypothetical criteria for the win in Colorado crashed. She climbed out of her milk pail with sour milk this time.

Three months after the stinging defeat in the Jayhawk state, Catt spoke to the national convention of NAWSA.

> "Catt blasted the convention delegates with a pithy summary of the movement's shortcomings. Although suffragists had been agitating for forty years, they had not turned the sentiment generated into success. Calling for sweeping tactical changes, she put before

> the convention a three-pronged plan: a special
> committee to raise money for state
> amendment campaigns; a new standing
> committee of organization to coordinate
> national, state, and local suffrage work; and a
> cadre of specially trained organizers to direct
> state campaigns."[11]

Another problem was the monothematic focus on voting. In earlier years, NAWSA writers boasted that their organization was the only women's organization "focused" on suffrage. This ignored the fact that local NAWSA affiliates would often become non-functional or even disband when long periods of inactivity occurred between suffrage events. In contrast, the "do everything" approach to help women here and now by the WCTU appeared to be wiser. The new organization being called for by Catt was sounding more like the WCTU in structure and effort. While not doing everything, NAWSA would push membership drives and raising money much more aggressively, and not allow local groups to wither from lack of activity.

In conclusion, the contrasting outcomes between Colorado and Kansas elections within a year helps to decrease the confidence that geographic proximity to a suffrage state, the Populist party, and the severe economic depression were the principal factors enabling suffrage to win in Colorado. The contrast of a much less active WCTU in the Kansas campaign serves to increase certainty that the WCTU was a real factor in the win for Colorado. The close cooperation of the state WCTU and CESA should have been a lesson for NAWSA in future campaigns, but this reality was not grasped at the time by the only national NAWSA leader on the scene, Carrie Chapman Catt.

The same can be said for the influence of Methodists. The per capita rate of members of the AMEC in 1894 Kansas was lower than in 1893 Colorado. Colorado had

10,792 Methodist Episcopal members in 1893 for a per capita rate in the general population of 2.6%.[1] Kansas had 25,798 AMEC members in 1894 for a per capita rate of 1.8%.[12]

The tiny population of Idaho (total 88,000) would pass women's suffrage in 1896 by a margin of 12,126 to 6,282. Women's suffrage then hit a wall. From 1896 to 1910, there would be no further advancement of suffrage at the state or federal level. One historian labeled this period as the "doldrums."[13] The 1893 achievement of men voting for women suffrage in Colorado was thus a remarkable victory. Wesleyans were part of the winning team.

References
Chapter 19

1. Minutes of the Annual Conference of Colorado. Minutes of the Annual Conferences of the Methodist Episcopal Church 1893; Fall 1893.
2. Carroll HK, United S. Report on Statistics of Churches in the United States at the Eleventh Census: 1890. Washington, D.C.: Government Printing Office; 1894.
3. WCTU. Fourteenth Annnual Convention of the Woman's Christian Temperance Union of Colorado. 1893, p. 48. (Colorado WCTU Archives, Norlin Library, Boulder, Colorado).
4. Van Ness JR, Van Ness CM. Spanish & Mexican Land Grants in New Mexico and Colorado: Sunflower University Press; 1980.
5. The Boston Tea Party. Woman's Journal 1893; 24; pp. 401-8.
6. Varnum GM. Denver Young Men's Christian Association. Woman's Journal 1894, p. 20.

7. Gittings EB. The Temperance Movement in Colorado. Woman's Journal 1894, p. 20.
8. Sabine J. Honor Due the Colorado W.C.T.U. Woman's Journal 1894, p. 40.
9. Editorial Reply. Honor Due the Colorado W.C.T.U. Woman's Journal 1894, p. 40.
10. Van Voris J. Carrie Chapman Catt: a Public Life: Feminist Press at CUNY; 1996, p. 37.
11. Graham SH. Woman Suffrage and the New Democracy. New Haven: Yale Univeresity Press; 1996, p. 7.
12. Methodist Episcopal C. Official Record and Minutes of the Annual Conference Session, Kansas Conference, Methodist Episcopal Church. Topeka, Kan.: F.M. Steves; 1894.
13. Graham, p. 33.

Chapter 20 The Church of the Nazarene

It is 33 AD. Day of Pentecost. Jerusalem. Disciples of Jesus, men and women, are praying for the blessing of God. The Holy Spirit comes and consecrates all those praying. The full participation of women on this first day of Christianity is clear.

In the 19th century, Wesleyan Holiness groups believed that they were following more closely the reforms of John Wesley than the mainline Methodist churches. John Wesley emphasized a return to what he called "primitive Christianity" or what we term "early Christianity" (first and second centuries AD).

Wesleyans encouraged public testimony after a person had received the blessing of the Holy Spirit. This admonition applied equally to women. Urged to testify in front of mixed audiences of their experience of grace, it was but a short step to the pulpit for women to preach. The 19th century saw many women in the Wesleyan Holiness movement become full-time ministers.

CHURCH OF THE NAZARENE AND MARY LEE CAGLE

The Church of the Nazarene is the largest denomination in the Wesleyan Holiness group. Its formation occurred at Pilot Point Texas in 1908 from three independent Wesleyan Holiness groups. It has the distinction of being the only denomination in the world that has started with explicitly written full ordination and ministerial rights for women.

Mary Lee Cagle (1864-1955) was one of the first woman pastors in the Church of the Nazarene. Her life typifies many of the Wesleyan Holiness women preachers in the late 19th and early 20th century. In a north Alabama revival, Mary Lee Cagle's committed herself to Christ. At 15, she joined her brother Frank at a Methodist mourner's bench. The experience of divine grace, so deep and powerful, created an evangelist's heart in her. Over the next year, Mary worked to bring her classmates to faith in Christ.

But in the hierarchical South, women were not to "step out of their place." Mary's desire to become a minister mortified her mother. Bowing to social pressure, Mary muted her testimony, and conformed by becoming a schoolteacher. Over the years, her conscience was uneasy about not following her call. The anxiety plagued her spiritual life.[1]

> "Mary was in her late 20s when a liberating path opened up. Robert Lee Harris (1861-1894), a Holiness revivalist, held meetings in Alabama. She heard his message, sought the experience of holiness, and found a deeper experience of grace. The next year, 1891, when Harris returned to the area, they married…She became her husband's constant companion and accompanied him everywhere. Contact with Nashville, Memphis, and other southern cities added new dimensions to her worldly understanding. She learned Robert Lee Harris' message and methods, absorbing the idioms and accent of Holiness revivalism."[1]

R. L. Harris left the Methodist Episcopal Church, South, in 1894 to organize a Wesleyan Holiness church with a congregational form of government in Milan, Tennessee. He then began to suffer from bouts of pulmonary tuberculosis. Mary watched his painful breathing and gasping for air that would strike for days at a time. When the bouts subsided, her 33-year-old husband was left with extreme physical weakness.

Mary's heart broke as she watched her husband of three years slipping away. She prayed for God to heal him and had persuaded herself that He would do it. However,

Robert told her all along that his work was done, and God was not going to heal him. In desperation, she earnestly prayed,

"Lord, if you will heal my husband, I will preach." But imagine her surprise when God seemed to speak back to her in thunderous tones, 'Whether I heal your husband or not, will you do what I want you to do?' And then came the bloodiest battle of all her life—it raged hot and long. She never said, 'I won't,' but 'I can't.' But after she had struggled long on her face before God on the floor, she looked up through her tears and said, 'Yes, Lord, whether my husband lives or dies, I will obey Thee.' It was said once and for all time. Of course, the glory fell, and she sprang to her feet, went bounding down the steps two steps at a leap, into her husband's room shouting, and threw her arms around him and said, 'Oh, husband, I am going to preach.' He looked up calmly and said, 'I have known that for some time.' He had prayed through on it before she did. She often says that all she is under God, she owes to that man's prayers, unwavering devotion and almost reckless faith in God. It has been an inspiration to her all through life. From that day of victory in the upper room she never wavered again about her call to preach, or her determination to do it."[2]

Robert L. Harris died shortly thereafter.

An extraordinary church planter, Mary Cagle organized several congregations in Tennessee, Alabama and Arkansas. By 1896, Mary had also planted congregations in west Texas. The Southern Holiness connection began to take structure. The first general meeting was held in Milan, Tennessee in 1899.

A Baptist preacher in Abilene, Texas described her ministry to audiences that were an estimated 800 to 1,000 people at a time,

> "Mrs. Harris knows how to preach. There is an absence of the usual excitement prevailing at most of the tent or camp meetings, but for deep feeling and willingness to respond to the invitation extended, it equals the best protracted meetings I ever attended in Abilene."[1]

In 1900, she moved her home to Buffalo Gap, near Abilene. She had other interests there too. That summer, she married Henry Cagle in front of hundreds gathered at the Buffalo Gap camp meeting. He was a rough-and-tumble cowboy converted, sanctified, and called to preach through her ministry.

Their work was not easy, as prejudice against women preachers ran high. Rumors circulated in Anson, Texas, that Mary had robbed the United States Mail, abandoned her four children, and once operated a bordello. These accusations only served to increase her audience size. Mary reported that it would be impossible to give away her children since she was childless! A preacher continued to perpetuate the house-of-ill-fame rumor until a Methodist official confronted him with the possibility of a libel suit. Folk culture labeled women who spoke publicly as unfit mothers or prostitutes.[3,4]

As congregations affiliated with the New Testament Church of Christ increased, so did the need for clergy to tend them. On December 12, 1899, the first congregational meeting of the Milan New Testament Church of Christ became a denominational business meeting. Mary Lee Cagle was ordained at this meeting.

> "In 1902, Mary Lee Cagle convened the first annual meeting of the Texas Council of the New Testament Church of Christ. Twelve churches were represented. From that point,

the Texas Council was differentiated from the
Eastern Council, composed of churches in
Tennessee and Arkansas. Cagle travelled
between the two councils to maintain some
focus of unity. An associate took her measure
in 1904, writing: 'She is here and there and
everywhere in the interest of missions and the
church generally.' A third of the New
Testament Church of Christ's ministers were
women, often called to preach under Mary
Cagle's ministry."[1]

Eventually several connections of congregational type
churches merged to form the Holiness Church of Christ.
Mary Lee Cagle was the leader of this large southern
contingent of congregations that would meet in 1908 at
Pilot Point Texas.

PHINEAS BRESEE

The second major leader of a group to merge at Pilot
Point, Phineas Bresee (1838-1915), was from Los
Angeles. Originally a Methodist Episcopal minister in
Iowa, Bresee moved to Southern California in 1883.
Pastoring an AMEC Methodist Church in Pasadena,
Bresee saw the membership increase from 130 to 700. For
the new building a huge, simple tabernacle was raised.
Bresee would incorporate this as a Nazarene model.
Churches were to be built without pretense in locations
that were accessible to all social classes.

He left the Methodist church in 1884 to work in a non-
denominational project for the poor and needy called the
Penial Mission. He had accepted the doctrine of holiness
and began promoting it. In addition, Bresee was invited to
start a new church where he could minister to the poor.
On October 15, 1895, the Church of the Nazarene
organized in Los Angeles. A founding tenet was the

ordination of women for the ministry and full rights for women.

Phineas Bresee was well-acquainted with the Wesleyan Holiness tradition of full involvement of women in the ministry. During one of his last Methodist pastorates, he brought Amanda Berry Smith, a black evangelist, to preach in his Los Angeles church in 1890.[5] After Los Angeles First Church of the Nazarene was organized, Bresee opened his pulpit to guest preachers on Sunday nights, and in this capacity, his list of guest preachers included women. He entrusted Phoebe Epperson with the primary preaching responsibility of Los Angeles First Church of the Nazarene during a period when he was travelling in other states.

Eventually, the two church connections, the southern holiness congregational contingent and the Church of the Nazarene, came to Pilot Point, Texas in October 1908 to form a single church.[a]

The merged national body would be called the "Church of the Nazarene." Bresee had chosen the name to designate his earlier group because it described the common people for whom Jesus lived and died.

During the convocation, Bresee spoke that the ministry of women, like men, was grounded in apostolic (i.e., early church) privilege. Asserting that the Church of the Nazarene had an apostolic ministry, he argued that women's right to preach and pursue ordination was safeguarded so long as apostolicity was the hallmark of the church's ministry.

Elsie Wallace (1868-1946) was the first woman minister to be ordained by Phineas Bresee in 1902 during

---

[a] The Church of the Nazarene had merged in 1907 with a New England Wesleyan-Holiness group called the Pentecostal Churches of America (at that time, the term "Pentecostal" did not refer to speaking in unknown tongues. In Acts chapter two the speakers are understood by everyone in the cosmopolitan audience. Nazarenes maintain it was a miracle of hearing not one of unknown utterances.

a visit to Spokane, Washington. Elsie and her husband, DeLance, led the John 3:16 Mission in "a block almost literally filled with saloons and places of wickedness."[6] The mission was to become the Spokane Church of the Nazarene. Elsie was also to become the first District Superintendent in the Church of the Nazarene in 1920.[b]

Women would become so essential in the early years that one entire conference of the Church of the Nazarene (Western Tennessee) consisted for a time of only women ministers. In the early decades of the church about 1 in 5 (20%) of the clergy were women.[7]

JOHNNIE HILL JERNIGAN

Johnnie Hill Jernigan (1862 to 1940) typifies another woman ordained in 1902 in one of the churches under Mary Lee Cagle's Leadership. Saved as a young woman in the Methodist Episcopal Church, her desire to share the Good News was immediate. Johnnie felt called to be a minister but did not see how that was possible in her church. Placed on the back burner in her life, the call receded.

One day she met her future husband, Charles B Jernigan, who became the "idol of my heart." She found herself "married to a man who, like Jonah, was running from a call to preach. Both shared the delusion that he would soon attend a medical college."[8]

She began to consider the future and see herself as a doctor's wife.

> "Then, I said, I'll get rich and drive a span of
> high-stepping bays to a carriage, and help
> husband at the sick-bed, and look after the
> poor, and that will settle this call to the
> ministry. I will then be happy. But, alas, God
> swept one prospect after another away, and no
> money was ever accumulated with which

---

[b] This position would be like a presiding elder in the AMEC.

husband could complete his education. One afternoon in August 1895, as I was sweeping the yard, husband came in with his face all aglow from his work. He had a brand-new experience that he called entire sanctification. His face shone with the love of God, till I knew that something out of the ordinary had happened to him."
He said, 'Wife, I promised God that I would preach, and I am now ready to go at it.'
She told herself, There it is; all my prospect of being a fashionable doctor's wife is gone, and I will be troubled with that call to be a woman preacher again. I turned away with a heavy heart, and for two weeks I fasted and prayed and struggled with that awful pride in my heart, until I was too weak to walk. Then, I yielded to God and said, here am I: send me, and in an instant the Holy Ghost came and sanctified me wholly."[8]

Soon the Jernigans conducted revivals as an evangelistic team. C. B. Jernigan encouraged his wife to develop her own preaching abilities, and both were ordained to the ministry by Seth C. Rees in 1902.

"Since then, I have wanted to tell the lost world of Jesus my Savior. I wanted to go to the low and the outcast, to those that no one else cared for, and tell them of a Savior that died for them. I wanted to tell the harlot of the Magdalene who washed the feel of Jesus with her tears of penitence, and in return he washed her and made her every whit whole and commissioned her to preach the first sermon of the resurrection."[8]

Her mission to "poor outcast girls" led her to the brothels, saloons, and street corners of Dallas, Ft. Worth, Waco, Little Rock, and other cities of the Southwest.

Johnnie witnessed and offered prostitutes a way out through the rescue homes she helped to staff. Drunks and saloon owners did not intimidate Johnnie. An angry brothel manager fired her revolver at Jernigan, angry that Jernigan was convincing "girls" to leave "the business."[9]

A story published in 1904 by a woman told how the Jernigans helped others,

> "When it was too late, I awoke to the fact that the man who called himself my friend, had been my hopeless ruin, and I was alone again in the cold, heartless world; still in poverty and with all that is sacred to a woman gone…About this time a holiness preacher and his wife came to the town where I lived, and began preaching a full and free salvation. A lady friend told me of these holiness preachers and asked them to take me and take care of me until the construction of rescue home at Arlington, Texas, was finished. I also had another friend tell me of a woman who might employ me until the rescue home opened. But when the lady saw my [pregnant] condition she did not want me. Then I put my little boys in the Orphan's Home at Peniel, Texas (Holiness Church); and went to stay with Sister Thompson.
> Here I was again in a strange town with no home and no money. I planned to end my wretched career by taking my own life; but, thank God someone telephoned Sister Jernigan to come see me. She encouraged me and prayed for me and went away to get a place for me to stay. Sister Jernigan tried several days but no one wanted a helpless woman. Then Sister Jernigan tried to raise money to pay my board and doctor's bill, but only got three dollars. She told me that she

would take me herself if she did not have a sick mother to wait on, who had been an invalid for some time. She said she was not able to wait on us both. Sister Jernigan went home and told Charles, her husband, that all her plans had failed; and that she did not know what to do next. She asked Charles to pray with her, for God to show them what to do; and while in the room alone with God He spoke to both hearts, 'Practice what you preach. You say your home is open to the fallen: here is your chance.' She then hitched her horse to her buggy and came out after me. She took me to her home and gave me her own bedroom. I stayed there until my baby Ruth was born. She paid all my bills and did my washing as she had no money to hire it done. Brother Jernigan sold his folding organ to help pay my bills.

One day some of her friends came in and found me in her bedroom, and said; 'Why, Sister Jernigan, would you give up your own good room to a fallen woman like this?' Sister Jernigan treated me like a mother until I was able to work, and then told me she would give me and little Ruth a home if she had one if I wanted it. I lived with her one year and a half. How many Christian women will open their home to a poor creature like me? I was converted in her home, and during the camp-meeting the next summer I was gloriously sanctified.

Then my mother's heart began to cry out for my little boys. I wanted to amend the past and raise them for God. I told Sister Jernigan about my desires, and she went to see the matron, and trustees of the Orphans' Home

and got my boys for me and rented me a
house. She bought furniture and provisions
enough to last me a month. My family, sons
and daughter, were united again. I am now
living in Peniel, Texas, taking in washing for
a living. I live happy even if I do have to
work hard. I thank God I can praise Him
while I stand over the wash tub and sing 'I
have been redeemed.' I feel like I owe my life
to Sister Jernigan, as she took me in when no
other person would have me. If it had not
been for her, I would have been in hell today
instead of writing this testimony to the
redeeming power of my Savior."
Marilla Gilliam, Peniel, Texas, December 4, 1904[8]
The Jernigans lived in Pilot Point, TX, and in 1908
Johnny Jernigan was hostess to Phineas and Maria Bresee
during the unification services. A few months later they
moved to join other couples to help create a new
community in Bethany, Oklahoma two years after
Oklahoma statehood. C.B. Jernigan had been appointed
district superintendent and Johnnie Jernigan administered
the Nazarene Home, a ministry for unwed teen mothers.
She helped over 700 women and girls during the seven
years of existence of the home. The home closed when
Johnnie's health began to decline. Johnnie Jernigan died
in 1940.

Returning to Mary Lee Cagle, the resilient minister
gave her last sermon at age 90. Blind and weak, two
strong men helped her stand as she delivered a 30-minute
sermon with "her usual vim and vigor." The religion of
the heart was everything to her. She died the next year.[1]

A THEOLOGY OF LOVE

Mildred Bangs Wynkoop (1905 to 1997) was a leading theologian for the Church of the Nazarene, professor of theology and specialist in John Wesley. In 1972, she wrote her magnum opus, *A Theology of Love*, to describe the central grounding that John Wesley had in theology, namely love.[10]

However, love is a "weasel" word (Wynkoop's choice) with many meanings and covers a wide gamut of behaviors in current society. To help distinguish a new type of love, the early Christians in the New Testament borrowed a seldom used Greek word "agape." Wynkoop defines agape-love as impartial goodwill. However, she also said that agape cannot be easily defined, but it can be more easily demonstrated by God giving us Christ: "while we were yet sinners, Christ died for us." (Romans 5:8)

Love is so central to John Wesley's total message according to Wynkoop that we cannot do better than to quote one of his strongest passages on this subject.

"It were well you should be thoroughly sensible of this, 'The heaven of heavens is love;' there is, in effect, nothing else; if you look for anything more than love, you are looking wide of the mark, you are getting out of the royal way, and when you are asking others, 'Have you received this or that blessing'? If you mean anything but more love, you mean wrong; you are leading them out of the way and putting them upon a false scent. Settle it in your heart, that from the moment God saved you from all sin, you are to aim at nothing more, but more of that love described in the 13th [chapter] of Corinthians."[11]

How do love and holiness relate? Wynkoop explains,

"When holiness and love are put together, the analogy of the two sides of a coin would be closer to the truth. Neither side can be both sides at the same time. Sides are not to be equated, but the obverse side is as essential to its existence as the face. Love is the essential inner character of holiness, and holiness does not exist apart from love. That is how close they are, and in a certain sense they can be said to be the same thing. At least Wesley consistently defined holiness, as well as perfection, as love…The dynamic of personal relationship is love. Love is a quality of response between persons. Love can exist only in freedom. It cannot be coerced. Freedom is the most fundamental ingredient of love. When love is spoken of, freedom is presupposed, and persons are involved. Love describes the kind of response that exists between persons. Love may link the persons into a fellowship or it may short-circuit about itself and reject other persons. In either case, it is the relation between persons that is at issue…Love, then, positively or negatively defines holiness or sin. Love, being dynamic and free, includes or excludes others in its search for fulfillment. When the object of love, that about which the total self-centers, is God, holiness is described. When, in this process, love centers in the self [exclusively], God is excluded, and sin is described. Holiness and sin are quality evaluations having to do with the kind of relationship the self sustains to God."[10]

Wynkoop, like Wesley was ever practical as she explained,

"When one becomes a Christian, or is born again, the ultimate in self-awareness and self-consciousness and personal identity is reached. God forgives the sin that has robbed the self of respect and security. The fear of God has changed to a sense of mutual love. In this experience every debilitating drag to self-identity is removed. The moment of release is an infinitely pleasant moment. We would like to preserve it, glory in it, live in it, retreat to it. But this is not spiritual health any more than arrested development is mental health. Personality is not static but dynamic…For the first time the person emerges as a true person and begins to function as a person. Self-interest—which is not of itself sin, but which has functioned out of perspective and, because it has shut God out, has been sinful—must now of its own free choice transfer its authority to God, and the object of its interest to others. Without relinquishing self-identity, it must identify itself with God and begin to live responsibly with others."[12]

Put in a different way, Diane Leclerc comments on Wynkoop: "Thus sin is not simply reduced to a set of broken rules and laws that can easily deteriorate into stagnant legalism. Sin is anti-relationship, anti-love."[13]

A contemporary theologian Elizabeth Johnson notes the positive correlation between a close relationship between God and autonomy, "Nearness to God and genuine autonomy grow in direct rather inverse proportion." Wesleyan Holiness women illustrate this autonomy as their relationship comes closer to God and they mature as Christians.[14]

CONCLUSIONS

Numerically, how have the Wesleyan Holiness groups compared to non-Wesleyan groups in terms of ordination? In 1920, one year after the 19th Amendment passed, an independent report listed 226 ordained women in ten non-Wesleyan Holiness denominations, while just one Wesleyan-Holiness group, the Church of the Nazarene, listed 350 ordained women ministers.[15]

The prior report was published by *The Woman Citizen*, a women's political journal. The basis of the information was derived from a questionnaire sent to a sample of 100 denominations in the United States; there was an excellent return rate of 75%. It asked "[Are] women ordained to the ministry? [Are they] given full laity rights as to voting? [Do they] hold all offices in the church on the same basis as men?"[15]

However, only 11 denominations listed ordained ministers. Sixty-four church groups did not report any ordained women ministers. Sorting the 11 denominations by Arminian or non-Arminian in belief (chapter three), there were 502 and 54 women ministers, respectively.[15] [c]

Boyd observes, "The returns show that until woman suffrage was assured there was little discussion of equality in most sects and the status of women remained

------

[c] For unknown reasons, The Salvation Army, also a Wesleyan-Holiness organization, was not included in this report. The 1920 World Almanac would suggest there were about 1,000 ordained women officers in the Salvation Army that year. This was calculated by dividing the total number of male and female officers by one-half—a proportion that the Army has typically had throughout its existence. Of course, since 1930, especially beginning in the 1950s, many denominations have elected to ordain women as ministers. The list is extensive. There are major hold outs. However, the latter topic is not relevant to this book. The purpose here is to show how some Wesleyan groups, particularly, the Wesleyan-Holiness groups and Salvation Army were out in front giving women equal status, long before it was fashionable.

high or low, according as it was laid down in the beginning."[15]

Boyd concludes, "These figures register the prevailing social disapproval of the ordination of women as 'servants of the servants of God;' yet the Church of the Nazarene bears witness that they perform the service well. "They are splendid preachers," says its official, "and excellent evangelists, and they are much honored as members of our governing boards."[15]

Both C.B. and Johnnie Jernigan were two of the four ministers that laid hands on J.B. Chapman during his ordination service to the ministry in 1903. Chapman later rose to be a general superintendent in the Church of the Nazarene. After criticism by some for ordaining women ministers, Chapman wrote a simple reaffirmation in 1930 for the denomination's journal,

> "The fact is that God calls men and women to
> preach the gospel; when he does so call them,
> they should gladly obey Him and members of
> the church and of the ministry should
> encourage them in the fulfillment of their
> task. This is the teaching of the New
> Testament, the new dispensation, and the
> position of the Church of the Nazarene."[16,17]

References
Chapter 20

1. Ingersol S. Nazarene Roots: Pastors, Prophets, Revivalists & Reformers: Beacon Hill Press of Kansas City; 2009, pp. 109-112.
2. Cagle ML. Life and Work of Mary Lee Cagle: An Autobiography: Nazarene Publishing House; 1928, p. 24.
3. Stanley SC. Holy Boldness: Women Preachers' Autobiographies and the Sanctified Self: Univ. of Tennessee Press; 2004, p. 121.

4. Laird R. Ordained Women in the Church of the Nazarene: Nazarene Publishing House; 1993, location 60%.

5. Bangs C. Phineas F. Bresee: His Life in Methodism, the Holiness Movement, and the Church of the Nazarene: Beacon Hill Press; 2013, location 54%.

6. Laird, location 32%.

7. Dayton D, Strong DM. Rediscovering an Evangelical Heritage: a Tradition and Trajectory of Integrating Piety and Justice. Second ed. Grand Rapids, Michigan: Baker Academic; 2014, location 67%.

8. Jernigan MJ. Redeemed Through the Blood or The Power of God to Save the Fallen. Digital Edition, CD ROM, 11/27/97 ed: Holiness Data Ministry, 1997 reprint; 1920, pp. 1-23.

9. Ingersol, p. 184.

10. Wynkoop MB. A Theology of Love: The Dynamic of Wesleyanism. Kansas City: Beacon Hill Press; 2015, location 4-5%.

11. John W. A Plain Account of Christian Perfection. Kansas City, MO: Beacon Hill Press; 1966.

12. Wynkoop, location 51%.

13. Wynkoop, location 98%.

14. Stanley, p. 11.

15. Boyd MS. Women Preachers. The Woman Citizen 1920; 29; pp. 794-6, 802.

16. Ingersol, p. 184.

17. Chapman JB. October Gleanings. Herald of Holiness 1930.

Chapter 21 Wesleyan Way of Reasoning

"If Mary can carry the Word of God in her womb, why can't I carry the Word of God on my lips?" Ida Robinson, a woman minister, aptly summarizes the logic for women in ministry.[1]

Many Wesleyans have asserted the extensive scriptural basis for women ministers. Excellent essayists have included Luther Lee, Catherine Booth, and Phoebe Palmer and Francis Willard.[2][a] The reader may think it strange to place a chapter on scriptural interpretation near the end of this book rather than at the beginning; but, readers needed to vicariously view the lives of these women and men as they argued for the abolition of slavery, temperance, and the rights of women. Moreover, there has been a focus on the accounts of the women themselves as they sensed a call of the Holy Spirit to preach. A call they were reluctant to accept since they knew they would face prejudice in secular society and intermittent opposition by church men and women.

Professor Cowles book, *A Woman's Place? Leadership in the Church*, is highly recommended. It is easy to read, yet thorough biblical exegesis of the topic. It represents the finest of Wesleyan scholarship on the topic.[3]

Wesleyans approach thinking about issues in Christianity using a fourfold approach. These are reason, tradition, experience and scripture.[4] When interpretation of scripture is at issue, the first three are used to illuminate understanding.

"Tradition" for Wesleyans refers especially to the practices of the early church. Earlier writers and John Wesley used the synonym "primitive" church. Later Wesleyan Holiness writers used the term "apostolic."

---

[a] The references to the essays of the first three in this list have been cited in earlier chapters. Frances Willard's is book length and is called Woman in the Pulpit.

Current readers more easily understand the term "early church" as referring to the events of the New Testament and the first two centuries of Christianity. Wesleyans assert that women enjoyed equal status with men in the New Testament. This is plainly seen at Pentecost where the Holy Spirit blessed both men and women. The Apostle Peter in the first message of Christianity referred to the Prophet Joel's prediction,

> "God says, I will pour out my Spirit on all people. Your sons and daughters will prophesy, your young men will see visions, your old men will dream dreams. Even on my servants, both men and women, I will pour out my Spirit in those days, and they will prophesy." Acts 2:17-18.

This is a crystal-clear assertion on day one of Christianity by the head of the church about the "prophetic" (i.e., speaking the good news of the kingdom of God, not predicting the future) status of men and women.

It bears repeating that when Thomas Doty, (chapter four) was asked about the legitimacy of women preachers, his succinct response was, "today is a Pentecostal day."

In context of Jewish rabbinical practice towards women, Jesus was radical in his practice. Jewish rabbis did not speak to women in public, yet we find Jesus speaking to many women in the gospels. His extensive discussion with the woman alone at the well in Samaria astonished his disciples. The Samaritan woman then returned to tell her town the good news of Jesus. It should be noted that there is not the least effort by Jesus to restrain this woman evangelist; indeed, he welcomes the crowd of people she has managed to convince through her preaching to return to listen to Him.

The Gospels of the New Testament tell us that women were last at the cross, first at the empty tomb, and the first to see the risen Christ. Peter and other men heard of the resurrection of Jesus from women. The risen Christ commissioned women to proclaim to men the most important news of the fledgling Christian faith—He is not dead but alive! The church at times has denied women an equal role in spreading the good news. Jesus had no such reluctance before His death or after His resurrection.

Paul issues a mountain top type assertion in Galatians 3:28. This has been considered a key ethic of Christianity ever since by Christians wishing to follow Biblical Christianity. Cowles provides a reasoned and sound Wesleyan approach to the verse. He and others have called it the "Magna Carta" of the New Testament.

Obviously, for those groups who oppose the ordination of women, Galatians 3:28 must be attacked, otherwise its obvious meaning wins the day.[b] The principal point that opponents of the Wesleyan position attempt to make about Galatians 3:28 is that the verse has only a "restricted" sense. Anti-equality arguments strive to curb the Gal. 3:28 by limiting the topic to personal salvation. They assert that the context of the verse is speaking only about salvation of the individual.[c]

---

[b] Opponents to the larger picture of Christian equality of men and women cited in Galatians 3:28 can be easily found with an internet search. The current author will not provide links, so the reader does not think I have "cherry-picked" the most egregious. I would say reading the illogical attacks induces sadness. Where is the sense of agape-love? I was privileged to take a class with the Wesleyan and Nazarene theologian, Robert Staples, a noted Wesleyan specialist. It was Professor Staples who helped inform me Nazarenes and Wesleyans are not "fundamentalists;" Wesleyans take the Bible seriously, but not literally. It is more a spirit of love and reason versus an unbending legalistic spirit. John Wesley was famous for his attitude that can be summed as "come let us reason together." It seems to the author, on the other hand, the fundamentalist's attitude is "my interpretation is the only possible one"

[c] The current author confesses that he cannot see that the immediate context of Galatians 3:38 is limited to salvation. The reader can judge for themselves. In any case, would not these arguments for a limited context also support the institution of slavery? (It was used in this sense to escape the obvious application to Christian slaves during the

But what about a larger context? Who decides where the line of surrounding context is made? Should "agape-love," as demonstrated by the fruit of the Holy Spirit mentioned only a few paragraphs later in Galatians (5:23), be included in the circle of context? What would an interpretation through the lens of love be? In any case, is not the Royal law of love the most important principle of Jesus and Paul? Since the nine fruits of the Holy Spirit define social interaction, an inclusive equality for Galatians 3:28 as outlined by C.S. Cowles and John Wesley is more consistent.

"Logical" Luther Lee's exposition of Galatians 3:28 cannot be improved (chapter eight),

> "The text fixes no limits, prescribes no
> bounds, names no places, occasions, subjects
> or duties, but affirms in general and
> unqualified terms, that there is neither male
> nor female, but that all are one in Christ
> Jesus; and this is by way an abrogation of the
> Mosaic Law, and it of necessity places males
> and females upon an equal platform of rights
> under the Gospel."

The calling of the Holy Spirit to individual women forms the basis of "experience" in the matter. When Wesleyans speak of experience, they mean the opinions of sanctified individuals who are living out the Royal law of love.

We must address the out of context and unclear passage in 1 Corinthians 14:34 about "women should remain silent in the churches." Out of context since Paul only a few verses later (14:39) tells the Corinthians, "My brothers and sisters, be eager to prophesy!" (i.e., preach). Many proof texters (those who hurl isolated verses around

---

Civil War). The "limited meaning" advocates cannot have it both ways. Thus, would slaves or Jews have a different social status in the church? This seems a slippery slope.

like lawyers in a courtroom) often cite the former but neglect to harmonize the latter admonition.

Wesleyan scholars believe the apparent contradiction is explained by some localized disturbance in the Corinthian church, a congregation that was felt to be immature (in 14:20 Paul says, "stop thinking like children"). This then was a temporary injunction for a specific disorder.

The same things about the Corinthian church also apply to the isolated verses of I Timothy or I Peter. Those who argue against women preaching do not seem to apply consistency to the strict silence imposed on women. That is, they avoid imposing these draconian restrictions on modern church attending women. For example, if the latter passages apply to modern women not being allowed to preach, then why do these same commentators allow women to sing or to teach Sunday School classes? Logic requires consistency. One cannot pick the meaning they wish out of a passage without thinking of its other applications. A little common sense, that is, rational thinking is needed here. How are these passages to be harmonized with the agape-love messages of Jesus and Paul?

The rational approach by Wesleyans requires harmonizing our entire outlook of the Bible and not getting mislead by irrelevant or obscure passages. Roger Hahn, was Dean of the Nazarene Seminary for many years in Kansas City.[d] Some have stumbled over the passage "a woman should not have authority over a man" in I Timothy 2:12. Dr Hahn's commentary on this passage is,

> "In [ancient Biblical] Greek, it is not clear at
> all; the structures are awkward and confusing,

---

[d] My mother and Roger's mother were friends for many decades and I thus know Roger, who is three years older than me. One can tell from the cited quotation that Roger graduated with a Major in Mathematics from college.

and there is more than one way to construct
the sentence. The key word translated to
'exert authority' or 'have authority' over men
is a word that we do not have the data to
define with precision. Four hundred years
before Paul writes it means "murder;" three
hundred years after he writes, it means to
'domineer' or 'take authority' over; but, what
did it mean in between when he wrote? We do
not have the kind of data to help us answer
the question…We simply do not have enough
data to exegetically to tie down what was
happening in First Timothy. So, we end up at
a state of 'could be this' or 'could be that,'
which is the best we can do. We just need to
remember that's what we are doing. Which
means this is not a text to make dogmatic
statements on women not being allowed to
teach or to have leadership positions, because
it is an unclear passage. Where you work
[from] are the clear passages.[5]

Rational systems of thought have lower and higher
laws. That is, there are descriptions of reality that apply to
an isolated purpose, but which are not part of a more
general truth. For example, a medicine which may work
to cure most patients with a disease may not work in a
particular individual. Or, under English common law, a
local ordinance in a town may be necessary, but may not
work as a national law. Thus, there are passages in the
Bible which may be advised in a peculiar setting, but not
serve as a universal recommendation. The understanding
of these differences are a part of wisdom and study rather
than a piecemeal viewpoint.

There is also room for humor here. The early
twentieth century Nazarene minister, Mary Lee Cagle
regaled listeners with,

"Why did God give women such a talent to talk, if not to be used for Him? If God did not intend for women to use their tongues for Him, He certainly did give the devil a great advantage in the beginning, for women can talk. The men are generally our superiors; but there are some things that we can excel them in. And one of them is talking: You can put a half-dozen women in one room and they can all talk at once and no one listen, and yet when they get out of the room each one can tell everything the other said. Men could not do that if their lives depended upon it. They must talk one at a time and then they can't tell it correctly across the street. How many men are there who never went downtown and phoned back and asked the wife what it was she told him to get? All that never did that keep your seats. It is no wonder to me why the devil has tried and in a large measure succeeded in keeping women from using their tongues for God, for he knows that if the women get filled with the Holy Ghost and turn their tongues loose on him he will have to hunt cooler quarters, or in other words will have to vacate."[6]

There is no rational reason why women should not be given complete ecclesiastical and civil rights. If one asserts that an isolated verse of the Bible should be interpreted as prohibiting women as full ministers for all time, then one is logically stating that there are systems of truth-one of rational reasoning and the other an interpretation of faith. This is very unsatisfactory. One cannot hide behind the mysteries of faith. Not when the issue involves at least half of the Christian body. At best, one must admit there is a contradiction and seek to resolve it. The Wesleyan way to think about apparent contradictions is to also use tradition and experience of Holy Spirit filled persons to help interpret the passage of scripture.

We have presented only a small part of the evidence of the early church tradition and intervening epochs where women were full-fledged ministers. Admittedly, women have never formed an equal number of ministers, but that is not necessary to carry the point.

Concluding questions: can we deny women called by God to preach the gospel? Assuming these women seek the proper credentials, and live a life above reproach, can we deny women called by God to preach the gospel? Can we deny women called by God to preach the Gospel?

References
Chapter 21

1. Knight HH. From Aldersgate to Azusa Street: Wesleyan, Holiness, and Pentecostal Visions of the New Creation. Wipf and Stock Publishers; 2010, location 72%.
2. Willard F. Woman in the Pulpit. D. Lothrop Company, 1888. Google ed: D. Lothrop Company; 1888.
3. Cowles CS. A Women's Place? Leadership in the Church. Kansas City, Kansas: Beacon Hill Press; 1993.
4. Thorsen D. The Wesleyan Quadrilateral: Scripture, Tradition, Reason, and Experience as a Model of Evangelical Theology. Emeth Press; 2005.
5. Metcalf JT. Ablaze with Love : a Video Documentary to Sensitize the Church of the Nazarene to its Heritage of Gender Mutuality in Ministry; 2002.
6. Cagle ML. Life and Work of Mary Lee Cagle: An Autobiography: Nazarene Publishing House; 1928, p. 171.

Chapter 22 Temperance

Temperance is a reform movement in the 19th and early 20th centuries ignored by most writers on women's suffrage. The direct relevance to women's suffrage is that all the first-generation women suffrage advocates (e.g., Susan B. Anthony, Elizabeth Cady Stanton, Lucretia Mott) started out in the temperance movement. More importantly, the issue remained important to them, even as they added anti-slavery or women's suffrage efforts. Many, but not all, second generation suffragists also started working in temperance and remained anchored within this movement; these included Frances Willard, Anna Shaw and Antoinette Brown.

Given the dependence women had to place on men during most of the 19th century, a wife married to a man who started drinking heavily suffered social chaos. The temperance movement responded to the cries by women for help.

PROBLEMS CAUSED BY ALCOHOLISM

In the United States the alcohol reduction movement began in the 1820s. Americans were attempting to deal with the new scourge of distilled alcohol beverages. The rapid distillation of grain slurry achieved by the new steam power in the 1700s allowed production of cheap whiskey and gin in copious quantities. The amount of alcohol contained in these beverages reached 80%. A gallon of gin in America or Britain circa 1800 cost as little as ten cents a gallon. Humankind had never experienced the easy availability of anything this toxic before.

Throughout history wine contained 1-10% ethanol, and it had a short shelf life of a few weeks when stored. Ethanol in wine is an unstable substance and quickly oxidizes to the stable compound acetic acid, known as vinegar. It had been known since the 13th century that the shelf life of wine could be extended longer if the wine was sterilized at hot temperatures, but this interfered with its final acceptability. In any case, by 1700, the price of wine was high, and the unspoiled product ingested only by the upper class. The most common beverage for the masses was ale, a watered-down form of beer containing only 1% ethanol. Beer usually contained around 2-4% ethanol.

It awaited the discovery of pasteurization of wine by Louis Pasteur in 1864, to enable bottled wine and beer to have a shelf life measured in decades. Heating beer and wine for a brief period to 140^0 F (60^0 C) was enough to kill most of the bacteria that caused spoilage, yet not ruin the product.

Society and churches were slow to respond to the epidemic of alcoholism caused by distilled spirits in the 18th century. This was partly because the lower classes were disproportionately afflicted; the upper class had more resources to mask their involvement. In any case, agreement existed among all political parties, social strata and Christians that drunkenness was undesirable since it disabled and destroyed men and women.

Historically, one important rationale existed for the of ale or beer. Namely, water drawn around human habitations often led to gastrointestinal infections, cholera, and bloodstream infections, such as typhoid. The understanding of infected water as the precise source of these problems was not prevalent until the mid-19th century. In 1854, the discovery by the physician John Snow that contaminated water, and not air, was the cause of the 1854 Broad Street cholera outbreak in London, did not require understanding of the newly debated germ theory.

However, physicians and lay persons before understanding the germ theory were not stupid. It was appreciated that ingestion of "bad" water (i.e., cloudy or smelly) caused severe diarrhea. Throughout history, accounts have described the idea of "living water;" a term indicating clear, fast flowing rivers or deep wells. These sources were usually safe.[a]

Even the small volume of ethanol present in ale served to sterilize the water. Even John Wesley admonished his preachers to "use a little ale" to treat their stomach problems. It was difficult to become drunk from ale of the time period.

On the other hand, it is easy to see how the introduction of cheap gin (10 pennies for a gallon in the 18th century) would lead to surge in alcoholism. Intoxication cost a penny.[1] It is quite possible that 18th century Britain was the most inebriated society in the history of the world. In 1743, in a nation of 6.5 million people, the British produced more than 18 million gallons of gin.[2] [b]

The problems in Britain were also in the New World. Social control developed slowly in the colonial period of the United States. The early decades of the 19th century found an epidemic of alcoholism for which little could be done.

Moral solutions were the obvious approach as the humoral theory for the medical treatment of diseases failed to help alcoholism.[c] The issues of voluntary aspect versus disease manifestation are still debated. The decision to take one's first drink and then later choose to

––––––––––––––––––––

[a] Pipelines providing cleaner water began in large cities in the mid-19th century. Thus, the need to drink ale because the ethanol sterilized the water began to disappear.

[b] The timing of this epidemic of alcoholism coincides with the life and ministry of John Wesley. Thus, Wesleyans were born in a time when alcoholism was the dominant social disorder. Yet, is it not still?

[c] The humoral theory reigned from about 400 BC to well into the 20th century. It is the idea that disease is caused by bad substances, i.e., humors, which need to have bloodletting or purging of the gut to get rid of the humors.

become inebriated are under voluntary control.[d] What is not clear is at what point the compulsion to keep drinking has its onset, and thus when the recreation (i.e., choice) turns into a medical disease.

The results of any contemporary organic disease model for treatment (i.e., psychiatry) can only be described as abject failure. The best results continue to emanate from patient help groups, such as Alcoholic Anonymous (AA), where the approach is essentially spiritual. AA focuses on voluntary control of relentless cravings. The latter would have been termed a "moral approach" in the 19th century. The disparity of results (i.e., long-term abstinence) from a purely psychiatric approach compared to AA remains about 5% versus 50%.

Chronic intoxication continues to be a major problem in the USA as 15% (1 in 6) adults meet criteria for alcoholism. American society in the first half of the 19th century likely faced an even higher rate of alcoholism that overwhelmed social resources.

JUSTICE VERSUS UTILITY

Justice is the idea that the vote should have been given to women because it was the right thing to do. It is only natural that women should have the same franchise rights as men. Utility, on the other hand, forms the basis as to what women voters would do if given the vote.

Justice was persuasive for some good men; examples would be B.F. Crary, Gilbert Haven and Matthew Simpson. There was also a core of male members in NAWSA that undoubtedly felt the weight of the argument for justice. Unfortunately, these men were few.

---

[d] The proponents of alcoholism consisting as a medical disease seem to muddle through the idea of its initiation. If one never takes his or her first drink, then a person will not become drunk for the first time. Certainly, the author, as a liver specialist, thinks alcoholism is a medical disease, but its genesis is indeed voluntary.

The artificial idea presented by many feminist historians is that NAWSA argued for the franchise based on justice. On the other hand, the WCTU argued for suffrage merely on the basis of utility; that is, the WCTU wanted the vote merely to be able to prohibit the sales of recreational alcohol. This idea is mentioned so many times in the non-WCTU suffrage literature that the maxim has come to be unquestioned.

The historical reality is much more complex. NAWSA expressed the idea in the 1880s, if not sooner, that giving the vote to women would help "clean up" the corruption of politics. A wording that sounds very like the concept of "home protection" advocated by the WCTU. However, WCTU speeches on suffrage, particularly after 1900, contain strong and frequent appeals to justice. NAWSA often employed speakers from the WCTU in local campaign efforts as the WCTU had the only pool of trained women public speakers in existence.

Aspects of the 1896 referendum in California serve to illustrate the tension over utility. The following anecdote also shows cooperation of the WCTU and NAWSA in their common efforts to obtain suffrage. Susan B Anthony placed an extraordinary request to her close friend Francis Willard to move the 1896 Annual National Convention of the WCTU scheduled to take place in California to out of the state. Willard countered with an inquiry about delaying the convention date until after the November referendum.

On January 23, Anthony replied with her worry that "less harm" would come of a union meeting after the election, but it would be better to move the event into another state.

Still in the Southern United States on March 15, Willard noted that her friend Anthony,

> "will not hear to our having it there this year
> even after the voting on suffrage amendment.
> On the contrary we think the liquor people

will vote against it any way and nobody can win the decent element like the WCTU. We believe our society has made more converts to woman's cause than any other; but Susan is 'set' and I think for good feeling's sake we would better change.' At a special meeting in Chicago on March 24, Willard prevailed over recalcitrant officers, and the union moved its meeting to St. Louis 'for Susan B. Anthony's sake.'"[3]

Suffragists also wanted to divorce the suffrage issue from the temperance issue at all levels. NAWSA's national headquarters dashed letters to the Californian women "urging them to keep the issues separate, which aroused much laughter, as nearly all the Californian suffragists were WCTU officials."[4]

The opposition was not idle. The Wholesale Liquor Dealers League met in San Francisco and resolved,

"to take such steps as were necessary to protect their interests.' Throughout the campaign the liquor lobby had repeatedly pressured the political parties not to support the amendment by threatening them with a denial of campaign funds and votes. Determined to defeat the suffrage amendment, the League issued a letter to all saloonkeepers, hotel proprietors, druggists, and grocers declaring: 'At the election held on November 3, Constitutional Amendment No. Six, which gives the right to vote to women, will be voted on. It is your interest and ours to vote against this amendment. We request and urge you to vote and work against it and do all you can to defeat it. See your neighbor in the same line of business as yourself and have him be with you in this matter.'

On election day the agents of the liquor lobby took hundreds of men from the San Francisco slums to the polls. Each man had a sample ballot showing him how to put an "X" against the suffrage amendment. Each had been informed if the referendum carried, there would never be another glass of beer sold in the city."[5]

The amendment failed by a 137,000 to 110,00 margin. Not close. NAWSA and the WCTU learned their lesson. Never again would NAWSA ask the national WCTU to desist from speaking about temperance.[e]

"Abstract arguments about expediency and justice flow easily from the pens of historians, yet most striking in the work of the WCTU is the difficulty of separating these concepts. For the WCTU's Clara Hoffman, who toured California in support of the suffrage referendum of 1896, expediency was pretending that women would not use the vote to oppose the sale of liquor. California suffragists had requested her not to wear the white ribbon while speaking in the campaign and to refrain from using temperance arguments. That the referendum failed merely reinforced Hoffman's conviction that 'the only people deceived were the suffragists themselves.'"[6]

Catt, who we have mentioned frequently in this text, was not a temperance or prohibition woman. Her analysis of why the Constitutional amendments for the prohibition of alcohol (18th Amendment) and women's suffrage (19th Amendment) gained nearly simultaneous approval deserves more widespread appreciation. The current author has redacted her 8100-word chapter on "The Unseen Enemy" to the following 3500 words below.[3] This is an extended quote without indications where breaks in the text occur.

____

[e] The amendment was resubmitted by Republicans in 1911 and this time barely passed with 50.7% of the vote. It was supported by rural counties. Opposition came mostly from the Bay Area where the liquor industry was well organized against it.

THE UNSEEN ENEMY BY CARRIE CHAPMAN CATT

Those invisible influences that were controlling elections; that invisible and invincible power that for forty years kept suffragists waiting for the woman's hour; for forty years circumvented the coming of suffrage; that power that made Republican leaders hesitate to fulfil their promises to early suffragists; restrained both dominant parties from endorsing woman suffrage; kept Legislatures from submitting suffrage amendments; was, manifestly, the power that inhered in the combined liquor interests.

Victorious movements record their history; vanquished ones rarely do. The men who buy or sell votes do not confess. Full knowledge, therefore, of the extent to which the liquor trade exercised a dominating influence over the politics of the United States for a generation will probably never be revealed. But enough indisputable evidence has been accumulated to establish the fact that it did wield that influence and to reveal also much of the general plan by which results were achieved.

When the first decision was made to include woman suffrage as an indirect menace to the liquor cause is unknown, but in 1867, during the Kansas suffrage campaign, suffragists noted that in all parts of the State local liquor men were conspicuous workers against the suffrage amendment.[f]

In 1873-4 an uprising of Christian women against the saloons of Ohio startled the church, the saloon and the nation. Groups of women, well known for their virtue and piety, appeared before the doors of saloons, or at times entered, read passages of Scripture, sang hymns and, kneeling, prayed fervently for the abolition of all "rum shops." Out of this, the Woman's Christian Temperance

---

[f] The reader should note that this opposition was in well in place before the WCTU was formed.

Union emerged in 1874. It grew in size and influence with astonishing rapidity and spread to all States of the Union.

Women thus became an unmistakable factor in the movement which was rapidly pressing forward the demand for 'total abstinence for the individual and prohibition for the State.' Their meetings filled churches, bridged denominational differences, enlisted the clergy and influential churchmen. More than all else, the organization aroused women and trained them for public work as no movement had yet done. Soon the Woman's Christian Temperance Union became the largest organization women had yet formed in any country. Its leader for many years, Frances Willard, was one of the world's greatest women, beloved by her followers and honored by all. She captivated audiences, disarmed their prejudices and enrolled them in her cause. It was doubtless because of these things that the press reports of the Brewers' Convention of 1881 included the adoption of an anti-suffrage resolution that the Brewers would *welcome prohibition as far less dangerous to the trade than woman suffrage, because prohibition could be repealed at any time, but woman suffrage would insure the permanency of prohibition* (italics by current author).

Meanwhile evidence had accumulated to prove conclusively that whether the brewers had staged their hostility to woman suffrage in resolutions or not, they had ceaselessly demonstrated it in practice. Three official investigations into the political activities of the brewers have been made and four large volumes of the evidence have been published. On January 9, 1915, the Attorney-General of the State of Texas filed suit against seven breweries in the State charging 'the use of their corporate means and assets in politics and elections' contrary to the laws of the State. In March 1916, indictments were brought against one hundred Pennsylvania brewing companies and the United States Brewers' Association by a Federal Grand Jury. The indictments charged the brewing companies with the unlawful expenditure of money in the election of federal officials. Rather than have the investigation proceed, the brewers chose to plead guilty and pay a fine of a million dollars.

The press reported that some tons of documents were taken on subpoena from various offices and bureaus. Although the evidence was fragmentary, it made clear that a national political agency, set up by the combined interests, had long existed and that it supervised or was active in both prohibition and suffrage campaigns throughout the United States.

This evidence, combined with the circumstantial and direct evidence supported by affidavits preserved by the National American Woman Suffrage Association during a period of fifty years, shows the liquor interests in active opposition to woman suffrage on the following counts:

1. The same man or men who conducted the anti-prohibition campaign directed the anti-suffrage contests in Legislatures, constitutional conventions and referenda campaigns.

2. Money to oppose woman suffrage was taken from the funds placed in the hands of the political committees organized by the liquor interests to fight prohibition.

3. A given quota of votes to be secured against woman suffrage was customarily assigned each saloon in referenda campaigns!

4. By definite agreement, in secret conferences, the liquor forces determined to conceal their opposition to woman suffrage so for as possible,

5. The liquor interests applied the boycott to men favoring woman suffrage as they did to those favoring prohibition.

6. By the same coercive means they sought contributions for anti-suffrage campaigns from firms with which they dealt.

7. In States reputed strong for both suffrage and prohibition, the attitude of Congressmen and State

legislators on both questions was reported to the national political committees of the liquor interests with equal care.

8. The allied organizations that were set up to oppose prohibition opposed woman suffrage by the same methods.

To carry on these numerous campaigns required great sums of money. The Brewers' officers, called on subpoena by the Government, admitted as little as possible and remembered nothing of importance, yet the evidence confirmed many suspicions and beliefs that had been based previously upon hearsay. It confirmed, for example:

1. That the United States Brewers' Association and the Pennsylvania Brewers' Association kept no minutes of their official proceedings.

2. That the practice of the United States Brewers' Association to destroy check stubs and cancelled checks with each bank balance was customary with State brewers' associations.

3. That a working agreement had existed for many years whereby the brewer's furnished two-thirds and the distillers one-third of the campaign funds.

4. That the United States Brewers' Association and the State Brewers' Associations each levied an annual tax of one-half cent to one cent per barrel on the output of member brewers, the amounts thus derived being dues, chiefly expended in administration of the national and State associations.

5. That funds for political campaigns were secured by making additional assessments as needed. In 1913 a contract was made whereby the brewers agreed to assess themselves three cents per barrel annually for a term of five years, the agreement to become operative when brewers representing twenty-five million barrels had subscribed. As more than that number entered into the agreement, the plan was carried out until the federal

prohibition amendment was submitted. This plan supported a national fund only. The State associations also assessed their member breweries according to State agreements to secure State campaign funds. That the largest known deposit of the United States Brewers' Association in any one year was $1,400,000 in the year 1914, and its known deposits from 1913 to 1918 were $4,457,941, although the records for a portion of this time were lost, so that the total was more.

From all of which it seems clear that the liquor funds spent in the political campaigns of the country ranged from four to ten million dollars a year. It was against such a Croesus foe as this that suffrage, with its pitiful but consecrated dimes and dollars, dared raise its head. 'I will pledge my car fare,' said a poor little woman at an upstate suffrage meeting in the New York campaign of 1915, when pledges of money to the suffrage campaign were being made. 'I will pledge my car fare. I can walk to and from my work.'[g]

Mr. Doyle of the Illinois State Brewers' Association wanted 'to suggest' and 'to implore' that 'female suffrage' be defeated at all hazards. 'As the result of experience, we have had with two different subjects, I want to suggest to the gentlemen who are here a very serious matter, that if you are living in liberal states which have not the initiative and referendum and have not female suffrage, I want to implore you to defeat these two things at all hazards.'

The struggle between temperance and liquor forces had reached its height in 1913. Statewide prohibition had been established in several States and the issue was a crucial one in the politics of many others. Court decisions were

---

[g] [(footnote by Catt) Chief of a Brewers' Bureau and President of the Association of Commerce and Labor, an organization set up by the brewers to give the appearance of voluntary outside protest against prohibition. Percy Andreae was under contract to receive $40,000 per year from the brewers].

notably friendlier to the temperance side of legal contests, but a far more important factor in the situation was the addition of many powerful manufacturers to the prohibition forces. The labor unions had striven long for employer's liabilities in cases of death and accident of employees, and such laws had been passed by many States. Manufacturers now discovered that accidents happened more often when men were under the influence of intoxicants and sought to protect themselves from this risk by advocating the legal removal of the cause. Another cogent factor pushing them toward prohibition was the argument that working forces would not be so depleted at the beginning of each work-week if working men had no Saturday night and Sunday sprees to sleep off on Monday morning. A tremendous impulse was given prohibition through the addition of this new ally. Legislators, sensing a changed public opinion, became more independent and daring. The liquor traffic recognized the need of more money and more intensive campaigning than ever before. Onlookers saw the final battle emerging from the half century struggle.

The brewers promptly entered into the five-year agreement previously noted to provide more money, and accepted the proposal of Percy Andreae, chief of a publicity bureau for the Brewers' Association, to increase organization. It was in an executive session of the United States Brewers' Association, held in Atlantic City in October 1913, that he urged this new policy. He did not take the brewers into his confidence as to how the plan was to be put into execution. 'I must have a free hand,' he said. 'No one who realizes the character and the magnitude of the work I have undertaken will believe that it could be accomplished under any other conditions. An army—and it is an army if you please, that is to be called into existence—must have a leader. What hope would there be for the success of an undertaking… involving alliances which the slightest misconstruction ... of our intentions would place in jeopardy if I were obliged to herald all details…to the world, which I would be doing if I confided them to the knowledge of several hundred men.'

The general plan, however, involved two main features:

1. To rely no longer upon contributions and favors as the sole means of controlling parties and politicians, but to add the threat of large blocks of voters which would go for or against the party or candidate who did not do the bidding of the trade.

2, To build up organizations, chiefly to be recruited from the foreign population, having the appearance of voluntary bodies with public-spirited aims; but, existing solely to defend the trade. These organizations were designed not only to join in the general propaganda, but to provide the army of voters which was expected to awe parties and politicians into a proper degree of subservience.

Mr. Andreae was authorized to proceed upon the policy that the foreign vote should be organized to control elections and legislation. The experiment about to be tried was not new and had already proved itself. It had organized the Russian vote against woman suffrage in the Dakotas, the German vote in Nebraska, Missouri and Iowa, the Negro vote in Kansas and Oklahoma, the Chinese vote in California.

The most important organizing done along this line was that which resulted in the National Association of Commerce and Labor. Mr. Andreae organized it and became its president. It appeared to be a businessman's organization and exerted great influence in consequence upon national and State political parties. Its staff salaries were $46,000 per year[h] and its workers were mainly ex-State Senators and Representatives.

---

[h] author's comment—'incredible.' the average working man's annual income was somewhere around $500 to $2,000; a Model A Ford cost

It should be plain by now why it was that when suffragists turned from the closed doors of Congress to seek justice by State action, they found that legislative doors were also closed; nay more—mysteriously locked! Suffragists approached their task with the exaltation of a belief that theirs was a righteous reform demanded by the great destinies of humanity. In the beginning they regarded the opposition they met as normal inertia to be overcome, but in later years the end of many campaigns left them prostrated with amazed despair, for with the years came the clearer comprehension of the invisible and devious but monstrous force against which suffrage was contending.

The legislative anti-suffrage work of the liquor interests began by simple processes. The first move was to 'fix' the committee to which a suffrage bill was referred and this they, or some other mysterious power, were able to do in nearly three-fourths of the suffrage legislative campaigns. An overworked committee, a crowded legislative calendar, were the explanation given to women workers, while the bargains which brought the result were made without witnesses behind closed doors. If the suffrage bill was likely to be reported out by the committee to which it had been referred, work was begun on the legislators.

Very often the legislative campaign was confined to the Senate, the smaller body where a single man or small group of men could be a sufficient balance of power to insure an adverse vote. The liquor lobbyist worked with economy and concentrated his efforts on a few men who held key positions in the Legislature. The member who believed that his political future depended upon getting a bill through the Legislature often traded his vote on suffrage for that of a liquor or railroad man who favored his pet measure.

$500.

Men who could not be bought were influenced by the knowledge that generous contributions were made to the State and national campaign committees of their party by representatives of the trade, and that blocks of voters alienated from party support would mean party defeat. With these thoughts in their minds, they were readily persuaded that women could wait for the vote. Cajolery, promises of assistance in coming campaigns, presents to wives, attentions to relatives and friends, business, financial and political preferment, were all among the methods employed. If the legislative poll showed a majority by these means, no others were applied. If, however, a few votes were still necessary to make the majority, the 'third degree' of politics was brought to bear. Intimidation, threats 'to make or break men' and out-and-out bribery were the methods used at this stage.

The women in time learned to know the signs, but they had incomplete proof to offer. The public neither knew nor wanted to know. After every legislative term, the reports of State suffrage auxiliaries to the National Suffrage Association bore a remarkable similarity of testimony. The full force of the statements of anyone became apparent only when taken relating to all the others. Men who wanted to go straight compromised with their consciences in that shady political borderland lying between honesty and dishonesty. An illustration chosen from many on file explains the difficulties of such men. It came from a State wherein manufacturers, railroads and liquor interests had each their great political battles and where all three worked together to secure the desired aims of anyone. Wrote the State suffrage officer February 1917:

'That the Senators meant to vote for the suffrage bill when they first came to ____, we believe. They said to us and to each other that they were pledged to it. The women antisuffragists who appeared at the hearing seemed to have made no impression. Various Senators told us so repeatedly. Yet gradually Senators began to weaken. One Senator, who spoke and voted for our bill, said 'You know I suppose, that it was the liquor interests which were responsible for the death of the bill.' Many others said the same thing, but no man will come out in the open and make a charge against the wet interests and back it up, for they are too afraid of those interests.

'A Senator who had openly espoused the bill in this Legislature and pledged himself to vote for it, not only voted, but made a speech against it. This was a matter of frequent occurrence, but this Senator gave an interview to the women to whom he had pledged his support, unusual for its frankness. Said he: 'The client giving me most business is a manufacturer who is tied up with the liquor interests. The most powerful newspaper in the town gives me all its legal business. But the newspaper is wet (i.e., pro-liquor) in policy and opposed to woman suffrage. If I become too pronounced as a champion of woman suffrage, the liquor interests would put the screws on the manufacturer and he in turn would notify me that he had found it convenient to seek legal counsel elsewhere. The newspaper would let me know that my services could be dispensed with. I have a nice home, a little Ford for business and pleasure, and two sons to educate. I cannot afford to lose the patronage of my two best-paying clients.' He added that he had often regretted that he was not a man of wealth and thus could be independent.'

The liquor trade also made allies of other special interests seeking legislative protection or privilege, and successes were frequently due to this combination. Liquor, railroad, manufacturers, cattle, sheep, and packers' lobbies were among the allied interests. None had 'trouble' in every State or in every Legislature but all had their big political campaigns, which frequently resulted in regularly employed counsel for the liquor intereests being nominated as representatives of the people by the controlling party—and being elected by unsuspecting voters to seats in the legislature. Within the legislative forum such men fought the battles of those who paid them. When two or three were engaged upon pleasures in the same Legislature, each having a group of legislators at command, it was usually easy to affect a union of forces whereby the trading of votes secured more certain results for all.

After the State of Washington, in 1910, and California, in 1911, had slipped into the suffrage column, an apparent challenging of the national brewers' admonition to keep to an underground policy on woman suffrage appeared in many States and the liquor forces more boldly displayed their hostility to woman suffrage. In the following year, 1912, when six States had referenda campaigns on suffrage amendments,   the trade so far abandoned its previous policy of 'the still hunt' as to become the most conspicuous opponent in each State. Consternation was aroused in the liquor camps when the press headlines, the morning after the first election in which women had participated in Illinois, announced that woman suffrage had closed one thousand saloons. Public expressions of liquor resentment became instantly bolder.

The open campaign of self-defense conducted by the liquor forces can be respected as the unquestioned privilege and right of all who seek to convince public opinion. The point at issue is that the liquor interests did not rely upon open propaganda but upon secret maneuvers for results, and in this field no moral law, no democratic principle, no right of majorities was recognized. While its activities were suspected by all observers of political events, proof was lacking, and its power was so intricately bound up with partisan politicos that none but the Prohibitionists, and not all of them, dared proclaim the truth.

In the end it defeated its own purposes. Men who conscientiously believed in moderate drinking found themselves aligned with a political condition they could not tolerate. Men who believed in total abstinence, but not prohibition, found their position equally untenable; women were aroused and made resentful by the attitude of the trade on the question of their enfranchisement. In the long run, the prohibition forces were augmented by the addition of thousands of men and women who came to protest the corrupt influences of the saloon in politics, methods it employed became the boomerang that gave the liquor power its final and mortal blow.[7] [i]

References
Chapter 22

1. Sournia J-C. A History of Alcoholism: Blackwell; 1990, p. 21.
2. Hansen DJ. Liquor in the 18th century: History of Distilled Spirits Timeline. In: https://www.alcoholproblemsandsolutions.org/liquor-in-the-18th-century-history-distilled-spirits-timeline/ State University of New York Potsdam, NY 13676: Sociology Department State University of New York Potsdam, NY 13676; 2017.
3. Gordon AD. The Selected Papers of Elizabeth Cady Stanton and Susan B. Anthony: An Awful Hush, 1895 to 1906: Rutgers University Press; 2013, p. 10.
4. Cooper DG. The California Suffrage Campaign of 1896: Its Origin, Strategies, Defeat. Southern California Quarterly 1989;71; p. 321.
5. Ibid, pp. 321-322.

[i] The current author is aware that contemporary efforts by the alcohol industry to avoid taxation and other control measures are still opposed by non-written directives. Stockholders of liquor companies are not being properly assessed for the damage their products cause; and, they walk away with higher profits than they should. Catt implies that, whether or not the WCTU was active, the liquor industry would have vehemently opposed suffrage. The church was not the enemy of suffrage – the furious foe was the alcohol industry.

6. Tyrrell I. Woman's World/Woman's Empire: the Woman's Christian Temperance Union in International Perspective, 1880-1930: UNC Press Books; 2014, p. 223.
7. Carrie Chapman C, Shuler NR. "The Invisible Enemy" chapter from Women Suffrage and Politics. The Inner Story of the Suffrage Movement. University of Washington Press; 1970, pp. 132-59.

Chapter 23 Wesleyans and Suffrage

Twenty-first century readers have difficulty understanding the dominant role religion played in late 19th century American society. One must imagine an era where only the written word, in the form of newspapers, provided information. Newspapers were everywhere; to be anything, even small towns had a weekly paper. Ruth Bordin captures this scenario with succinctness,

> "The tone of American society was still overwhelmingly Protestant. The attention paid to the activities of the various denominations by the newspapers bears witness to this fact. The secular press, both in small towns and major cities, reported the Sunday sermons delivered from local pulpits in impressive detail. The politics of Protestantism-the machinations of its ecclesiastical bodies, the quarrels among the luminaries who composed its hierarchies, its doctrinal disputes within and between denominations—found full, amazingly objective, and sometimes witty coverage in the public press, to say nothing of the fact that dozens of weekly and monthly church periodicals were read in America's parlors. The reading public was deluged with church-related news that nearly rivaled politics and much outdistanced sports in the competition for the public's attention."[1]

To reiterate a quote from a non-Methodist church historian concerning the period of the last half of the 19th century and first half of the 20th century, "the Methodists were not only the largest denomination numerically, they convinced half of the rest of the Protestants (and some Roman Catholics) to act like Methodists; thus, becoming the country's most culturally influential religious tradition."[2]

The AMEC, Wesleyan Methodists, the Salvation Army, and the assemblage of Wesleyan Holiness groups were used in this book to report the activities supporting suffrage; the Church of the Nazarene, the denomination with the largest number of members, was chosen to represent the Wesleyan Holiness viewpoint, though the Wesleyan Methodists were the first chronological member of this collection.

Surprisingly, the various Wesleyan groups differed little, if any, in doctrine or theology. They all accepted John Wesley's approach to understanding theology, the Bible, and the egalitarian role of all peoples. The groups differed in method, like The Salvation Army; or, Wesleyan Methodists concerning church government; or in emphasis, where Holiness groups stressed Wesley's doctrine of perfect love.

Wesleyan Holiness groups are to be distinguished from Pentecostals since they do not "speak in (unknown) tongues." Moreover, the meaning of the word "Pentecostal" started to change in the early 20th century to become strongly identified with the worship practice of unknown spoken utterances. However, in the 19th century, the "Pentecostal" simply referred to the first occurrence of the visitation of the Holy Spirit in the early church recounted in Acts chapter two of the New Testament. This is the recounting of the initial event of the Christian church where both men *and women* were endowed with the manifestations of the Spirit of God.

Three main issues were investigated in the Wesleyan groups examined. Examination of their stance on secular franchise for women; the voting privileges within the organization; and whether ordination for women was allowed. This last issue reflects the idea of complete ecclesiastical equality, a status that Wesleyans would assert was present in an equivalent way during the early church and New Testament. However, the use of the term "ordination" was not present in the early church for men or women.

METHODIST EPISCOPAL CHURCH

The contributions of the American Methodist Episcopal Church to the advancement of the status of women were many. A few are reviewed here. Laywomen joined their brethren in voting in the local church by at least the 1870s. Neither men nor women had any voting privileges above the local level. Only ministers, who were all men, could vote at the annual (i.e., regional) conferences and General Conference. The General Conference of the Methodist Church was the only body that could change the rules of the church. Bishops could not make new laws but had judicial-like responsibility in applying the rules. Starting in the 1860s, support started for lay representation on the regional electoral committees to determine delegates to the quadrennial General Conference started. The AMEC was bedeviled with the lack of a gender-neutral pronoun and this created confusion as to whether women could join the general conference as full delegates. True, this franchise was not the same as suffrage for women in secular politics; however, it certainly represented a strong surrogate sentiment that the AMEC supported voting privileges for women.

The national vote taken by Methodists to change this church rule (i.e., women voting at the General Conference) represents a remarkable statistical cross-section of a social group in America in 1892. There is no numerical sample even remotely approaching this in the 19th century on voting for women. To reiterate: 235,668 members of individual churches voted for the eligibility of women to be full delegates at the General Conference; and 163,843 were against (a 60% majority in favor!);

while 5,609 ministers were in favor of women delegates, and 5144 against (54% in favor!). And while this failed in the three-quarters majority required to change the *Discipline*, the leadership saw the handwriting on the wall and moved to change procedural rules that prevented women from becoming full-fledged Conference delegates. Women were then seated at the 1904 General Conference. This process occurred during a twelve-year background in American society where there were very few gains in the franchise issue for women.

Bishop Simpson was a towering figure in Methodism and secular women's suffrage. His prestige as a bishop among bishops gave the suffrage movement moral and persuasive support in the early decades of the 1860s and 1870s when there were few national leaders of any type willing to assert women's suffrage. Similarly, Bishop Haven was honored for his principled positions against slavery, where he did not let bitter Southern denunciation deter him. He was also a firm advocate of women's suffrage. Haven was also an advocate of ordination for women.[3] These two Methodist men undoubtedly swayed many Methodist men to convert to the franchise in church and state.

On the other hand, the AMEC did not institute the privilege of ordination for women until 1954. However, the approval and use of women lay preachers waxed and waned from the Revolutionary War period until 1954. Moreover, AMEC allowed women to increasingly take a visible and aggressive role in church affairs and foreign missions. The liberty Methodist women experienced within the AMEC was equaled by few other denominations.[4]

WESLEYAN METHODISTS

The Wesleyan Methodists simply considered women equal. Hosting the Seneca Falls convention in 1848, when no other facility or church in town would have them, speaks of their earliest and staunch support of secular suffrage for women. It is hoped this text will help future historians to not treat the Seneca Falls Wesleyan Chapel as a happenstance venue.

Women could vote in the Wesleyan Methodist Church from the beginning.

Wesleyan Methodists were more than social reformers. They were on fire, but not burned out, with radical ideas combined with personal piety. Piety is a term seldom used now with negative connotations. The 19th century usage is entirely opposite as it reflected a person who loved God and their neighbor as themselves. The Wesleyan Methodists refused to substitute social reform for piety. In 1845, Orange Scott warned the young church that "deep Experience in the things of God is essential to the peace and usefulness of all Christians; but it is essential to any class of Christian Reformers."[5]

Rev. Antoinette Brown Blackwell's ordination by the Wesleyan Methodist, Rev. Luther Lee, in 1853 during a Congregational church service represents the first of ordination of a woman minister in the modern period. The next evidence we have for a woman preacher being ordained in America was through the Wesleyan Methodist Church. In 1861, the Illinois conference of the Wesleyan Methodist Church ordained Mrs. Mary A. Will.

The Wesleyan Methodists would have probably had a woman ordained earlier but for the fact that there may not have been any qualified women in their smaller denomination who met the rigorous education requirements of ordination. It took time for a woman to meet all the educational requirements in the co-educational secondary and college system of the Wesleyans Methodists.

SALVATION ARMY

The Salvation Army was (and is) one of the most unique Wesleyan efforts in history. An officer in the Salvation Army was ordained as part of their job description. In the 19th century, there were more than a thousand female Salvation officers and their number exceeded the number of male officers. The Army may represent the earliest egalitarian organization, either ecclesiastical or secular, in modern world history after early Christianity.

It could not be discovered whether the Army ever made a public stance on secular suffrage for women. Instead, they asserted a new role for women singing and preaching on the street; this aggressiveness even went so far as to suffer physical injury and death. The example of the Army women gave secular suffragettes courage to step out in a similar radical manner and march in the streets.

FRANCES WILLARD AND THE WCTU

On the morning of February 18, 1898, the news flashed around the earth "Frances Willard is dead." Condolences poured in from worldwide reform leaders and followers. Dying in New York City, arrangements were made to send her body back to Evanston, Illinois by train. When news of her death reached Evanston, the city lowered the flags to half-mast. In Washington D.C., Des Moines, Iowa, Chicago and many other places, flags were also lowered to half-mast, a symbol of a farewell salute; an honor never accorded an American woman.

Despite rain and storms, more than 2000 people attended her funeral in New York City at the Broadway Tabernacle. When her casket reached the Women's Temple in Chicago, one of the worst storms in the history of the Windy City was taking place with sheets of snow and sleet coming off the Lake Michigan.

Despite the tempest, mourners swamped the WCTU headquarters.

"Then the police interposed and formed the waiting multitude into a line four deep. This extended from the entrance on Monroe Street to the middle of La Salle Street, then turning past the front of the Temple it extended for nearly a block. All day long that sad procession never flagged, and, though twenty thousand people viewed the remains, at four o'clock in the afternoon, when it was necessary to take the body to the train for Evanston, the police were obliged to disperse five hundred people who were still waiting to see for the last time the beloved face. Such world-wide honors were never before accorded any woman; such universal grief has not touched humanity since Abraham Lincoln died."[7]

Seven years later, a statue of Frances Willard was donated by the state of Illinois to the National Statuary Hall in the old House of Representatives room of the U.S. Capital building. A Congressional Act in 1864 provided that each state could provide two statues of important citizens to adorn the hall. By the year 1905, only 39 statues had been provided, all men. Frances Willard was the first woman to be so honored.

The day the statue was formally accepted by Congress many speeches were given in honor of Frances Willard. The senior Senator from Illinois, Shelby Cullom, also a Regent of the Smithsonian, said in part,

"Miss Willard was not only an advocate of temperance, but of all other beneficial, progressive reforms—purity in politics, equal rights for women, and, to secure political

315

reform, woman suffrage. She believed 'that
there is such a power in the influence of
women as, if it were exerted right, would
shake the kingdom to the center.' She was
recognized as an able public speaker, perhaps
the greatest woman speaker in the country.
She had a rare gift of eloquence and
magnetism which drew thousands into the
temperance ranks. During her years of active
life, she probably addressed a larger number
of public audiences than any man or woman
of her time."[8]

That day, the newspaper reporters and members of
Congress were all men. Why should the honor have
accorded Francis Willard matter to us? The quote from
the first popular vote to give women suffrage in Colorado
is at the core of the matter,

"We thank the men of Colorado who showed
the world yesterday that they were neither
afraid nor ashamed to give their women equal
rights with themselves…This was the first
time in history [in which] the class in power
enfranchised a class not in power without
being forced to do it."[9]

Simply put, men had to give the power of voting to
women. To this end, men needed to be convinced that
women could vote responsibly. What was looked for was
an articulate, yet non-threatening woman. One who had
no tinge of misandry. Francis Willard fit that description
better than any woman in America in the final decades of
the 19th century; and, whose influence extended for the
early decades of the 20th century.[a]

---

[a] Contrast this with Elizabeth Cady Stanton who called men
"monsters." She also created her own version of the Bible without
knowledge of Greek or Hebrew. Third, she promoted the "fake"
science history of the conflict of science and religion. All this was an
insult to the predominant Protestant viewpoint of the era. The author

The Woman's Christian Temperance Union was largely a Wesleyan parachurch organization. The first two national leaders during the initial 22 years were Methodists.[b] The WCTU did not have membership categories by denomination, so the composition cannot be determined. When Ruth Borden did a small-scale study of WCTU leaders (n=184), she found that 45% were Methodist affiliated.[10]

The WCTU was the giant in supporting women's suffrage in the last quarter of the 19th century. They had a large presence in every state and territory in the Union as opposed to the few chapters in a limited number of states for NAWSA. In reading the literature, without knowing the numbers, the person new to the subject would think the WCTU had very little role in the working for the franchise while NAWSA was the giant.

Because of the lack of state and local NAWSA chapters, many women, whose only interest was in suffrage, joined the local WCTU to have a group that would support their interest in suffrage. Moreover, one reads time and time again of NAWSA in Western states hiring WCTU speakers to represent the franchise issue. NAWSA had virtually no training program to develop women speakers, whereas the WCTU raised and maintained a battalion of eloquent women speakers.

Any effort to portray the WCTU as a single-issue organization distorts the facts. In fact, Frances Willard's "do everything" approach with 37 departments showed the organization's efforts to improve the lot of women in many practical ways; these included such efforts as literacy, job training, day care and refuge houses.

---

speculates that she may have delayed the time to getting suffrage for women.

[b] The author could not determine the denominational affiliation of the third national leader of 15 years, Lillian Stevens. That she was a Protestant with a deep Christian faith is not to be doubted.

The irony here is that secular sources often satirize evangelicals in the 19th century for waiting for "the pie in the sky" millennial return of Christ to make all things right in the world. However, NAWSA, with their limited membership, was determined to stay focused on the single issue of the franchise. This led to the secular organization's constant hope that once women got the vote, they would be able to correct all the problems of women. Or, in other words, the secular millennium will come, so to speak, with the franchise. For example, the following exchange occurred at the 1894 NAWSA convention,

Kate Field: "My dear friend Miss Anthony thinks that the millennium will come when women get the suffrage."

Miss Anthony: "Yes, [I do]."[12]

That paradise did not unfold after the 19th amendment does not seem to faze historians who poke fun at Christian aspirations for the heavenly millennium. The problem with this hope-for-the-future position by NAWSA was twofold. One, the single-issue focus led to long periods of inactivity in any given locale between referendums for the franchise; during the idleness, some local chapters would dissolve from dormancy. Two, the suffragettes always hoped for a convincing win in the next state election; moreover, this anticipated victory would then start an avalanche of franchise approval.[c]

In defense of NAWSA, since their numbers were small, and this necessitated having men as members, they were always strapped for cash. Unfortunately, this caused them to gravitate to upper class women and men who could give large amounts and influence others to do so. This strategy limited membership numbers.[d]

---

[c] If secular suffragette supporters had known that 72 years would intervene between Seneca Falls and the 19th amendment, we can speculate that they might have buckled down to the hard labor of improving the lot of women in the here and now.

[d] Since there are so few rich people as a percentage of the total

In contrast, the WCTU set up a class and chapter organization very similar to what John Wesley and the Methodist's did. In the 18th century, Methodist class members contributed a penny every week. The penny was quite affordable for lower-class men or women to bring. Any one chapter's amount did not amount to much, but the contribution of thousands of classes allowed the Methodists to administer gargantuan social help.

The WCTU did the same. The dues were small and quite possible for women to give, but together in mass, and with local women volunteers, the local and state chapters could achieve unthought of help for women. This combined with the brilliant national leadership strategy of avoiding top down projects, gave women in any local chapter the freedom to pursue projects to meet local need. Examples would be day care or agitating for women jail matrons in districts where the justice system was available for males only.

All this kept WCTU women active. These women could then be marshaled for duty to support women's suffrage when the four year or longer cycle returned with an opportunity. Indeed, this was a secret of the Colorado victory. A t the September 1893 state chapter meeting, the leadership asked women in every local Colorado chapter to drop all their other activities and focus efforts on getting support from men for the November referendum.[13]

Frances Willard may easily be the most famous Methodist of the 19th century. Her recruitment of women into the world's largest women's group and her keen interest in suffrage from a young age, make her one of the most influential women in achieving the franchise. She was the first woman in America to have flags flown at half-mast when she died. She is the first woman to be honored in the Statuary Hall of Congress. Willard did not live to see the day, but she inspired thousands of women

---

population.

and converted many men to the just cause of suffrage for women.

SECULAR SOURCES NOTING WESLEYAN SUPPORT

There are numerous allusions to the fact that Methodists were supporters of the franchise for women. During the 1890 South Dakota referendum, Catt stated, "Now what have we? 1st.—The Lutherans, both German and Scandinavian, and the Catholics are bitterly opposed. The Methodists, our strongest friends everywhere else, are not so here. 2d.—We have one party [i.e., political] openly and two others secretly against us."[14] [e]

In the 1877 Colorado referendum vote, the poll observer in Georgetown noted uniform approval of suffrage by Methodist men. She could tell us because the secret ballot had not yet been instituted and observers could see the color of the voting ticket placed in the glass bowl.

Bishop Matthew Simpson, of the Methodist Church, was a strenuous advocate for this great reform.[15] The *History of Woman's Suffrage* is full of references to the famous Methodist leader expressing his backing of women's suffrage.

Another Bishop, Gilbert Haven is also cited in the *History*.[15] Unfortunately, his early death in 1879, at age 58, deprived the women's movement of an outspoken advocate. Had he been able to live through the 1894 General Conference, it seems he would have been able to

---

[e] the quotation serves to highlight the general opposition everywhere in South Dakota during this election and emphasizes unequivocal Wesleyan support elsewhere. The current author could not determine why Methodists (AMEC) were an exception in the Dakota campaign. One possibility is that there were no strong local leaders such as the Presiding Elder BF Crary had been for Colorado.

swing the Bishops and Delegates into the immediate seating of Francis Willard and her four companions.

CONCLUSIONS

Data and events in this book demonstrate the contributions of those who adhered to John Wesley's theological tradition. The data have been both quantitative and qualitative. In the 19th century Wesleyans were steadfast supporters of women's suffrage when most other social or religious groups were non-committal or in active opposition. Methodists were one of many reasons for the stunning plebiscite giving the early and isolated win in Colorado. The latter victory enabled a showcase for the nation that women were interested in voting and did contribute to a better atmosphere for politics.

Bishop Matthew Simpson wrote the forward to Thomas Webster's 1873 book, *Woman Man's Equal*. In it Simpson stated ideas that were a hundred years ahead of what even the most ardent reformer might have dreamed,

> "She may preach, orate, lecture, teach,
> practice medicine or law or politics; may
> vote, marshal armies, navigate ships, and go
> sailoring or soldiering to her heart's content,
> and at her own good-will and pleasure, if she
> only proves to the age that she has ability to
> do and dare in all these directions."[16]

Simpson had no doubt of these eventual achievements of women. Simpson personifies the best attitude in the many Wesleyan men who wanted to see women have the franchise.

References

Chapter 23

1. Bordin R. Frances Willard: A Biography: UNC Press Books; 2014, p. 171.
2. Dayton D. The Global Impact of the Wesleyan Traditions and their Related Movements. In: C Yrigoyen Jr. C, ed. The Global Impact of the Wesleyan Traditions and their Related Movements. Lanham, Maryland: Scarecrow Press, Inc.; 2002, pp. 6-7.
3. Willard F. Woman in the Pulpit, D. Lothrop Company, 1888. Google ed, p. 93.
4. Keller RS. Spirituality and Social Responsibility: Vocational Vision of Women in the United Methodist Tradition: Abingdon Press; 1993.
5. Dayton D, Strong D. Rediscovering an Evangelical Heritage: a Tradition and Trajectory of Integrating Piety and Justice. Second ed. Grand Rapids, Michigan: Baker Academic; 2014, location 54%.
6. Caldwell W, ed. Reformers and Revivalists: History of the Wesleyan Church. Indianapolis, Indiana: Wesley Press; 1992, p. 59.
7. Parks IW. Frances Elizabeth Willard, the "White Ribbon Chieftain". Methodist Review 1898, pp. 849-62.
8. Willard FE. Statue of Miss Frances E Willard: Erected in Statuary Hall of the Capitol Building at Washington. Proceedings in the Senate and House of Representatives on the Occasion of the Reception and Acceptance of the Statue from the State of Illinois: US Government Printing Office; 1905, p. 22.
9. Leonard S. Bristling for Their Rights: Colorado's Women and the Mandate of 1893. Colorado Heritage 1993; Spring 1993; p. 14.
10. Bordin RBA. Woman and Temperance: The Quest for Power and Liberty, 1873-1900: Temple University Press; 1981, p. 169.
11. Ibid, p. 88.

12. National American Woman Suffrage A, Upton HT. Proceedings of the Twenty-sixth Annual Convention of the National American Woman Suffrage Association, held in Washington, D.C., February 15, 16, 17, 18, 19, and 20, 1894. Washington, D.C.: The Association; 1894, p. 159.
13. WCTU. Fourteenth Annnual Convention of the Woman's Christian Temperance Union of Colorado. 1893, p. 48. (WCTU Archives, Norlin Library, Boulder, Colorado).
14. Van Voris J. Carrie Chapman Catt: a Public Life: Feminist Press at CUNY; 1996, p. 24.
15. Stanton EC, Anthony SB, Gage MJ, Harper IH. History of Woman Suffrage, Volume 3, 1886, p. 236, 460.
16. Ibid, pp. 236, 268, 277, 391, etc.
16. Webster T. Woman Man's Equal: Hitchcock and Walden; 1873, p. 4.

Chapter 24 Epilogue

The 18th Amendment to the United States Constitution prohibiting the use of alcohol became effective January 16, 1920.

The 19th Amendment to the United States Constitution became the law of the land on August 26, 1920. The key point: "The right of citizens of the United States to vote shall not be denied or abridged by the United States or by any State on account of sex."

A sweet victory for justice. Disappointing in that it took 72 years since the convention at the Wesleyan Chapel in Seneca Falls. Our story largely ends in 1908 with the formation of the Church of the Nazarene. It would take another volume to describe the events from 1908 to 1920.

Wesleyans continued to support women's suffrage, but their contributions were diluted by many other streams of support. The numbers tell the story. During the first decade of the 20th century, the WCTU continued to grow in membership to 250,000 women. However, NAWSA expanded to 500,000 men and women.

One theme in this volume has been the interrelatedness of the reforms of temperance, anti-slavery, and women's suffrage. It was not by accident that the 18th and 19th Amendments were passed nearly simultaneously. The exposure of the corrupt alcohol industry in the second decade of the 20th century was crucial. Carrie Chapman Catt is surely right. Buying and bullying of legislators shocked the public. The actions of the alcohol industry were so ugly that even moderate drinkers were disgusted. A groundswell of support led to the passage of both the 18th and 19th Amendments. Motivating moderate drinkers was essential as the group supporting prohibition was never large enough to win passage of the 18th Amendment alone.

Wesleyans Help Women's Suffrage

Wesleyans were a key group in their longtime support of women's suffrage. Offspring of the 18th century theologian do not believe they have a monopoly on truth; but consider themselves one branch of the true tree of Christianity.

The tradition Wesleyans hold to is the early church as exemplified by the New Testament interpreted holistically, not in bits and pieces.

One of Christianity's greatest thoughts is that the ground at the foot of the cross is level for all people. This idea should make a difference.

Appendix A Quakers and Wesleyans

The Society of Friends was founded by George Fox (1624-1691) in England. In his famous tract of 1656, *The Woman Learning in Silence*, Fox proclaimed,
> "If Christ be in the Female as well as in the Male, is not he the same? And may not the Spirit of Christ speak in the Female as well as the Male? Is he there to be limited? Who is it that dare limit the Holy one of Israel? For the Light is the same in the Male, and in the Female, which cometh from Christ."[1]

How did the Society of Friends, or Quakers as they are better known, differ from Wesleyan Methodists? While generalizations may be misleading, a comparison of the two groups may be useful to the reader. Timothy Smith estimated the Society of Friends in 1855 to stand at 75,000 members, of which 10,000 were Hicksite Quakers. The Friends were so predominantly rural that only 4 of 400 churches in Philadelphia in 1861 were Quaker. In contrast, when the Wesleyan Methodists organized their "Connection," their preferred name for the new denomination, in 1843, there were 3,000 members in nine states. By the mid-1850s, they had grown to an estimated 25,000 members in 16 states. The Connection was much more concentrated in cities and towns in the East than the Society of Friends.[2]

In terms of doctrine and beliefs in the 18th and early 19th centuries, the Friends and Methodists were nearly identical. Timothy Smith places both in the American Protestant stream of Evangelical Arminianism. In John Wesley's time, one critic of both movements even lumped them together as "Quakero-Methodism."[4] Both believed in free will, salvation, and importance of the inspiration of the Holy Spirit. While the members of each group had a variety of views, both assemblies were predominantly interested in the social reforms of antislavery, temperance and women's rights. Moreover, each group had women lay preachers.

The similarities led to competition and cooperation between the churches. Competition occurred when members were proselyted from the other group; or, when individuals merely chose the other group. This did not lead to any degree of being considered tainted by the receiving church.

A prominent example is Dr John Whitehead, a Methodist lay preacher and physician, who attended John Wesley in the days before the founder of Methodism died on March 2, 1791. Whitehead had recently returned to Methodism after spending 20 years with the Quakers. Moreover, he was authorized to write a biography of Wesley, the first using official documents from Wesley's estate.

Cooperation also took place. Critics may think that the new denomination took their antislavery stance easily by remaining in the less hostile North. Not so. The work of the Wesleyan Methodists in the South was started by a 23-year-old minister, Adam Crooks, who volunteered for the start of church planting in North Carolina in 1847. He wrote in his diary, "I turned my face to go to the far south, to pronounce the Gospel which proclaims liberty to the captives, and the opening of prisons to them that are bound." Crooks was thrown in jail for disturbing the peace, poisoned on two occasions, and nearly assassinated twice. Another Wesleyan Methodist pastor was lynched. Nonetheless, the Wesleyan Methodists continued to labor in Virginia and North Carolina; by 1851 they numbered 500 persons in the two-state area.[5,6]

Adam Crooks went to establish the first churches of the Wesleyan Methodists in the unfriendly state of North Carolina in 1850. The Quakers in the Piedmont area of North Carolina, known as the "Quaker Belt" were natural allies for Crooks and provided help for the fledging Wesleyan movement in the area.[5]

George Pegler (first pastor of Seneca Falls, chapter six) started a Wesleyan Methodist Church in New Salem, New York in 1858. In the community, there were both Orthodox (Quaker) and Hicksite meeting houses that were well attended.

> "I continued to preach to and visit among this people. I had many friends among the Quakers, who always gave me a hearty welcome to their peaceful and comfortable homes; and some of them allowed me to hold social meetings with their families. The following winter we held a protracted meeting, and the good Lord poured out his Spirit upon the people. A number professed to experience religion, among them some who were birth-right members of the "Friends;" and some of their lady preachers kindly and Christianly aided in the meeting by prayer and exhortation. I cannot forbear to make mention of the kindness of Joseph C. Hathaway, and his brother Lorenzo, and their sister Phoebe, and their excellent families, and some others, who it would seem went a little beyond their established views in administering to our necessities. But they invariably said, "Friend Pegler is not a hireling priest."[7] [a]

The Underground Railroad was another area of cooperation. If black refugees from the South arrived in an area where there were Wesleyan Methodists or Quakers, they knew they could count on help: "it came to be said of the Wesleyans, as of the Quakers, that almost every neighborhood where a few of them lived was likely to be a station of the secret Road to Canada." There is evidence to suggest that Wesleyans cooperated with

---

[a] Traditional Quaker beliefs involved not paying the pastor

Quakers in Wilmington, and Urbana, Ohio in helping freedom seekers.[8]

Differences between the two groups were more in polity and practices. The Society of Friends were completely under local control with few rules. The result of a local governing format is that practices of different congregations vary widely. On the other hand, the reformed Wesleyans, while they had departed from the authoritarian status of bishops and instituted lay representation, still gave significant authority to the annual and general (national) conferences. National supervision led to a uniformity of practice.

The Friends did not have a plan of their services. Waiting for the inspiration of the "Inward Light" with all worshippers remaining quiet until the stirring of their spirit was a unique and common practice of early Quakers. In contrast, the Wesleyans had a plan of their worship service such as what songs would be sung and the scripture reading for the day. If the Holy Spirit moved on the service, previous plans could be discarded.

Quakers, especially early on, were barred by their own convictions from participating in law and politics. As time went on, a few entered politics in the 19th century. Edward Pease was the first Quaker elected to Parliament in 1832. This attitude helps the reader understand the reluctance of the 1848 Women's Rights Convention to include in the resolutions of *Sentiments* voting as an issue for women. The Wesleyan Methodists had no such compunction against participation in law and politics. Indeed, antebellum leaders urged members to vote the Liberty Party ticket (chapter seven).

Elias Hicks (1748-1830) was an early antislavery Quaker. After helping to rid slavery amongst the Quakers, he continued to promote abolition. Hicks became the focal point of the "great separation" of 1827-28 amongst The Society of Friends. Briefly, a two-thirds majority who were principally rural, became known as the "Hicksite" group; they emphasized the Inner Light in guiding their faith and conscience; while the remaining third, known as "Orthodox," espoused a more Protestant emphasis on Biblical authority and the atonement.[9]

The Hicksites had a strong presence in New York State. The group made a solid contribution to women's rights as four of five women leaders of the 1848 Seneca Falls Convention were Hicksite. Susan B Anthony was also a Hicksite Quaker.[b]

> "The minutes of the Hicksite Women's Yearly
> Meeting in Philadelphia after the schism
> reveal a new spirit of liberation. The Hicksite
> women became more assertive, initiating
> actions and undertaking concerns without
> waiting for the approval of the men. The
> corresponding Orthodox women's minutes
> show no such change."[10]

The Orthodox branch did produce feminists. Hannah Whitall Smith and the Grimke sisters remained in this group. Many of the evangelical Quaker women of the Midwest were leaders in suffrage and women's rights. But the wealthy, urban Quaker men who dominated the Orthodox absorbed from their non-Quaker business colleagues the nineteenth-century concept of the special sphere of woman. Wealth and power tended to undercut gender equality within Quakerism. By sharing responsibilities between husband and wife on the farm or shop, the rural Hicksites were less influenced by the new ideas of separate roles for men and women and more loyal to the traditional Quaker tradition.

> "Yet the Hicksites were by no means united.
> Quietism remained strong, and members were
> discouraged from mingling with outsiders in
> the reform movements. Several prominent
> Friends were disowned for taking part in the

---

[b] A common misconception about Susan B Anthony is that she was at the Seneca Falls Convention. She was not.

antislavery movement, and small groups of antislavery Friends separated from the main Hicksite meetings. . . Liberty of conscience was their major theme.' Lucretia Mott heard the following saying and made it famous: 'Truth for authority, not authority for truth.'[10]

For many reasons, after the formation of the Hicksite assembly, the Quaker sub-group began a century long decline in numbers. From 1840 to 1920, the number slid from 35,000 to 17,000 before eventually stabilizing in the 1940s. In 1919, the upstate New York Meeting had dwindled to a few hundred members.[11]

Hannah Whitall Smith (1832-1911) was the most famous of all Quaker women in the 19th Century. Moving outside the circle of Friends, she worshiped with the Methodists and became a popular Holiness writer and speaker. Her devotional classic, *The Christian's Secret of a Happy Life*, has sold millions of copies in numerous languages and is still in print today. She authored over a dozen other books as well. She and her husband, Robert Pearsall Smith, were the major forces in the extension of the "Holiness Revival" to England and the Continent.

Hannah Whitall Smith was deeply involved in the temperance movement as a close friend of Frances Willard for nearly a quarter of a century. Smith held several national offices in both the American and British branches of the WCTU She spoke at suffrage conventions and was an advocate of women's education.

She was so busy with advancing Holiness and women's rights, she joked that her epitaph would have to be, "Died of too many Meetings."[12]

Hannah Whitall Smith must also be remembered for her discussion of "God as our Mother." In 1885, she devoted an entire chapter in one of her books, *The Open Secret*. Citing Isaiah 66:13: "As one whom his mother comforts, so will I comfort you; and ye shall be comforted in Jerusalem," she argued,

"There are many other ways in which God is like a mother, and a comparison of these points will, I trust, open our eyes to see some truths concerning Him, which have been hitherto hidden from our gaze."[13] c

Comparing the love, comfort, and sacrifice of a mother to that of God she cited verses in scripture which refer to God in traditional feminine imagery (Deuteronomy 32:11 and 12; Isaiah 40:11; Matthew 23:37, etc.) She concluded,

> "If God is only as good as the mothers He has
> made, where can there be any room left for a
> thought of care or of fear? And if He is as
> much truer to the ideal of motherhood than an
> earthly mother can be, as His infiniteness is
> above hers, then what oceans and continents
> of bliss are ours for the taking!"[14]

In 1908, three years before her death, Smith wrote to her daughter,

> "Thy account, Ray, of your enthusiasm over
> the suffrage victory thrilled me through and
> through. I wept some tears of joy to think that
> you girls have embraced the cause of
> Women's Liberty with such enthusiasm. I feel
> now that I can die in peace and leave the
> Cause to your fresh and eager young
> hands."[15]

It is difficult to properly gauge the impact of the Quakers or Wesleyan Methodists on social reform of the

---

c Comfort was surely needed by women that same year of 1885, after W.T. Stead authored his expose: "The Maiden Tribute to Modern Babylon: The Report of the Pall Mall Gazette's Secret Committee in England". It described the horrors of the London brothel scene and international prostitution trade, or "white slavery," as it was called. Stead's four-part newspaper series is available online, but it is not a comfortable read even today as it documents true stories of involuntary involvement by young women sold and traded as flesh. Frances Willard and Hannah Whitall Smith, under the auspices of the WCTU, among others, began to organize internationally and campaign against "the traffic in women."

19th century. Quakers were key in starting the first women's rights convention in Seneca Falls that proved to be a springboard for further conventions. They had equality of the sexes within the meeting house and assisted others without regard to religion. Relatively few, Timothy Smith noted that "their interest in social problems" gave them more "significance" than the small numbers might otherwise indicate.[2]

On the other hand, the location of the Wesleyan Methodists in the Eastern cities and towns and their willingness to engage in politics represent factors for their influence. Women had complete rights to voting within the church at all levels. In the matter of slavery, Wesleyan Methodists wagged the tail of the Methodist Episcopal Church. In 1844, the American Methodist Episcopal leadership feared further secession of churches after the exodus of the Wesleyan Methodists in 1843. The concern of the AMEC over further losses led to a return to the outspoken antislavery roots of the mainline denomination.

References
Appendix A

1. Fox G. Gospel-truth Demonstrated: In a Collection of Doctrinal Books: T. Sowle; 1706, p. 81.
2. Smith TL. Revivalism and Social Reform. Baltimore: John Hopkins University Press; 2004, pp. 20-22.
3. Chilcote PW. John Wesley and the Women Preachers of Early Methodism. Lanham, Maryland: Scarecrow Press; 1991, p. 10.
4. Ibid p. 60.
5. Black R, Drury K. The Story of the Wesleyan Church. Indianapolis: Wesleyan Publishing House; 2012, pp. 47-50.

6. Dayton D, Strong D. Rediscovering an Evangelical Heritage: a Tradition and Trajectory of Integrating Piety and Justice. Second ed. Grand Rapids, Michigan: Baker Academic; 2014, location 55%.
7. Pegler G. Autobiography of the Life and Times of George Pegler. https://archive.org/details/autobiographyofl00pegl; 1875, location 86%.
8. Siebert WH. The Underground Railroad from Slavery to Freedom: Reprint Services Corporation; 1898, p. 95.
9. A Brief History of the Branches of Friends. http://www.quakerinfo.org/quakerism/branches/history 2011. (Acessed Novembeer 30, 2015)
10. Bacon M. Mothers of Feminism: The Story of Quaker Women in America. San Francisco: Harper and Row; 1986, pp. 93-94.
11. Thomas H. The Quakers in America. New York: Columbia University Press; 2003, p. 55.
12. McFadden M. The Ironies of Pentecost: Phoebe Palmer, World Evangelism, and Female Networks. Methodist History 1993; 31; pp. 63-75.
13. Smith HW. The Open Secret. Whitaker House; 2012, location 75%.
14. Ibid, location 87%.
15. Strachey R. A Quaker Grandmother, Hannah Whitall Smith: Fleming H. Revell Company; 1914, p. 133.

Appendix B Soviet Science and Suffrage

Historians like to compare. To what other system of thought may we compare the interaction of Christianity and science? Elizabeth Cady Stanton thought the ideas of communism were fine. In her 1890 NAWSA convention address she opined – "It is justice, and that alone that can end the impossible conflict between freedom and slavery going on in every nation on the globe. That is all the Nihilists, the socialists, the Communists ask"[1]

If White, Draper and Stanton could have waited a few years, the Soviet Union would arise as the only avowed atheistic political system in world history. "Religion is the opiate of the masses" was Karl Marx's phrase.[a] Let us examine what absence of religion does to science.

The drumbeat of Communism contended that it was the only "scientific society" in the world. Joseph Stalin recognized that the process of science required free and unrestrained discussion. However, criticism of the Communist Party, which controlled scientific activities, would not be tolerated. Absurd logic.[2]

THE LYSENKO AFFAIR

Trofim Lysenko (1898 to 1976) was minimally educated in agriculture; but, dogmatic in his assertion that acquired physical traits could be inherited even in the first-generation offspring. An example of this anti-Mendelian theory would be removing the tail from a rat and then expecting the next generation to be born without a tail. In like manner, Lysenko vowed quick

---

[a] Review of current day internet apologists for communism deny that Marx's quote is anti-religious! Not so. For the author, who lived through the cold war with communism, the phrase was used as justification to savage the church. Clergy and members of the Russian Orthodox Church were brutalized and executed by the thousands.

improvements to the chronic poor production of grain. Specifically, Lysenko promised the Soviet hierarchy a breakthrough in developing a variety of wheat that would thrive in the winter. One approach was to merely subject wheat seed to alternating periods of cold and heat! His Machiavellian rise to the top of Agriculture science and remaining there for 35 years is a fascinating story of cunning deceit told in *The Lysenko Affair*.

An example of Lysenko's bizarre talk: "In order to obtain a certain result, you must want to obtain precisely that result; if you want to obtain a certain result, you will obtain it…I need only such people as will obtain the results that I need."[2] [b]

Lysenko saw to it that those who disagreed lost their jobs or worse. The practical effect was the Soviet Union's repression of more than 3,000 biologists during Lysenko's 35 years in power.[3] Repression in this context is defined as being executed, sent to Siberia for hard labor, or merely losing their job (with little hope of using their scientific skills in the future)[2] In a secretive society, it is hard to ascertain what happens when a scientist disappears.

The repression led to a chronic failure to develop new varieties of plants, and most importantly, winter wheat. This led to poor wheat harvests, famines, and a hidden embarrassment to the "scientific society" that had to often import grain from the "decadent" West for more than 30 years.

Meanwhile, in contrast, the best winter wheat variety, *Triumph*, was developed over 13 years in Oklahoma and introduced in 1940. The use of *Triumph* and its genetically derived hybrids were produced using the

---

[b] Another author, a former Soviet biologist, Vadim Birstein, assures us that Lysenko's statements sound as bad in Russian as they do in English. Birstein V. (The Perversion of Knowledge: The True Story of Soviet Science. Cambridge, Massachusetts: Westview Press; 2001. Location 10%).

standard science of Mendelian genetics. The use of hardy winter wheat became widespread in the Western World; growing crops during the winter led to a doubling of the basic food supply. In doing so, the new varieties were responsible for eliminating famine worldwide.[4]

It was not only the field of biology that suffered in the Soviet Union during its brief 72-year existence. Physics, geology and chemistry in different time periods also suffered from pseudo-scientific party officials who "eliminated" critics of their approach. What could be taught in schools about science was severely restricted.

The foregoing is only a minor evil compared with the crimes of Communism. In the 1970s, when two Communist party members in France attempted to take their seats in French Parliament, outcries against the evils of communism were shouted. The two candidates were denied their seats. Because of this incident, two French academicians set out to document the abuses of Communism.

The reader is urged to read *The Black Book of Communism: Crimes, Terror, Repression* (Harvard University Press, 1999).[5] Careful, irrefutable documentation in their encyclopedic book shows that Communism caused 100 million human beings to have been executed, allowed to die in prison, or forced to starve. Intense chilling comes when the authors say that, in their opinion, probably 200 million people were victims; it is just that the second 100 million did not meet their documentation standards! Of course, what this means is that 50-100 million women were killed for a religion-free political philosophy.

The famous Russian writer Dostoyevsky foreshadowed the future Soviet regime's license to kill in his 1880 novel, *The Brothers Karamazov*. Dostoyevsky's theme was, "If there is no God, then murder is permissible."

The issue of universal suffrage granted in 1918 was a sham. Elections in Communism routinely returned 99%

approval for the single party slate of candidates. What kept this high rate of approval, in part, was that the 1% of voters who were naysayers never seemed to make it to the next election. Thus, women's "equality" in Communism was a mockery.

Birstein gives us a poignant example of the Soviet scientific approach on the well-being of women,

> "Each time when I read about the achievements of Soviet physics in the late 1940s-1950s, I recall materials from the Memorial Archive. Old, poor-quality photos show women prisoners somewhere in the Dalstroi labor camps. These prisoners are sitting at tables on which there are heaps of ore. It is uranium ore, and the [enslaved] women are working with the ore with their bare hands. It is difficult even to imagine how short the life of these women was and how terrible their death was after the radiation they had been exposed to."[6]

In conclusion, the Lysenko affair demonstrates the irrationality of Soviet science. Voting in Communism was a mockery. The killing of 50-100 million women has no comparator in history. These were the outcomes of an avowedly atheistic political system that gained absolute power. One wonders what White, Draper and Stanton would think about Soviet science, ethics and Communism now.

References
Appendix B

1. Graham SH. Woman Suffrage and the New Democracy. New Haven: Yale Univeresity Press; 1996, p. 44.
2. Joravsky D. The Lysenko Affair. Cambridge Massachusetts: Harvard University Press; 1970, pp. 110-112.
3. Birstein V. The Perversion of Knowledge: the True Story of Soviet Science. Cambridge, MAssachusetts: Westview Press; 2001, location 48%.
4. Carver B. Early Triumph Wheat. In: http://www.okhistory.org/publications/enc/entry.php?entry=EA003 ed. February 15, 2018: Oklahoma Historical Society; 2009
5. Kramer M. The Black Book of Communism: Crimes, Terror, Repression: Harvard University Press; 1999.
6. Birstein, location 38%.